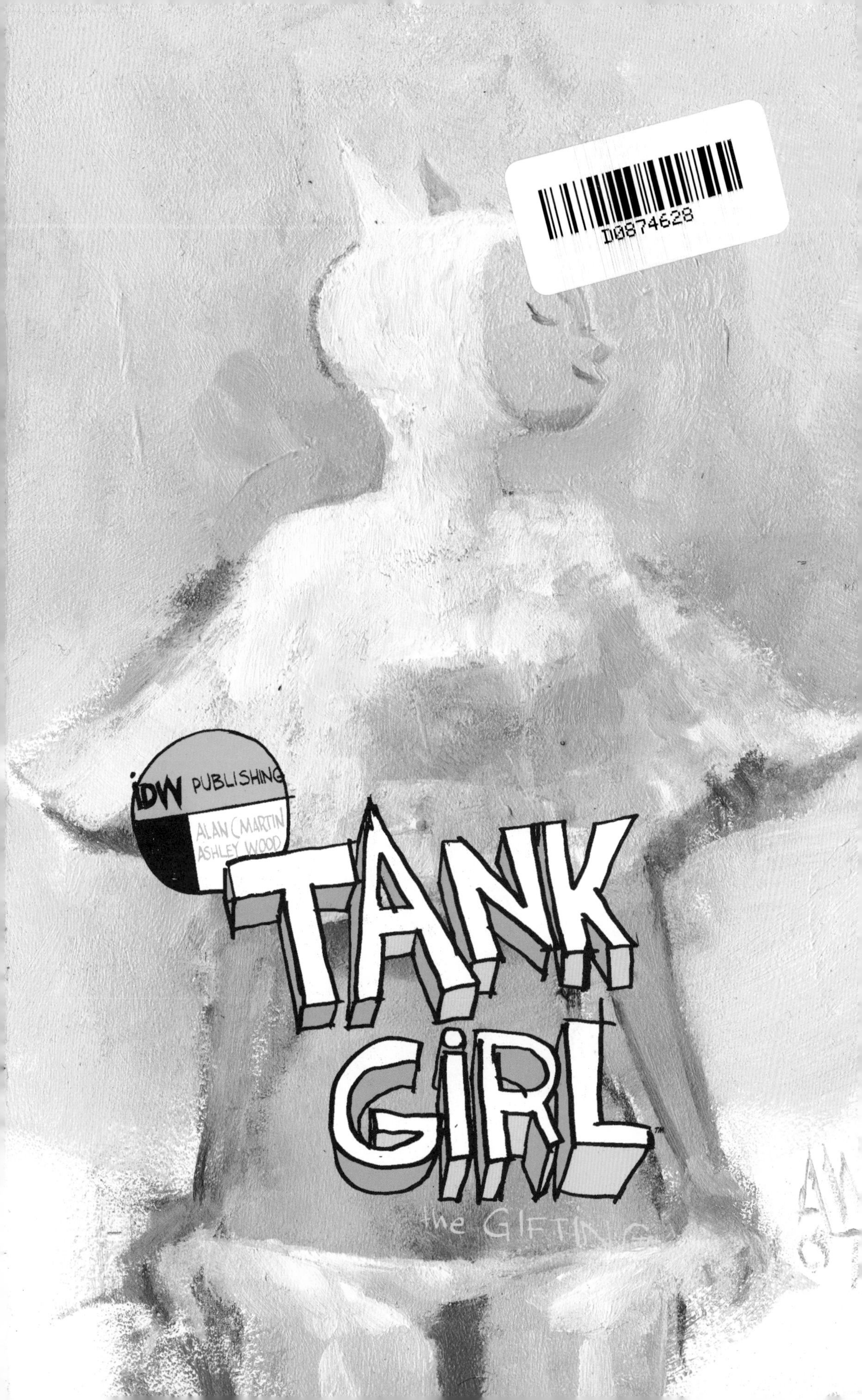
IDW PUBLISHING
ALAN C MARTIN
ASHLEY WOOD
TANK GIRL™
the GIFTING

written by: **alan martin**
art by: **ashley wood** for 7174 pty ltd
layouts by: **rufus dayglo**

letters by: **robbie robbins**
edits by: **chris ryall**

IDW Publishing is:
Ted Adams, President
Robbie Robbins, EVP/Sr. Graphic Artist
Clifford Meth, EVP of Strategies/Editorial
Chris Ryall, Publisher/Editor-in-Chief
Alan Payne, VP of Sales
Neil Uyetake, Art Director
Justin Eisinger, Editor
Tom Waltz, Editor
Andrew Steven Harris, Editor
Chris Mowry, Graphic Artist
Amauri Osorio, Graphic Artist
Matthew Ruzicka, CPA, Controller
Alonzo Simon, Shipping Manager
Kris Oprisko, Editor/Foreign Lic. Rep.

INTRODUCTION

If you were to lock a mad woman in a closet for twelve years, what would you expect her to do and say when you finally let her out? Would you be hoping for divine wisdom and solitary insights, or would you be bracing yourself for an even madder, angrier, sadder shell of a human being?

We locked Tank Girl away back in 1995; it was a merciful act benefiting the comic-reading public, our own sanity, and Tank Girl's tattered and whored character. Jamie Hewlett and I had driven the tank since its debut in 1988, and when the brick wall of a Hollywood movie rose up on the horizon, we put the peddle to the metal and drove straight into the fucker. It hurt bad. Disillusioned and disorientated, we walked away from the whole mess and gave Tank Girl up for a goner.

But old comic characters never die, they just get new hairstyles. And stuck on a hanger in her own personal closet through the rough ride of the mid/late 90's and the scary opening years of the new millennium, Tank Girl didn't die and fade away, she just sobered up, festered, and went a bit smelly.

In 2001, Titan Books in the UK came a-knocking and, over the course of a couple of years, re-vamped and re-published the whole back catalogue. Suddenly people were talking about *Tank Girl* again—people wanted to know where the hell she had disappeared to—so I turned the key and let her out.

And here she is. Different, of course, from when you last saw her, and wild as all hell, but still, deep down, the same ol' gal that we loved and hated and cheered and jeered all those years ago.

Sir Ashley Wood and his noble squire Rufus Dayglo have performed magical rites with my cranky, surreal scripts, and what they have delivered is nothing short of a blizzard of dazzling-mayhem-genius.

This has been a lot of fun for us, and we hope you will enjoy the bumpy ride, too. Keep a look out; we could be driving the tank along this road again soon.

Peace, love, and rock and roll,

Alan C. Martin
Hethpool Stone Circle
College Valley
Northumberland
England
September 2007

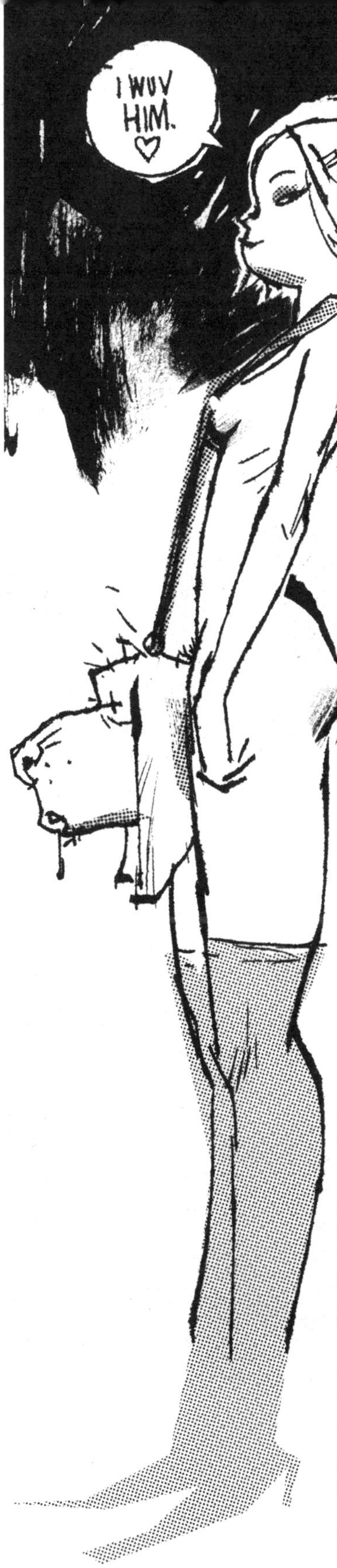
I WUV HIM. ♡

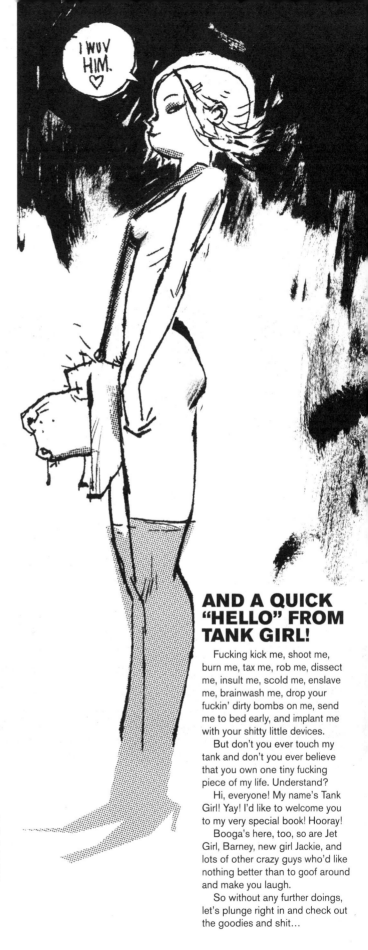

AND A QUICK "HELLO" FROM TANK GIRL!

Fucking kick me, shoot me, burn me, tax me, rob me, dissect me, insult me, scold me, enslave me, brainwash me, drop your fuckin' dirty bombs on me, send me to bed early, and implant me with your shitty little devices.

But don't you ever touch my tank and don't you ever believe that you own one tiny fucking piece of my life. Understand?

Hi, everyone! My name's Tank Girl! Yay! I'd like to welcome you to my very special book! Hooray!

Booga's here, too, so are Jet Girl, Barney, new girl Jackie, and lots of other crazy guys who'd like nothing better than to goof around and make you laugh.

So without any further doings, let's plunge right in and check out the goodies and shit...

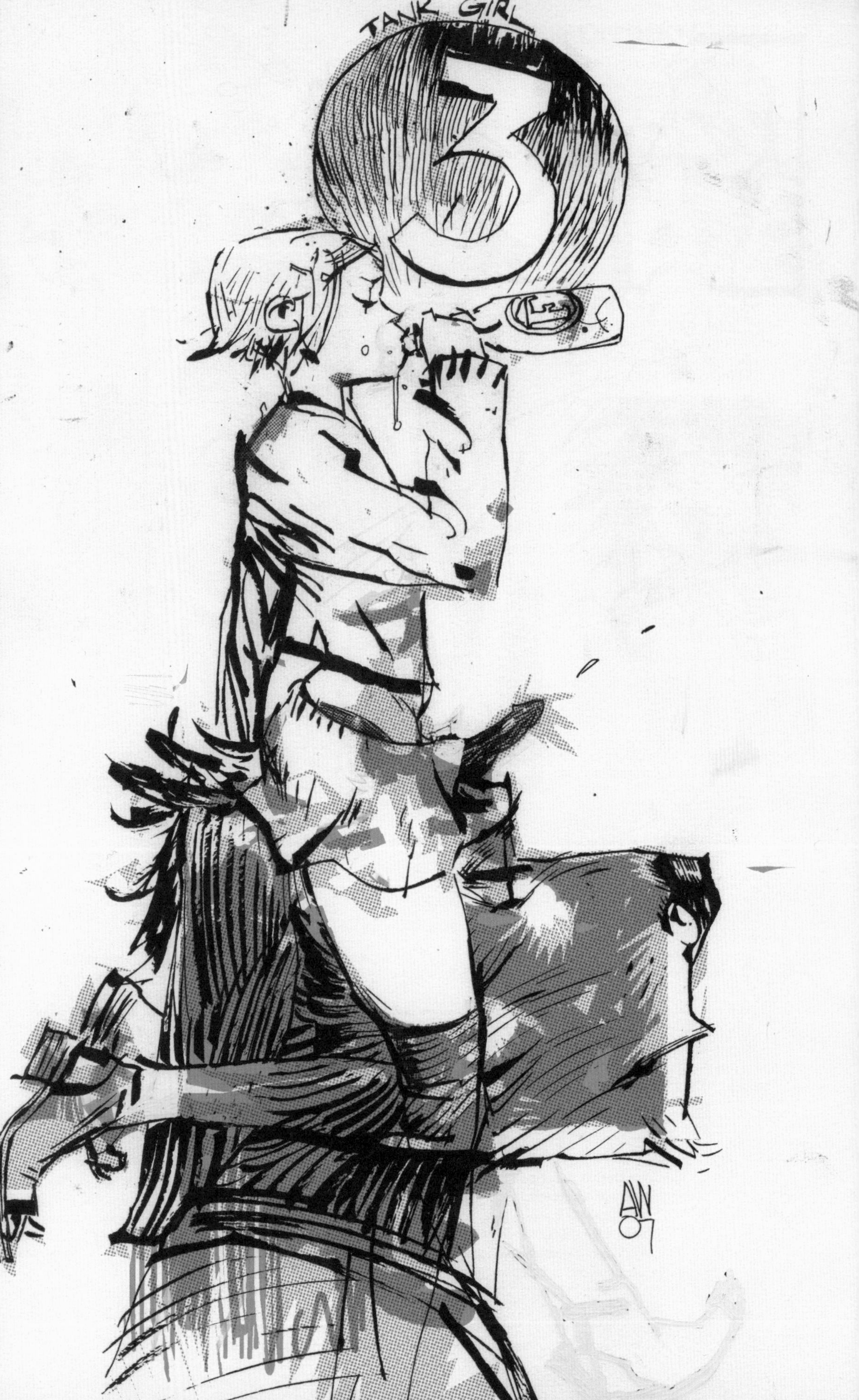
TANK GIRL

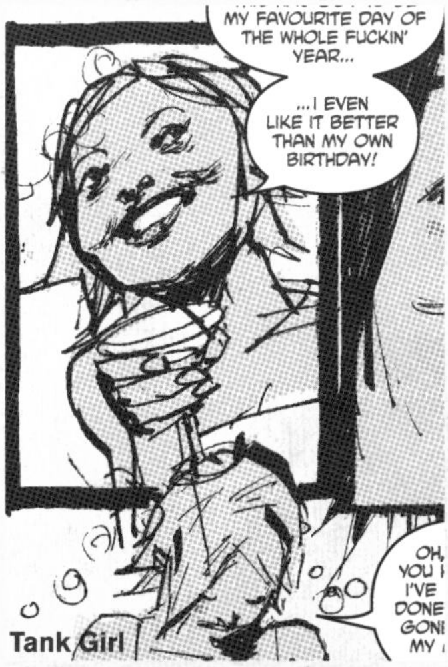
MY FAVOURITE DAY OF THE WHOLE FUCKIN' YEAR...
...I EVEN LIKE IT BETTER THAN MY OWN BIRTHDAY!
Tank Girl

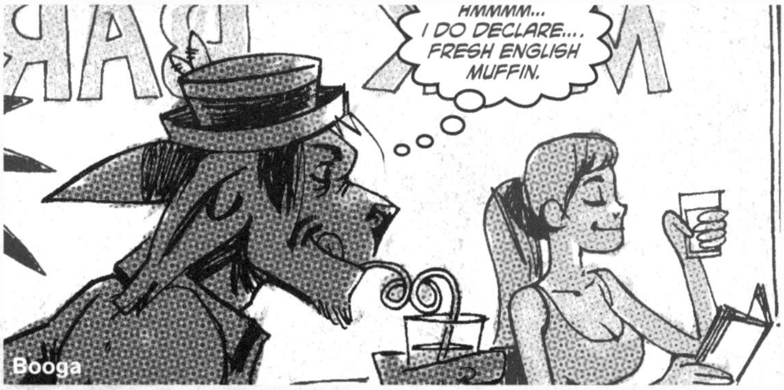
HMMMM... I DO DECLARE.... FRESH ENGLISH MUFFIN.
Booga

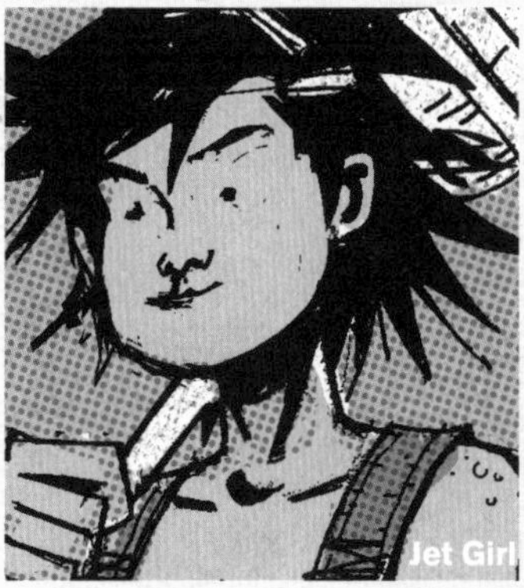
Jet Girl

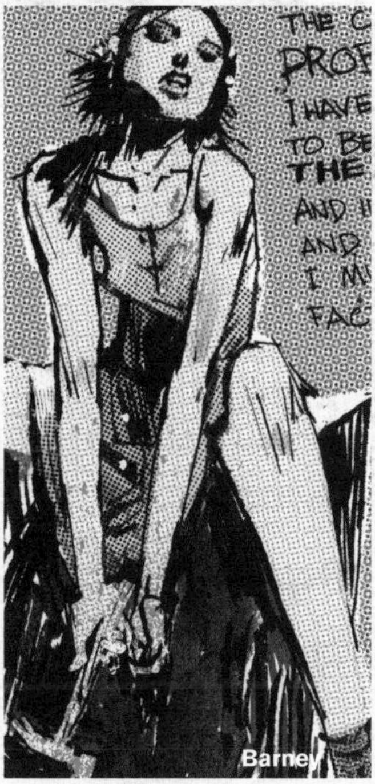
Barney

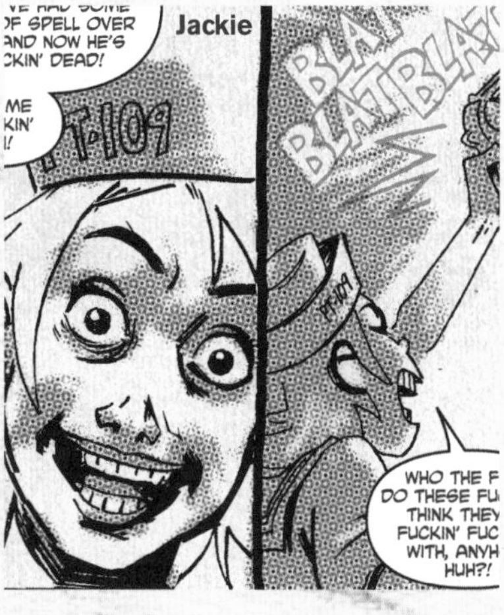
Jackie

Tank Girl n. proper: 1. a girl in a tank. 2. a foul-mouthed, booze-driven maniac with a crappy hair-do and a grenade pin between her teeth.
(from the Oxford Underarm Dictionary)

Welcome.

For the uninitiated we would like to introduce…

Tank Girl – a feisty, sexy, angry, overly fashion-conscious, renegade tank-pilot with a particularly bent sense of humour. She left the army some time ago and took their best tank with her. Likes '76 punk rock, David Niven films, expensive champagne, and tea parties. Collects door knobs. Unsavoury.

Booga – Tank Girl's dopey kangaroo boyfriend. Moved into the tank one day without being invited and has stayed ever since. Often the butt of Tank Girl's jokes, he is always well-meaning and eager to join in on any ridiculous scheme that comes his way. An avid Ramones fan. Randy.

Jet Girl – Tank Girl's best friend. A keen flying enthusiast, she has often broken the sound barrier whilst stoned out of her mind. Owns lots of property and never seems to be short of a few bucks. Dark-haired and skinny, looks good in a jump suit. Likes Yoko Ono. Flaky.

Barney – an escaped mental patient. Ostensibly a pretty, cuddly, and charming girl, she can suddenly turn into a dangerous psychopath. Tank Girl likes to keep her around to add a certain "spice" to her life. Favourite dish – grilled tomatoes. Favourite band – Adam and the Ants. Fishy.

Jackie – Barney's "hairdresser." Has a mess of personal problems to work through, but makes friends easily. Owns a greatly modified World War II motor torpedo boat. Hates Torvill and Dean. Likes Julian Cope. Has an extensive knowledge of antique toy robots. Touchy-feely.

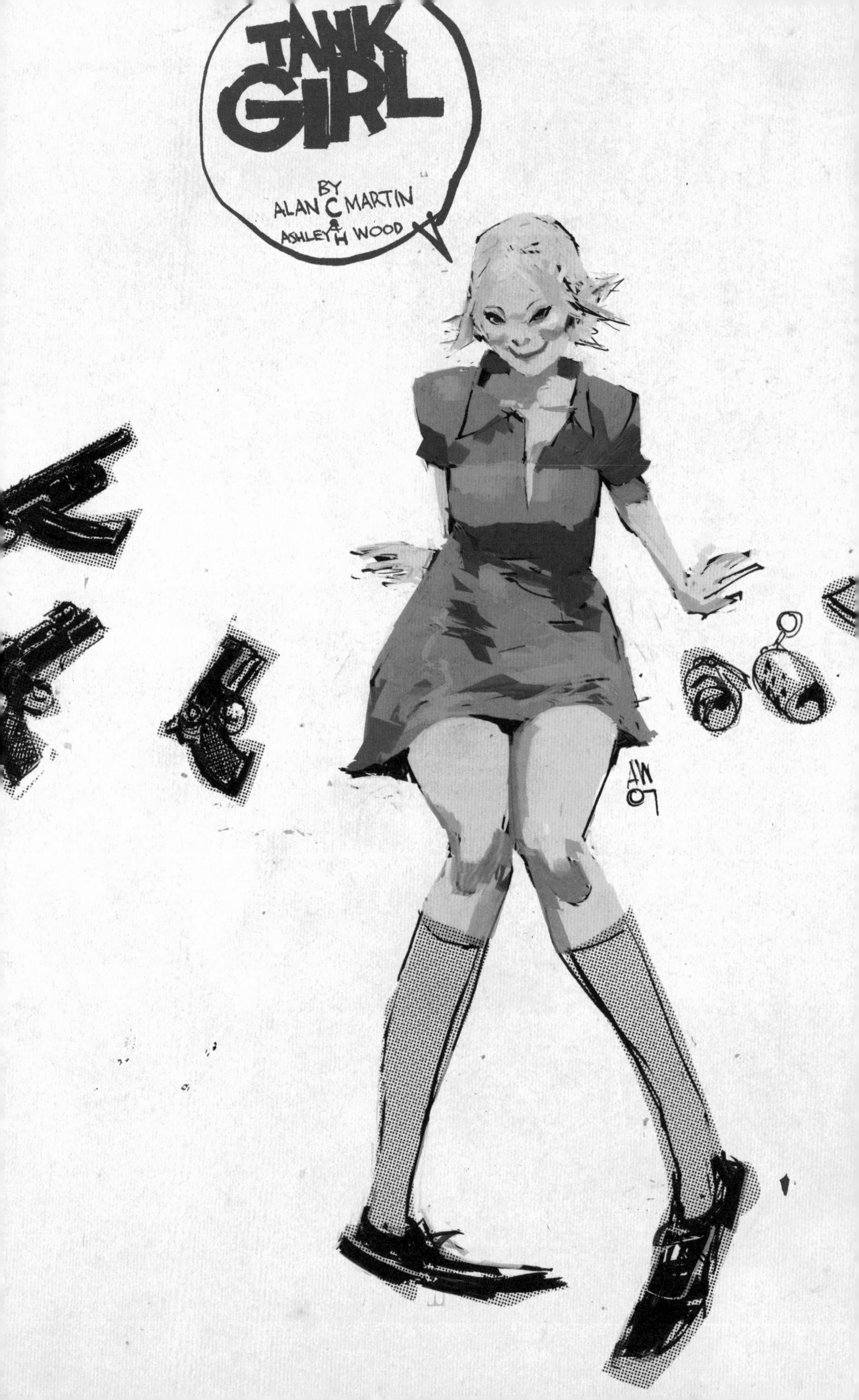
TANK GIRL
BY ALAN C MARTIN & ASHLEY H WOOD
AW 07

ALAN C MARTIN ★ ASHLEY WOOD

TANKGIRL IN THE FUNSTERS WILL PLAY.

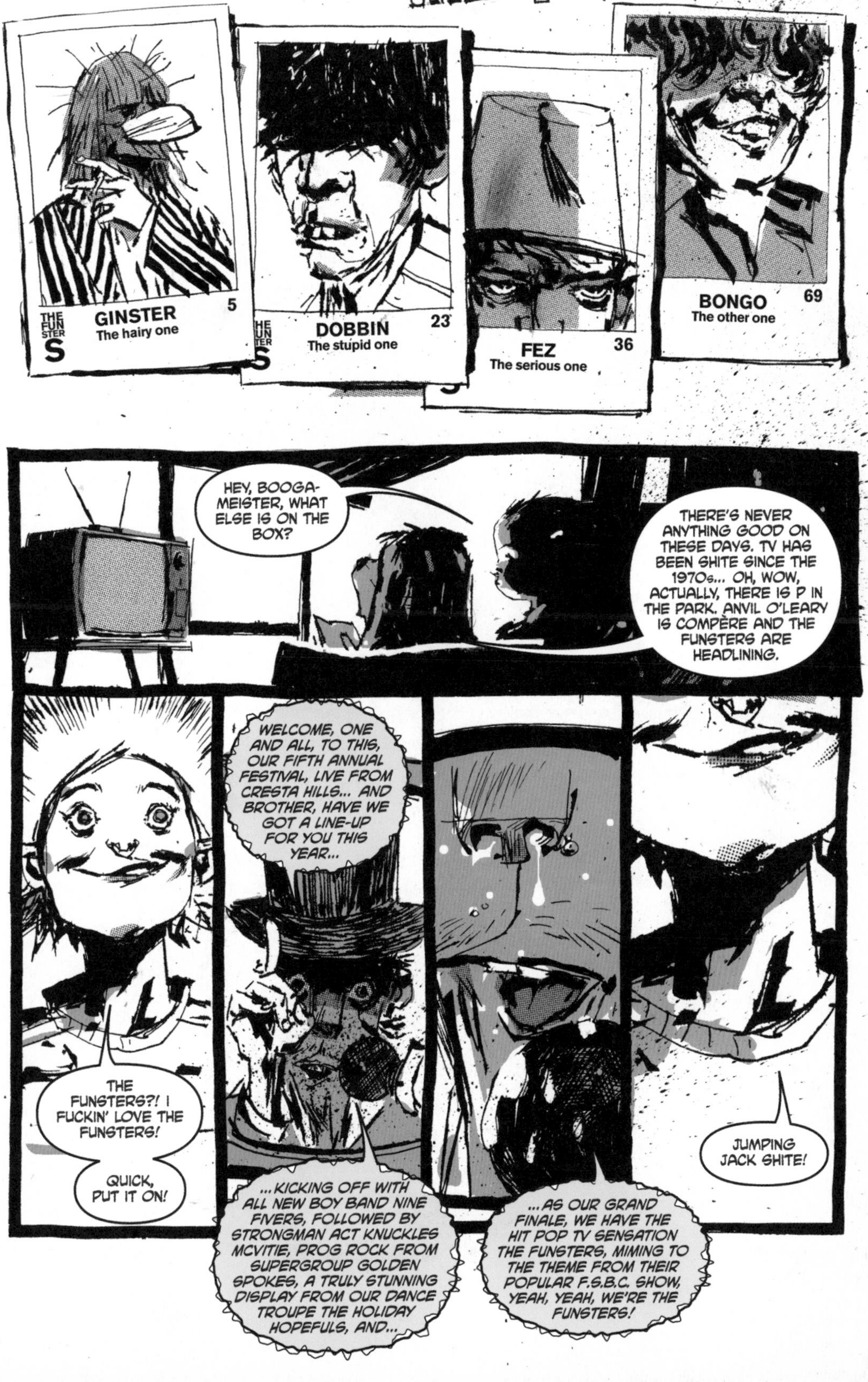
THE FUNSTERS
GINSTER 5
The hairy one
DOBBIN 23
The stupid one
FEZ 36
The serious one
BONGO 69
The other one
HEY, BOOGA-MEISTER, WHAT ELSE IS ON THE BOX?
THERE'S NEVER ANYTHING GOOD ON THESE DAYS. TV HAS BEEN SHITE SINCE THE 1970s... OH, WOW, ACTUALLY, THERE IS P IN THE PARK. ANVIL O'LEARY IS COMPÈRE AND THE FUNSTERS ARE HEADLINING.
THE FUNSTERS?! I FUCKIN' LOVE THE FUNSTERS!
QUICK, PUT IT ON!
WELCOME, ONE AND ALL, TO THIS, OUR FIFTH ANNUAL FESTIVAL, LIVE FROM CRESTA HILLS... AND BROTHER, HAVE WE GOT A LINE-UP FOR YOU THIS YEAR...
...KICKING OFF WITH ALL NEW BOY BAND NINE FIVERS, FOLLOWED BY STRONGMAN ACT KNUCKLES MCVITIE, PROG ROCK FROM SUPERGROUP GOLDEN SPOKES, A TRULY STUNNING DISPLAY FROM OUR DANCE TROUPE THE HOLIDAY HOPEFULS, AND...
...AS OUR GRAND FINALE, WE HAVE THE HIT POP TV SENSATION THE FUNSTERS, MIMING TO THE THEME FROM THEIR POPULAR F.S.B.C. SHOW, YEAH, YEAH, WE'RE THE FUNSTERS!
JUMPING JACK SHITE!

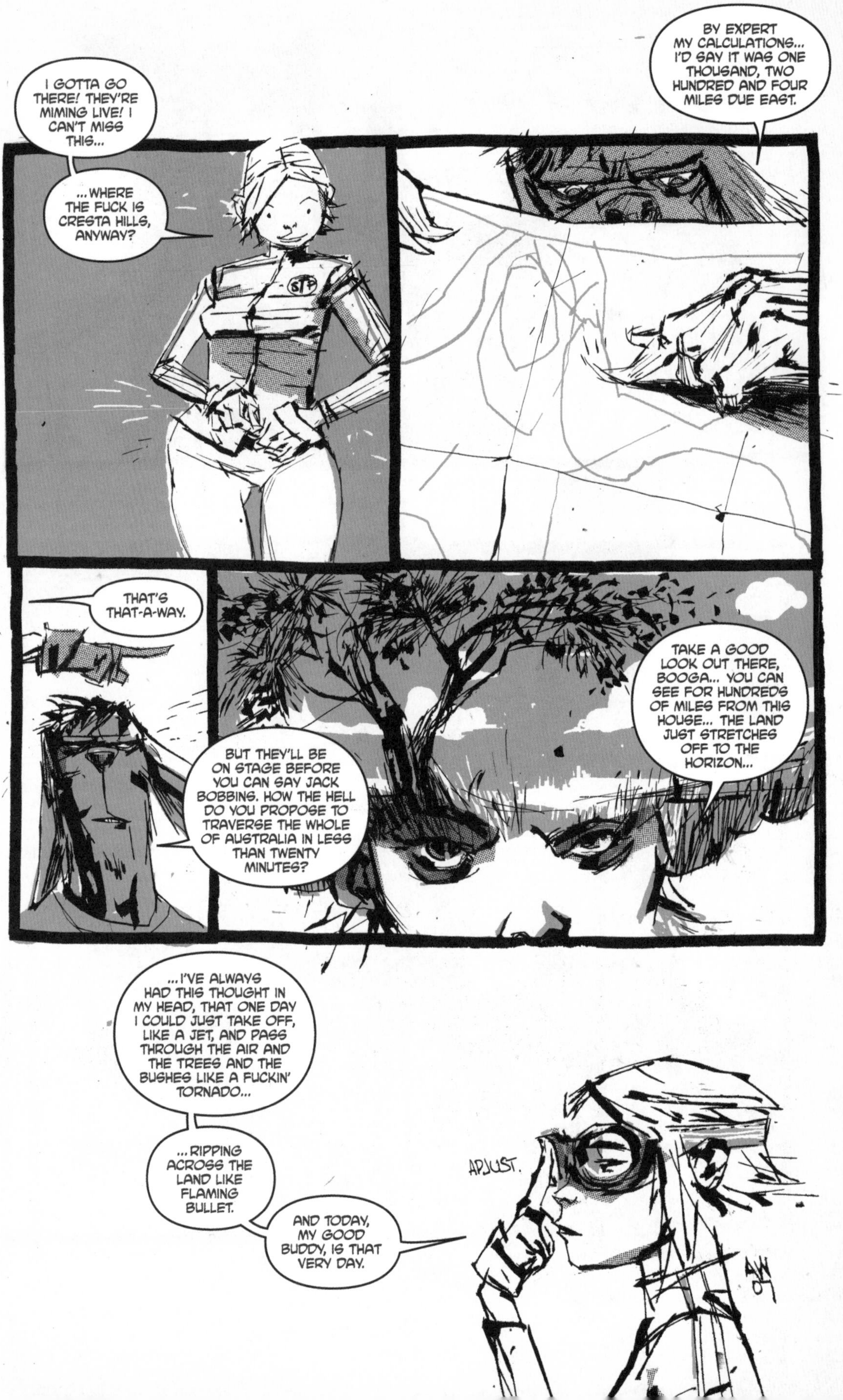
I GOTTA GO THERE! THEY'RE MIMING LIVE! I CAN'T MISS THIS...
...WHERE THE FUCK IS CRESTA HILLS, ANYWAY?
BY EXPERT MY CALCULATIONS... I'D SAY IT WAS ONE THOUSAND, TWO HUNDRED AND FOUR MILES DUE EAST.
THAT'S THAT-A-WAY.
BUT THEY'LL BE ON STAGE BEFORE YOU CAN SAY JACK BOBBING. HOW THE HELL DO YOU PROPOSE TO TRAVERSE THE WHOLE OF AUSTRALIA IN LESS THAN TWENTY MINUTES?
TAKE A GOOD LOOK OUT THERE, BOOGA... YOU CAN SEE FOR HUNDREDS OF MILES FROM THIS HOUSE... THE LAND JUST STRETCHES OFF TO THE HORIZON...
...I'VE ALWAYS HAD THIS THOUGHT IN MY HEAD, THAT ONE DAY I COULD JUST TAKE OFF, LIKE A JET, AND PASS THROUGH THE AIR AND THE TREES AND THE BUSHES LIKE A FUCKIN' TORNADO...
...RIPPING ACROSS THE LAND LIKE FLAMING BULLET.
ADJUST.
AND TODAY, MY GOOD BUDDY, IS THAT VERY DAY.
AW 07

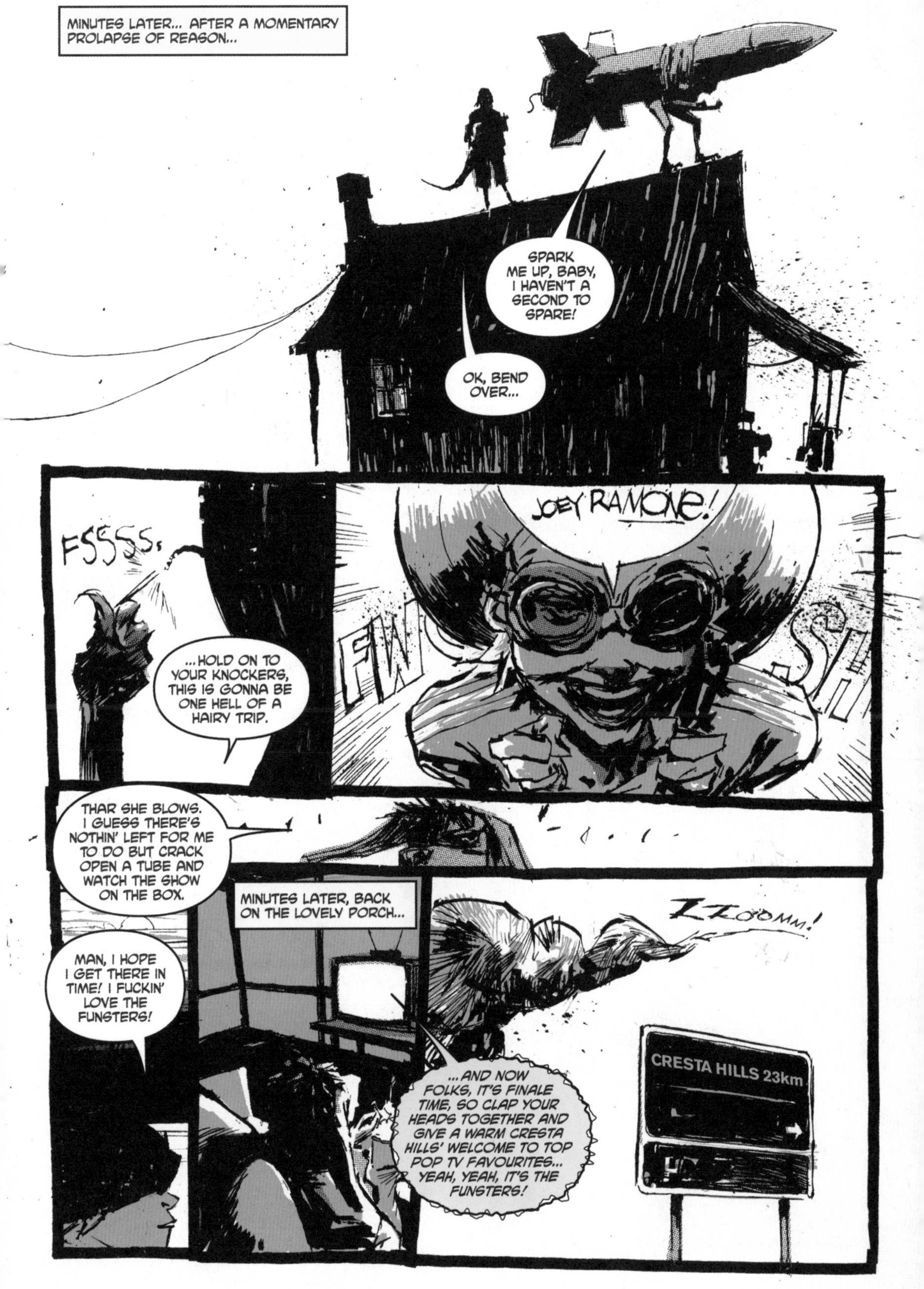
MINUTES LATER... AFTER A MOMENTARY PROLAPSE OF REASON...
SPARK ME UP, BABY, I HAVEN'T A SECOND TO SPARE!
OK, BEND OVER...
FSSSS.
...HOLD ON TO YOUR KNOCKERS, THIS IS GONNA BE ONE HELL OF A HAIRY TRIP.
JOEY RAMONE!
THAR SHE BLOWS. I GUESS THERE'S NOTHIN' LEFT FOR ME TO DO BUT CRACK OPEN A TUBE AND WATCH THE SHOW ON THE BOX.
MINUTES LATER, BACK ON THE LOVELY PORCH...
MAN, I HOPE I GET THERE IN TIME! I FUCKIN' LOVE THE FUNSTERS!
...AND NOW FOLKS, IT'S FINALE TIME, SO CLAP YOUR HEADS TOGETHER AND GIVE A WARM CRESTA HILLS' WELCOME TO TOP POP TV FAVOURITES... YEAH, YEAH, IT'S THE FUNSTERS!
ZZOOMM!
CRESTA HILLS 23km

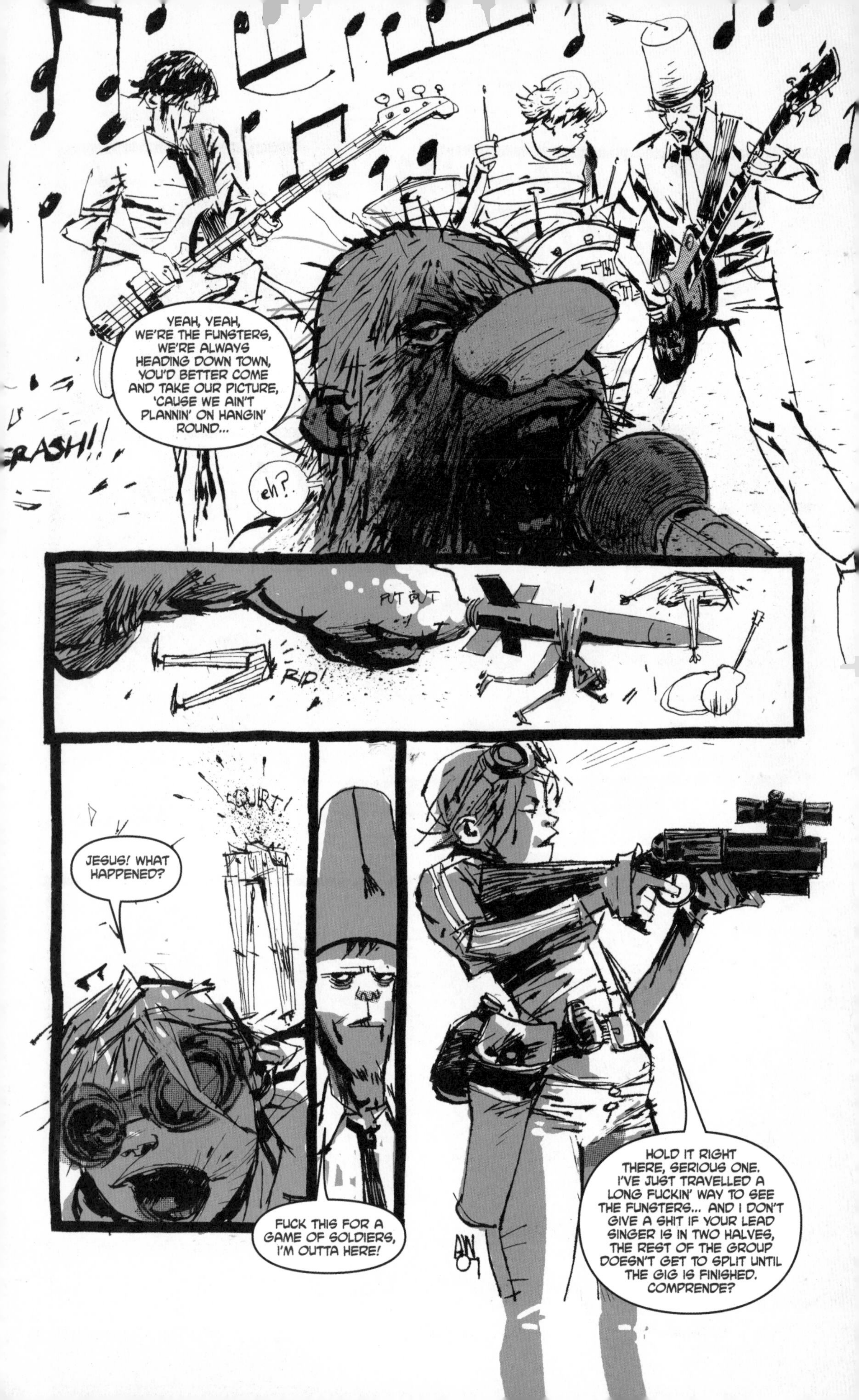

YEAH, YEAH, WE'RE THE FUNSTERS, WE'RE ALWAYS HEADING DOWN TOWN, YOU'D BETTER COME AND TAKE OUR PICTURE, 'CAUSE WE AIN'T PLANNIN' ON HANGIN' ROUND...
RASH!!
eh?
PUT PUT
RIP!
SQUIRT!
JESUS! WHAT HAPPENED?
FUCK THIS FOR A GAME OF SOLDIERS, I'M OUTTA HERE!
HOLD IT RIGHT THERE, SERIOUS ONE. I'VE JUST TRAVELLED A LONG FUCKIN' WAY TO SEE THE FUNSTERS... AND I DON'T GIVE A SHIT IF YOUR LEAD SINGER IS IN TWO HALVES, THE REST OF THE GROUP DOESN'T GET TO SPLIT UNTIL THE GIG IS FINISHED. COMPRENDE?

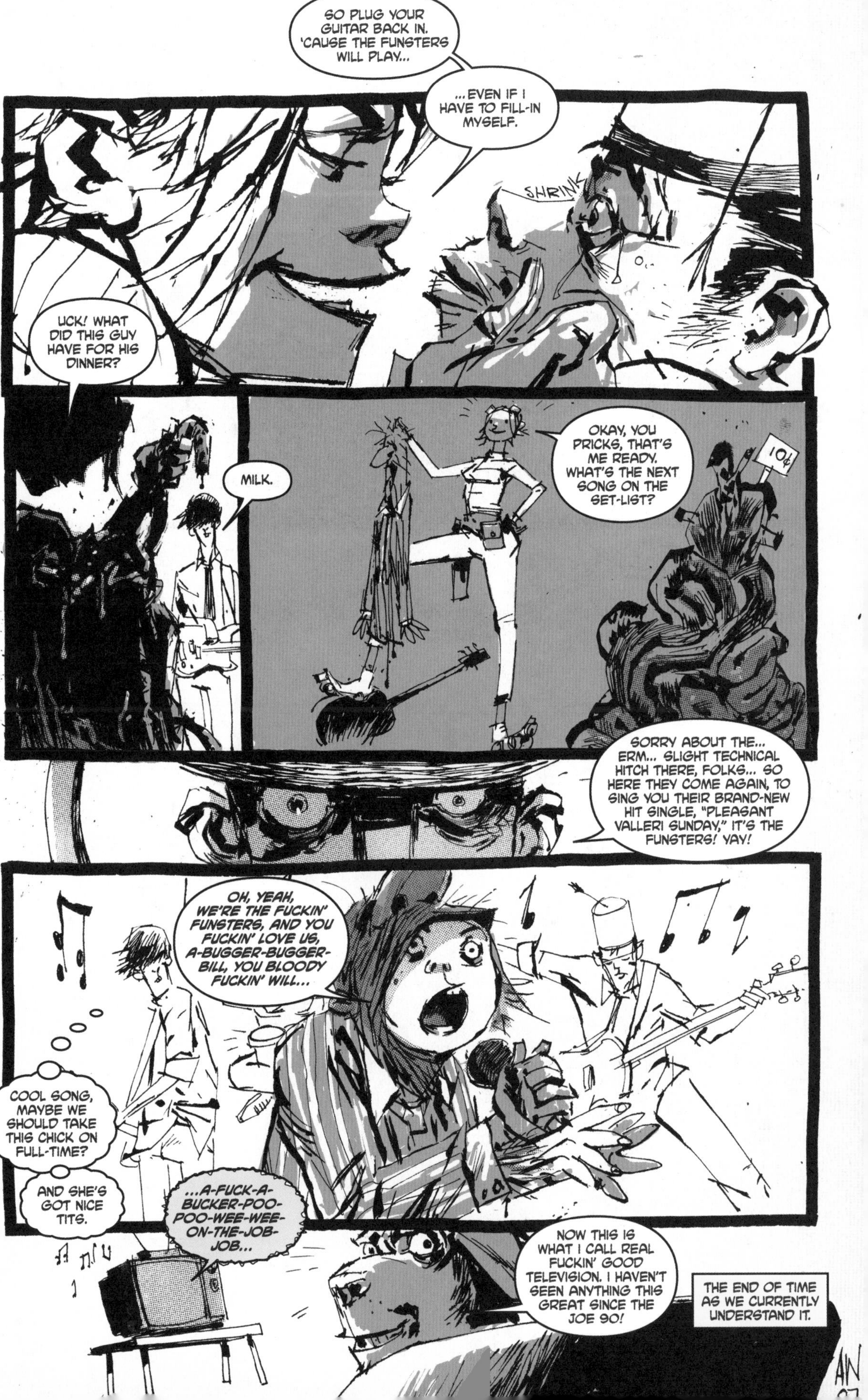

SO PLUG YOUR GUITAR BACK IN. 'CAUSE THE FUNSTERS WILL PLAY...
...EVEN IF I HAVE TO FILL-IN MYSELF.
SHRINK
UCK! WHAT DID THIS GUY HAVE FOR HIS DINNER?
MILK.
OKAY, YOU PRICKS, THAT'S ME READY. WHAT'S THE NEXT SONG ON THE SET-LIST?
10¢
SORRY ABOUT THE... ERM... SLIGHT TECHNICAL HITCH THERE, FOLKS... SO HERE THEY COME AGAIN, TO SING YOU THEIR BRAND-NEW HIT SINGLE, "PLEASANT VALLERI SUNDAY," IT'S THE FUNSTERS! YAY!
OH, YEAH, WE'RE THE FUCKIN' FUNSTERS, AND YOU FUCKIN' LOVE US, A-BUGGER-BUGGER-BILL, YOU BLOODY FUCKIN' WILL...
COOL SONG, MAYBE WE SHOULD TAKE THIS CHICK ON FULL-TIME?
AND SHE'S GOT NICE TITS.
...A-FUCK-A-BUCKER-POO-POO-WEE-WEE-ON-THE-JOB-JOB...
NOW THIS IS WHAT I CALL REAL FUCKIN' GOOD TELEVISION. I HAVEN'T SEEN ANYTHING THIS GREAT SINCE THE JOE 90!
THE END OF TIME AS WE CURRENTLY UNDERSTAND IT.

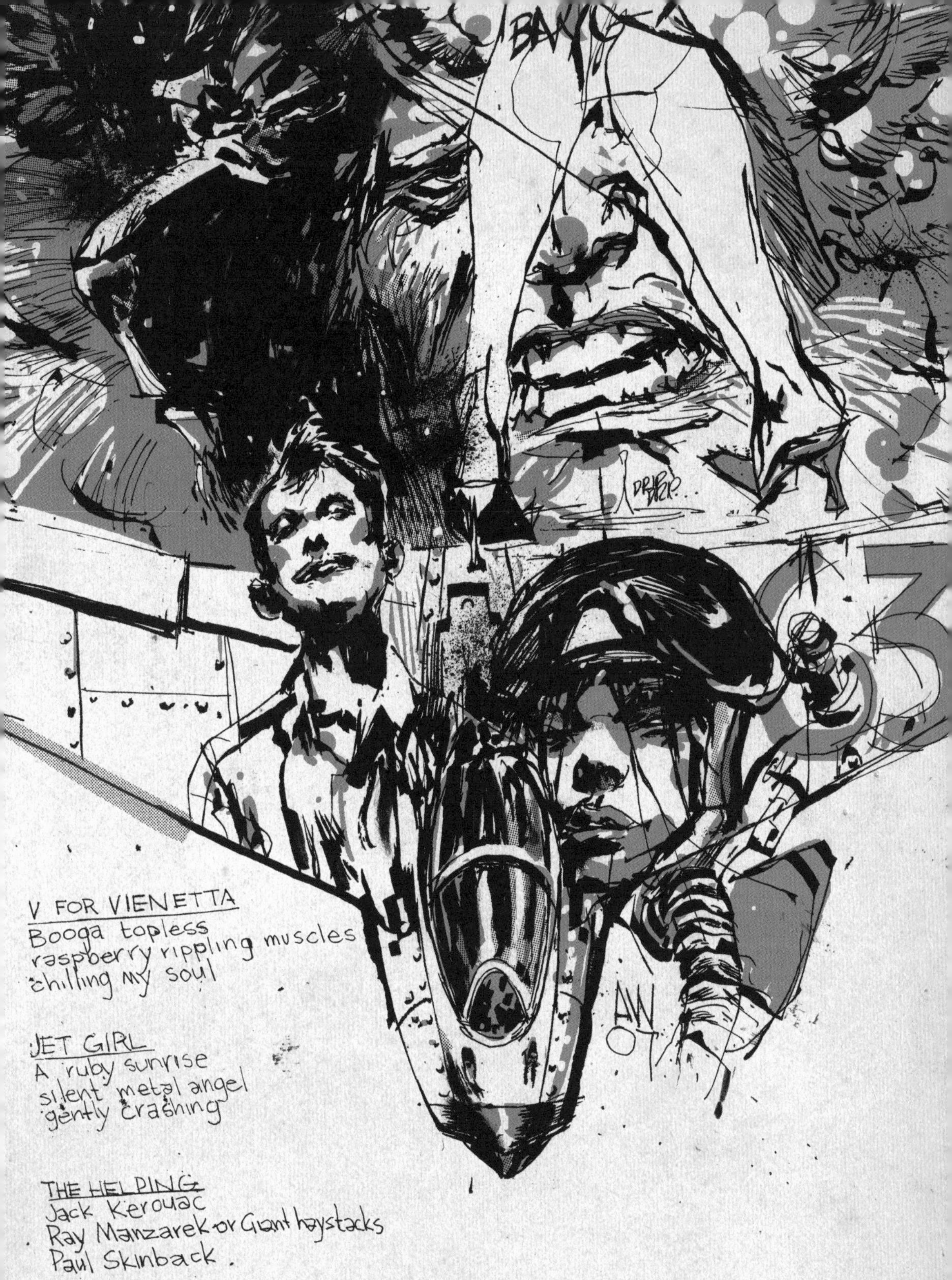

V FOR VIENETTA
Booga topless
raspberry rippling muscles
chilling my soul

JET GIRL
A ruby sunrise
silent metal angel
gently crashing

THE HELPING
Jack Kerouac
Ray Manzarek or Giant haystacks
Paul Skinback.

BARNEY
DRUNKEN SUNSET
empty bottle hits stone
still pissing

THE BLUE MICRODOT
Undercover
the man with two shits-
blowing my mind to bits

TANK GIRL HAIKU

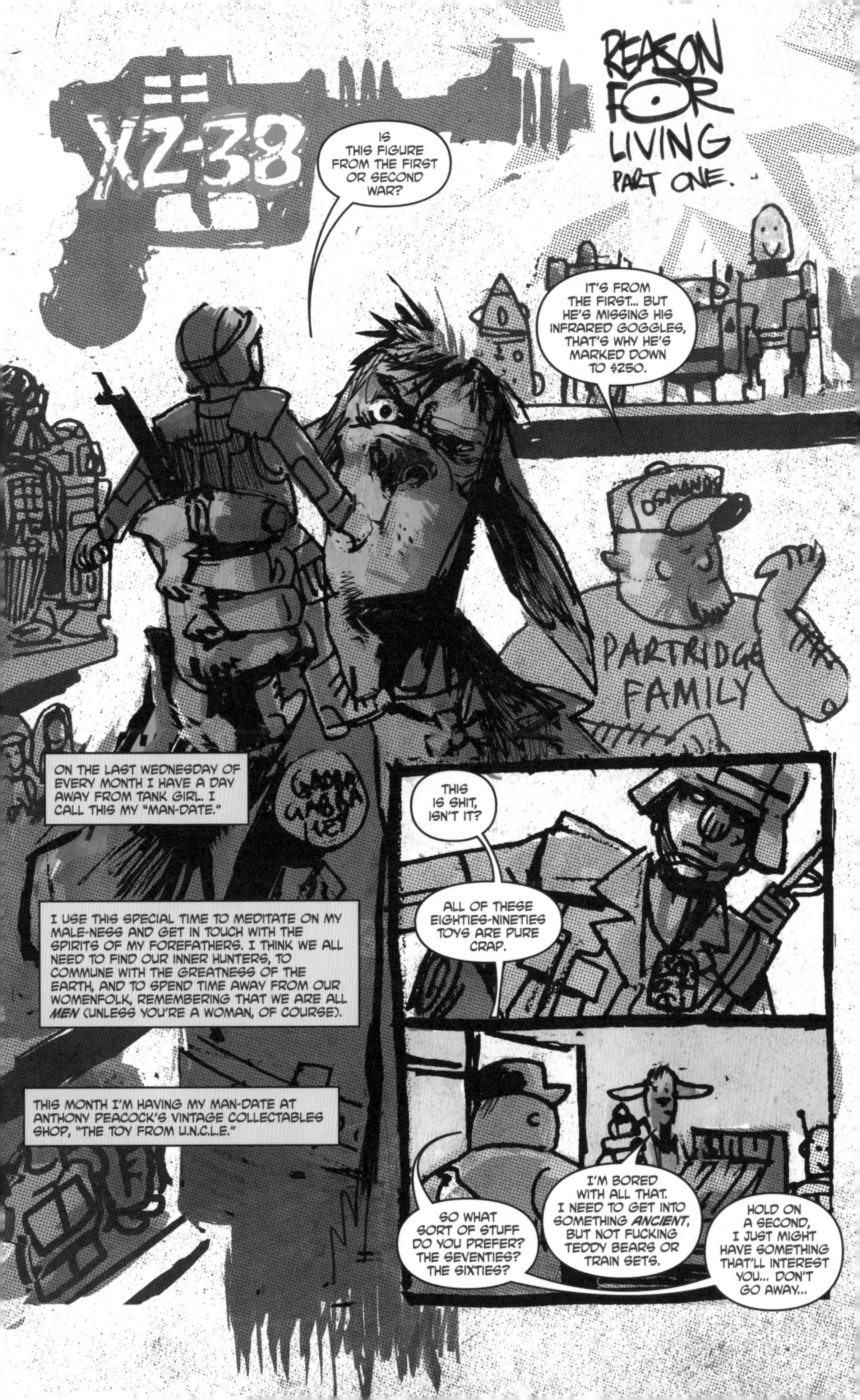
XZ-38
REASON FOR LIVING PART ONE.
IS THIS FIGURE FROM THE FIRST OR SECOND WAR?
IT'S FROM THE FIRST... BUT HE'S MISSING HIS INFRARED GOGGLES, THAT'S WHY HE'S MARKED DOWN TO $250.
PARTRIDGE FAMILY
ON THE LAST WEDNESDAY OF EVERY MONTH I HAVE A DAY AWAY FROM TANK GIRL. I CALL THIS MY "MAN-DATE."
THIS IS SHIT, ISN'T IT?
ALL OF THESE EIGHTIES-NINETIES TOYS ARE PURE CRAP.
I USE THIS SPECIAL TIME TO MEDITATE ON MY MALE-NESS AND GET IN TOUCH WITH THE SPIRITS OF MY FOREFATHERS. I THINK WE ALL NEED TO FIND OUR INNER HUNTERS, TO COMMUNE WITH THE GREATNESS OF THE EARTH, AND TO SPEND TIME AWAY FROM OUR WOMENFOLK, REMEMBERING THAT WE ARE ALL *MEN* (UNLESS YOU'RE A WOMAN, OF COURSE).
THIS MONTH I'M HAVING MY MAN-DATE AT ANTHONY PEACOCK'S VINTAGE COLLECTABLES SHOP, "THE TOY FROM U.N.C.L.E."
SO WHAT SORT OF STUFF DO YOU PREFER? THE SEVENTIES? THE SIXTIES?
I'M BORED WITH ALL THAT. I NEED TO GET INTO SOMETHING *ANCIENT*, BUT NOT FUCKING TEDDY BEARS OR TRAIN SETS.
HOLD ON A SECOND, I JUST MIGHT HAVE SOMETHING THAT'LL INTEREST YOU... DON'T GO AWAY...

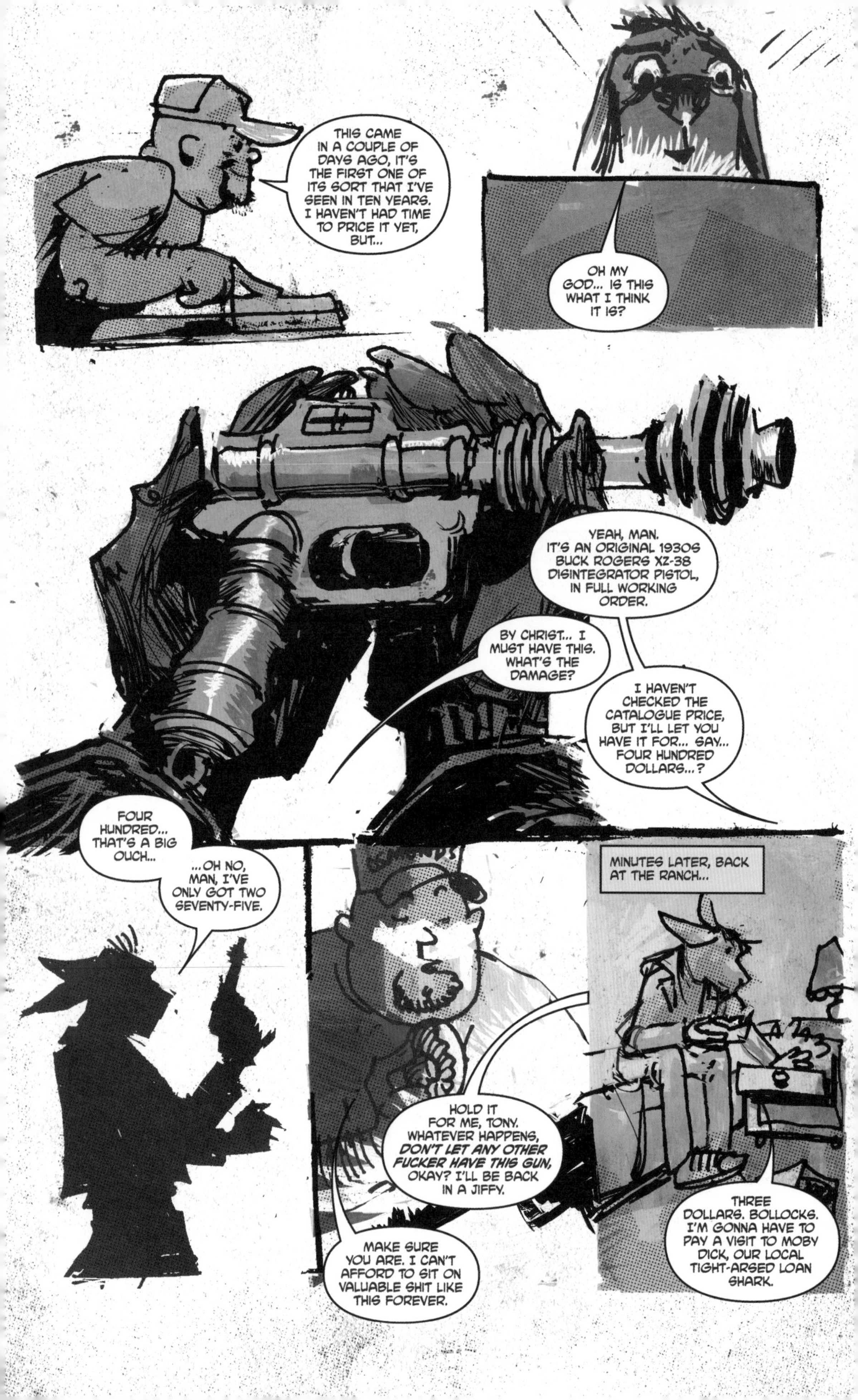
THIS CAME IN A COUPLE OF DAYS AGO, IT'S THE FIRST ONE OF ITS SORT THAT I'VE SEEN IN TEN YEARS. I HAVEN'T HAD TIME TO PRICE IT YET, BUT...
OH MY GOD... IS THIS WHAT I THINK IT IS?
YEAH, MAN. IT'S AN ORIGINAL 1930S BUCK ROGERS XZ-38 DISINTEGRATOR PISTOL, IN FULL WORKING ORDER.
BY CHRIST... I MUST HAVE THIS. WHAT'S THE DAMAGE?
I HAVEN'T CHECKED THE CATALOGUE PRICE, BUT I'LL LET YOU HAVE IT FOR... SAY... FOUR HUNDRED DOLLARS...?
FOUR HUNDRED... THAT'S A BIG OUCH...
...OH NO, MAN, I'VE ONLY GOT TWO SEVENTY-FIVE.
HOLD IT FOR ME, TONY. WHATEVER HAPPENS, *DON'T LET ANY OTHER FUCKER HAVE THIS GUN,* OKAY? I'LL BE BACK IN A JIFFY.
MAKE SURE YOU ARE. I CAN'T AFFORD TO SIT ON VALUABLE SHIT LIKE THIS FOREVER.
MINUTES LATER, BACK AT THE RANCH...
THREE DOLLARS. BOLLOCKS. I'M GONNA HAVE TO PAY A VISIT TO MOBY DICK, OUR LOCAL TIGHT-ARSED LOAN SHARK.

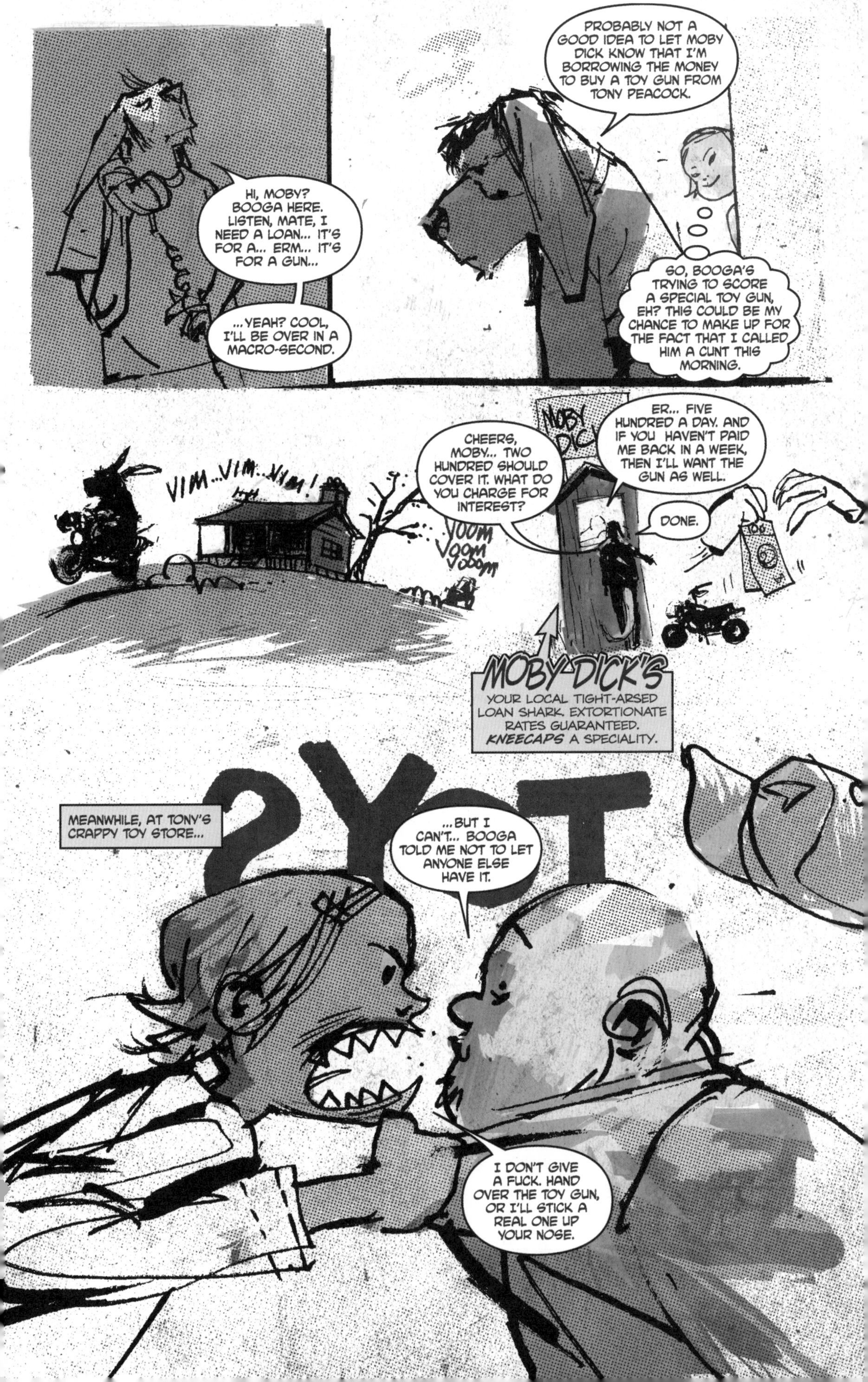
HI, MOBY? BOOGA HERE. LISTEN, MATE, I NEED A LOAN... IT'S FOR A... ERM... IT'S FOR A GUN...
...YEAH? COOL, I'LL BE OVER IN A MACRO-SECOND.
PROBABLY NOT A GOOD IDEA TO LET MOBY DICK KNOW THAT I'M BORROWING THE MONEY TO BUY A TOY GUN FROM TONY PEACOCK.
SO, BOOGA'S TRYING TO SCORE A SPECIAL TOY GUN, EH? THIS COULD BE MY CHANCE TO MAKE UP FOR THE FACT THAT I CALLED HIM A CUNT THIS MORNING.
VIM...VIM...VIM!
MOBY DICK
CHEERS, MOBY... TWO HUNDRED SHOULD COVER IT. WHAT DO YOU CHARGE FOR INTEREST?
ER... FIVE HUNDRED A DAY. AND IF YOU HAVEN'T PAID ME BACK IN A WEEK, THEN I'LL WANT THE GUN AS WELL.
DONE.
VOOM VOOM VOOM
MOBY DICK'S
YOUR LOCAL TIGHT-ARSED LOAN SHARK. EXTORTIONATE RATES GUARANTEED. KNEECAPS A SPECIALITY.
MEANWHILE, AT TONY'S CRAPPY TOY STORE...
...BUT I CAN'T... BOOGA TOLD ME NOT TO LET ANYONE ELSE HAVE IT.
I DON'T GIVE A FUCK. HAND OVER THE TOY GUN, OR I'LL STICK A REAL ONE UP YOUR NOSE.

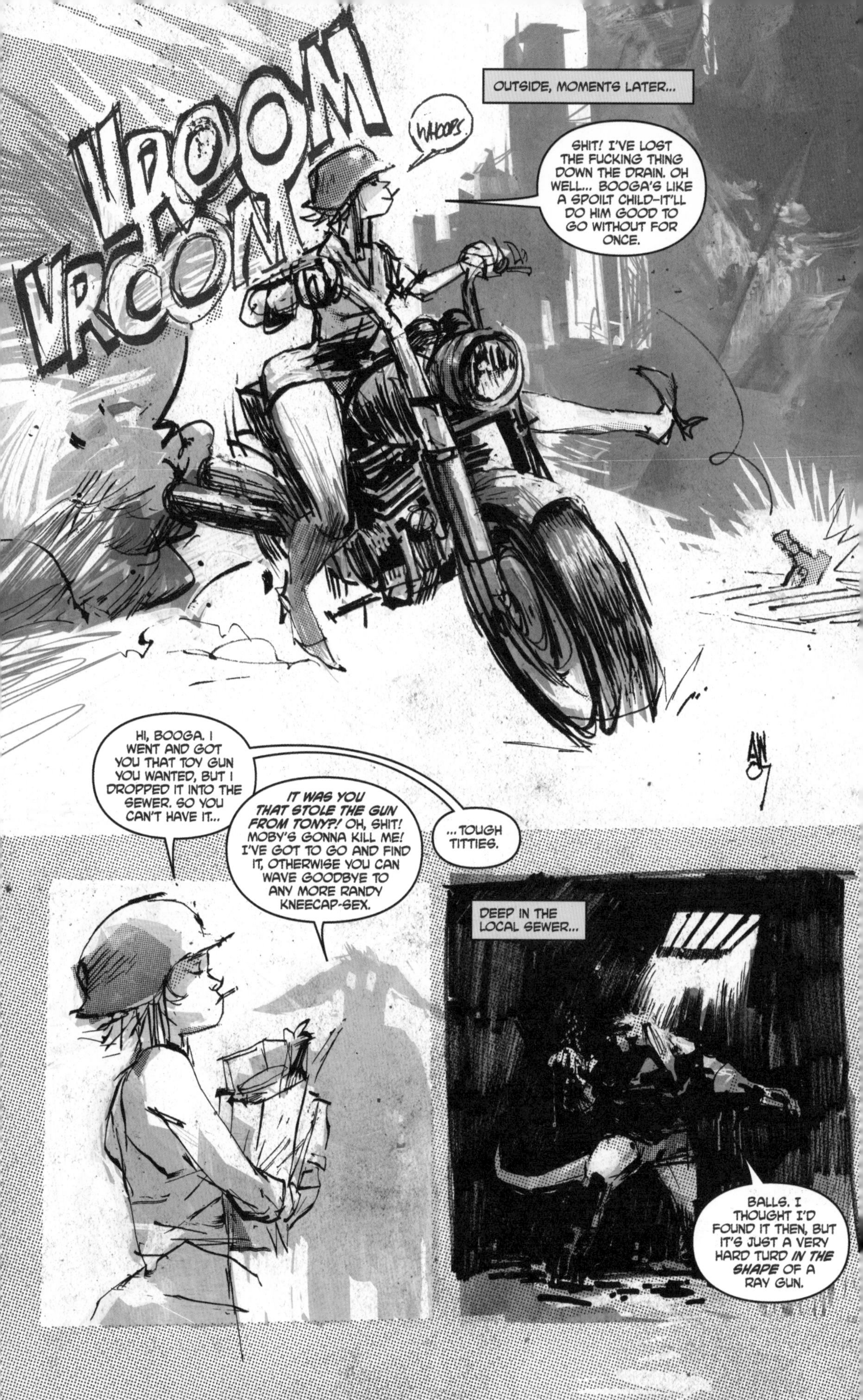
OUTSIDE, MOMENTS LATER...
VROOM
VROOM
WHOOPS.
SHIT! I'VE LOST THE FUCKING THING DOWN THE DRAIN. OH WELL... BOOGA'S LIKE A SPOILT CHILD–IT'LL DO HIM GOOD TO GO WITHOUT FOR ONCE.
HI, BOOGA. I WENT AND GOT YOU THAT TOY GUN YOU WANTED, BUT I DROPPED IT INTO THE SEWER. SO YOU CAN'T HAVE IT...
IT WAS YOU THAT STOLE THE GUN FROM TONY?! OH, SHIT! MOBY'S GONNA KILL ME! I'VE GOT TO GO AND FIND IT, OTHERWISE YOU CAN WAVE GOODBYE TO ANY MORE RANDY KNEECAP-SEX.
...TOUGH TITTIES.
DEEP IN THE LOCAL SEWER...
BALLS. I THOUGHT I'D FOUND IT THEN, BUT IT'S JUST A VERY HARD TURD IN THE SHAPE OF A RAY GUN.

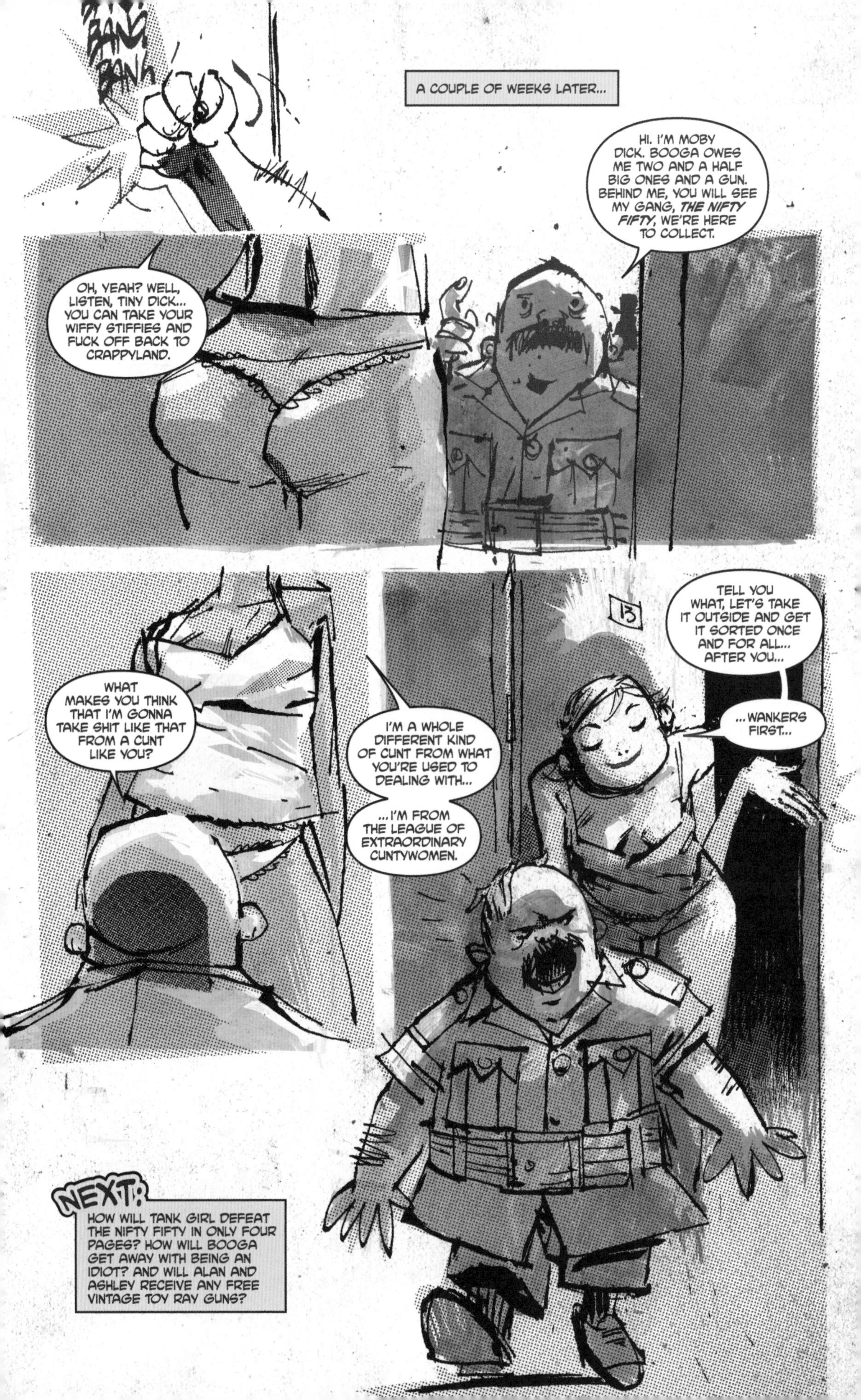
BANG
BANG
A COUPLE OF WEEKS LATER...
HI. I'M MOBY DICK. BOOGA OWES ME TWO AND A HALF BIG ONES AND A GUN. BEHIND ME, YOU WILL SEE MY GANG, *THE NIFTY FIFTY*, WE'RE HERE TO COLLECT.
OH, YEAH? WELL, LISTEN, TINY DICK... YOU CAN TAKE YOUR WIFFY STIFFIES AND FUCK OFF BACK TO CRAPPYLAND.
WHAT MAKES YOU THINK THAT I'M GONNA TAKE SHIT LIKE THAT FROM A CUNT LIKE YOU?
I'M A WHOLE DIFFERENT KIND OF CUNT FROM WHAT YOU'RE USED TO DEALING WITH...
...I'M FROM THE LEAGUE OF EXTRAORDINARY CUNTYWOMEN.
13
TELL YOU WHAT, LET'S TAKE IT OUTSIDE AND GET IT SORTED ONCE AND FOR ALL... AFTER YOU...
...WANKERS FIRST...
NEXT:
HOW WILL TANK GIRL DEFEAT THE NIFTY FIFTY IN ONLY FOUR PAGES? HOW WILL BOOGA GET AWAY WITH BEING AN IDIOT? AND WILL ALAN AND ASHLEY RECEIVE ANY FREE VINTAGE TOY RAY GUNS?

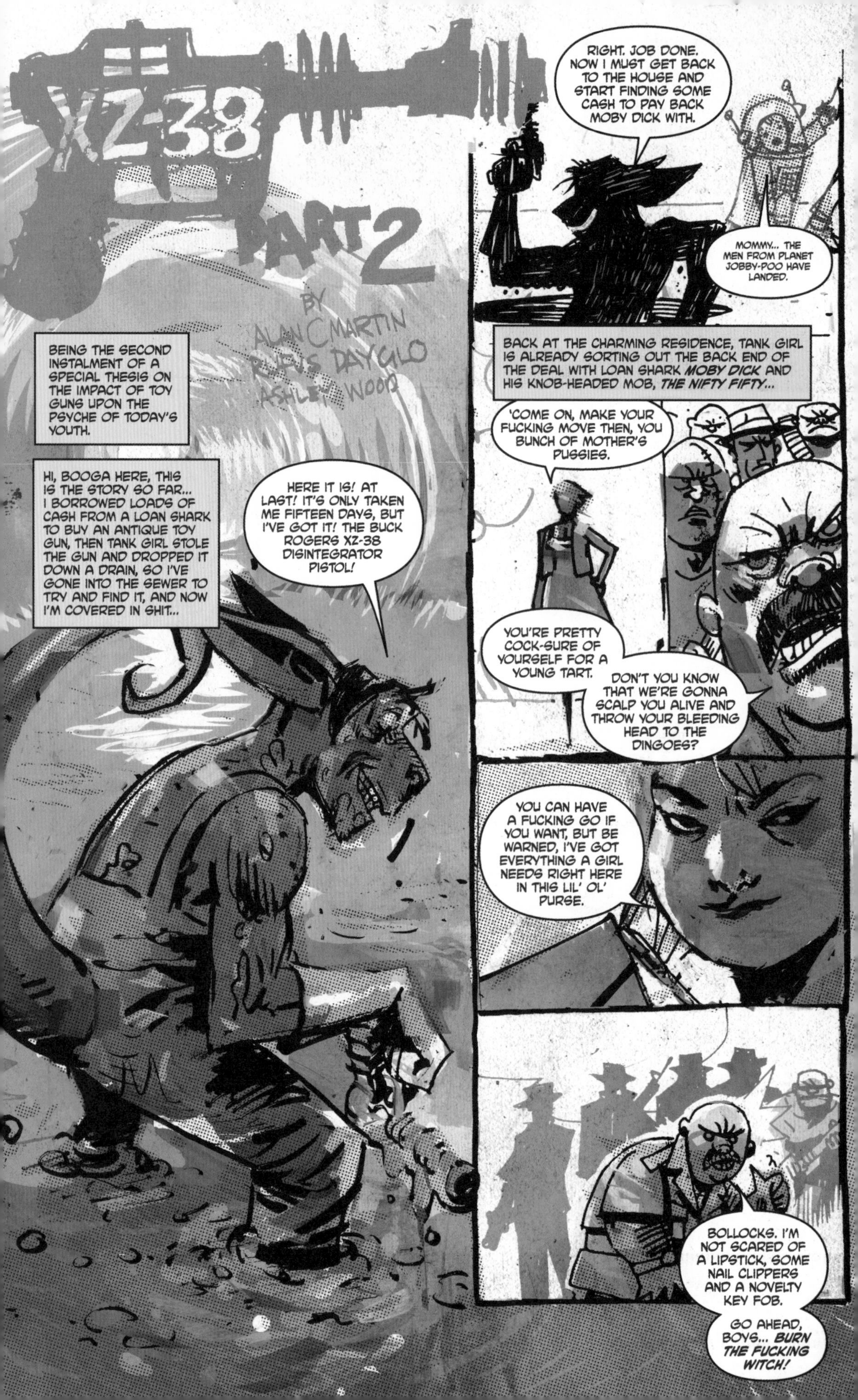
XZ-38
PART 2
BY ALAN C MARTIN RUFUS DAYGLO ASHLEY WOOD
BEING THE SECOND INSTALMENT OF A SPECIAL THESIS ON THE IMPACT OF TOY GUNS UPON THE PSYCHE OF TODAY'S YOUTH.
HI, BOOGA HERE, THIS IS THE STORY SO FAR... I BORROWED LOADS OF CASH FROM A LOAN SHARK TO BUY AN ANTIQUE TOY GUN, THEN TANK GIRL STOLE THE GUN AND DROPPED IT DOWN A DRAIN, SO I'VE GONE INTO THE SEWER TO TRY AND FIND IT, AND NOW I'M COVERED IN SHIT...
HERE IT IS! AT LAST! IT'S ONLY TAKEN ME FIFTEEN DAYS, BUT I'VE GOT IT! THE BUCK ROGERS XZ-38 DISINTEGRATOR PISTOL!
RIGHT. JOB DONE. NOW I MUST GET BACK TO THE HOUSE AND START FINDING SOME CASH TO PAY BACK MOBY DICK WITH.
MOMMY... THE MEN FROM PLANET JOBBY-POO HAVE LANDED.
BACK AT THE CHARMING RESIDENCE, TANK GIRL IS ALREADY SORTING OUT THE BACK END OF THE DEAL WITH LOAN SHARK *MOBY DICK* AND HIS KNOB-HEADED MOB, *THE NIFTY FIFTY*...
'COME ON, MAKE YOUR FUCKING MOVE THEN, YOU BUNCH OF MOTHER'S PUSSIES.
YOU'RE PRETTY COCK-SURE OF YOURSELF FOR A YOUNG TART.
DON'T YOU KNOW THAT WE'RE GONNA SCALP YOU ALIVE AND THROW YOUR BLEEDING HEAD TO THE DINGOES?
YOU CAN HAVE A FUCKING GO IF YOU WANT, BUT BE WARNED, I'VE GOT EVERYTHING A GIRL NEEDS RIGHT HERE IN THIS LIL' OL' PURSE.
BOLLOCKS. I'M NOT SCARED OF A LIPSTICK, SOME NAIL CLIPPERS AND A NOVELTY KEY FOB.
GO AHEAD, BOYS... *BURN THE FUCKING WITCH!*

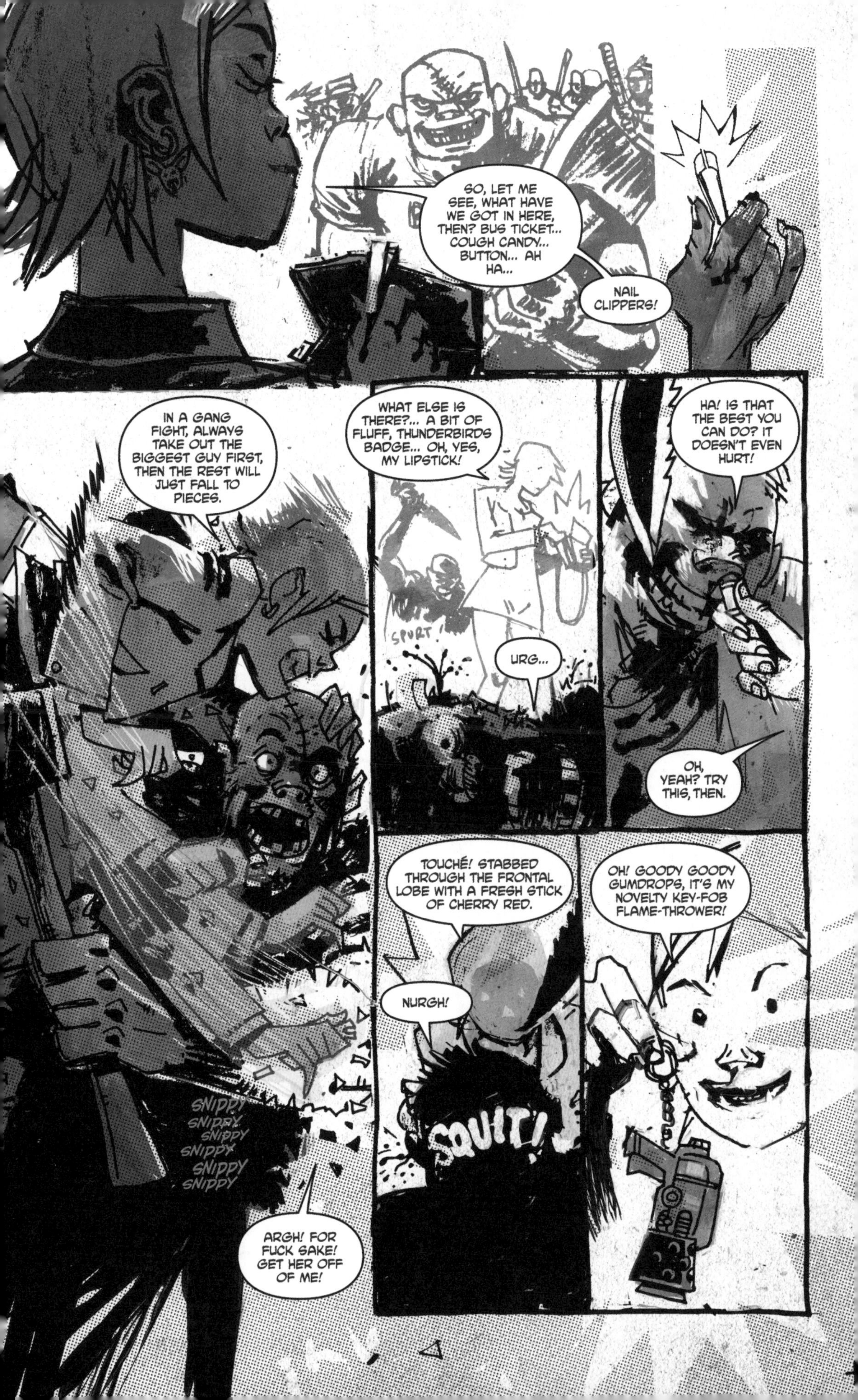
SO, LET ME SEE, WHAT HAVE WE GOT IN HERE, THEN? BUS TICKET... COUGH CANDY... BUTTON... AH HA...
NAIL CLIPPERS!
IN A GANG FIGHT, ALWAYS TAKE OUT THE BIGGEST GUY FIRST, THEN THE REST WILL JUST FALL TO PIECES.
SNIPPY SNIPPY SNIPPY SNIPPY SNIPPY SNIPPY
ARGH! FOR FUCK SAKE! GET HER OFF OF ME!
WHAT ELSE IS THERE?... A BIT OF FLUFF, THUNDERBIRDS BADGE... OH, YES, MY LIPSTICK!
SPURT!
URG...
HA! IS THAT THE BEST YOU CAN DO? IT DOESN'T EVEN HURT!
OH, YEAH? TRY THIS, THEN.
TOUCHÉ! STABBED THROUGH THE FRONTAL LOBE WITH A FRESH STICK OF CHERRY RED.
NURGH!
SQUIT!
OH! GOODY GOODY GUMDROPS, IT'S MY NOVELTY KEY-FOB FLAME-THROWER!

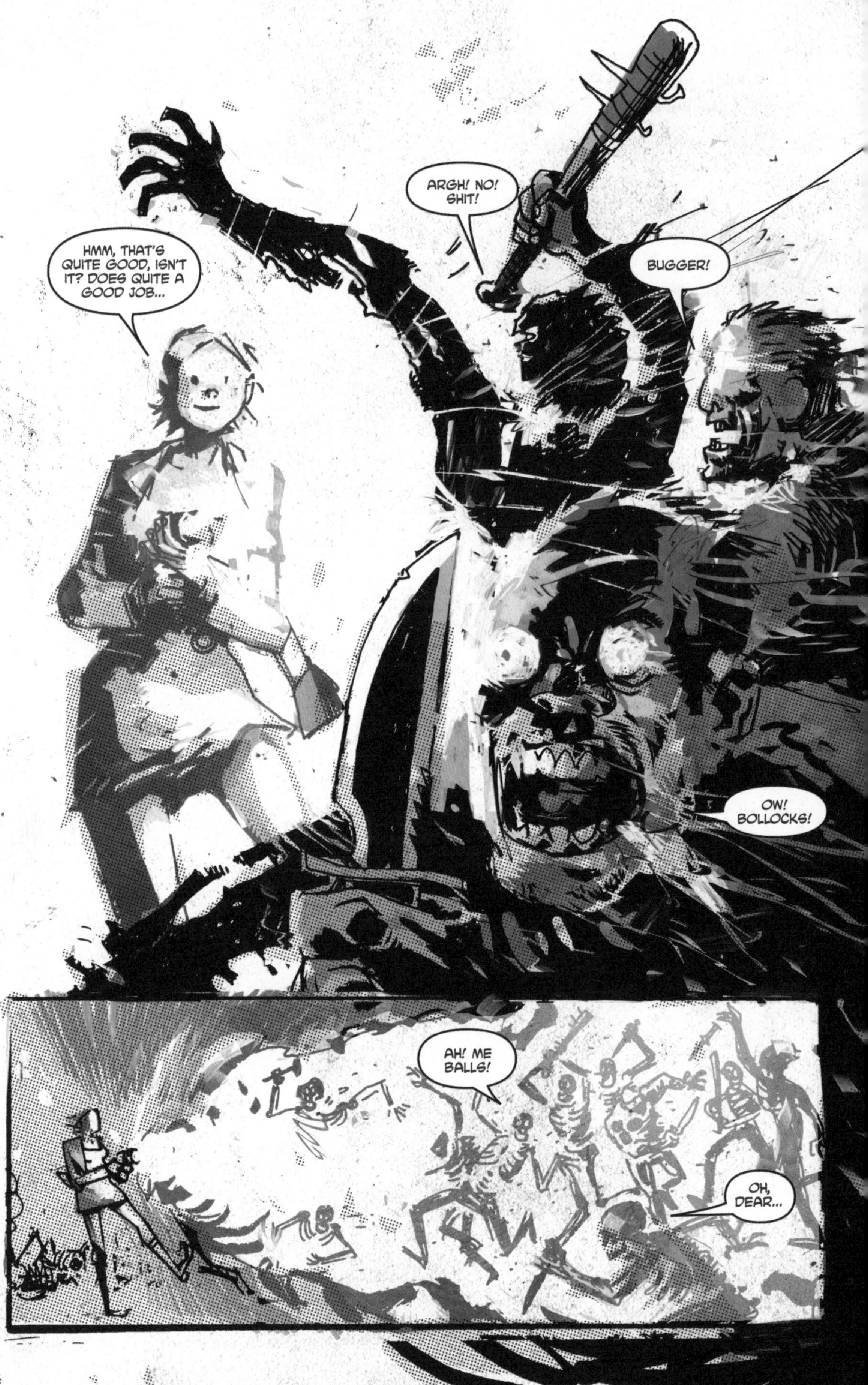
HMM, THAT'S QUITE GOOD, ISN'T IT? DOES QUITE A GOOD JOB...
ARGH! NO! SHIT!
BUGGER!
OW! BOLLOCKS!
AH! ME BALLS!
OH, DEAR...

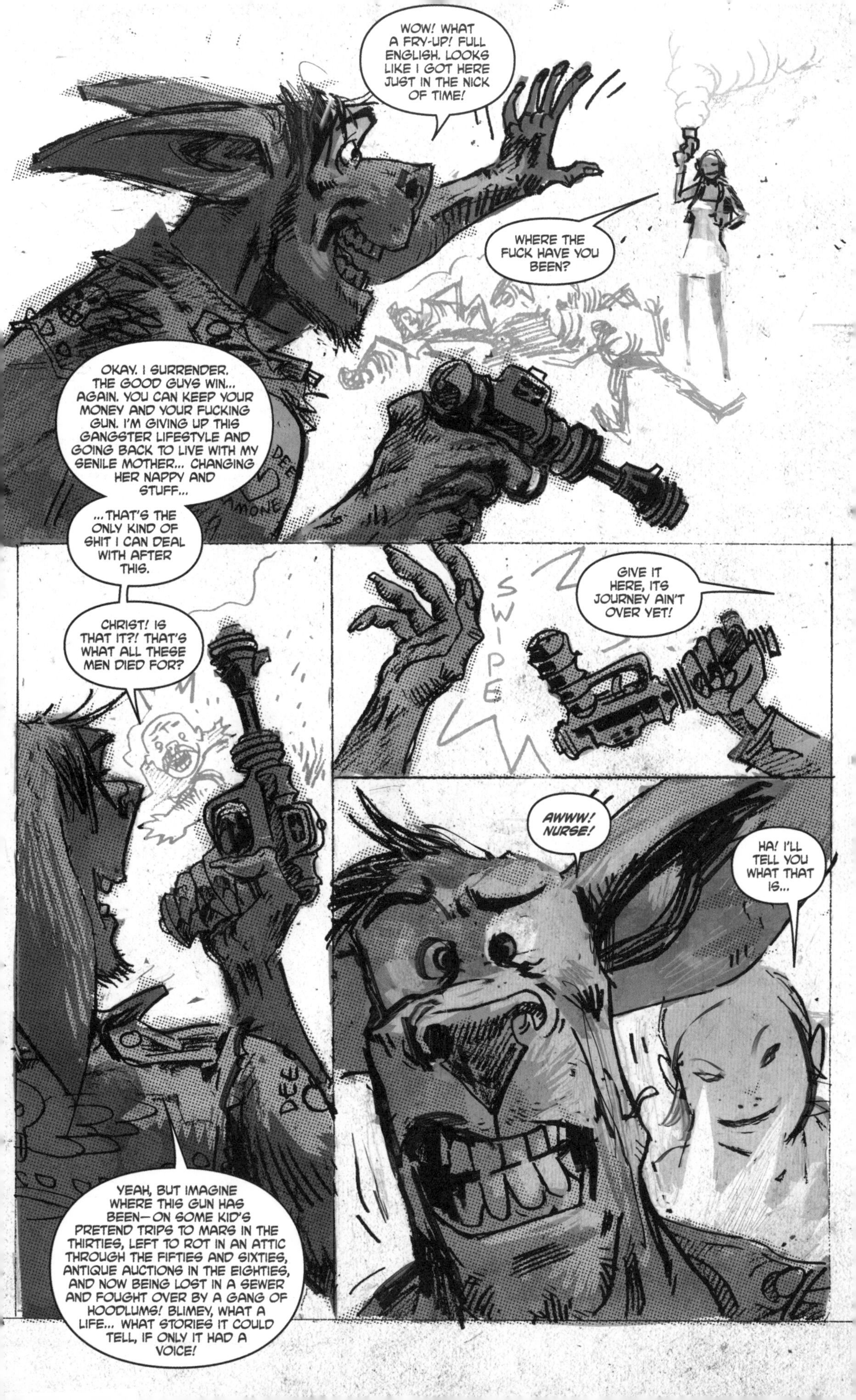

WOW! WHAT A FRY-UP! FULL ENGLISH. LOOKS LIKE I GOT HERE JUST IN THE NICK OF TIME!
WHERE THE FUCK HAVE YOU BEEN?
OKAY. I SURRENDER. THE GOOD GUYS WIN... AGAIN. YOU CAN KEEP YOUR MONEY AND YOUR FUCKING GUN. I'M GIVING UP THIS GANGSTER LIFESTYLE AND GOING BACK TO LIVE WITH MY SENILE MOTHER... CHANGING HER NAPPY AND STUFF...
...THAT'S THE ONLY KIND OF SHIT I CAN DEAL WITH AFTER THIS.
CHRIST! IS THAT IT?! THAT'S WHAT ALL THESE MEN DIED FOR?
YEAH, BUT IMAGINE WHERE THIS GUN HAS BEEN—ON SOME KID'S PRETEND TRIPS TO MARS IN THE THIRTIES, LEFT TO ROT IN AN ATTIC THROUGH THE FIFTIES AND SIXTIES, ANTIQUE AUCTIONS IN THE EIGHTIES, AND NOW BEING LOST IN A SEWER AND FOUGHT OVER BY A GANG OF HOODLUMS! BLIMEY, WHAT A LIFE... WHAT STORIES IT COULD TELL, IF ONLY IT HAD A VOICE!
SWIPE
GIVE IT HERE, ITS JOURNEY AIN'T OVER YET!
AWWW! NURSE!
HA! I'LL TELL YOU WHAT THAT IS...

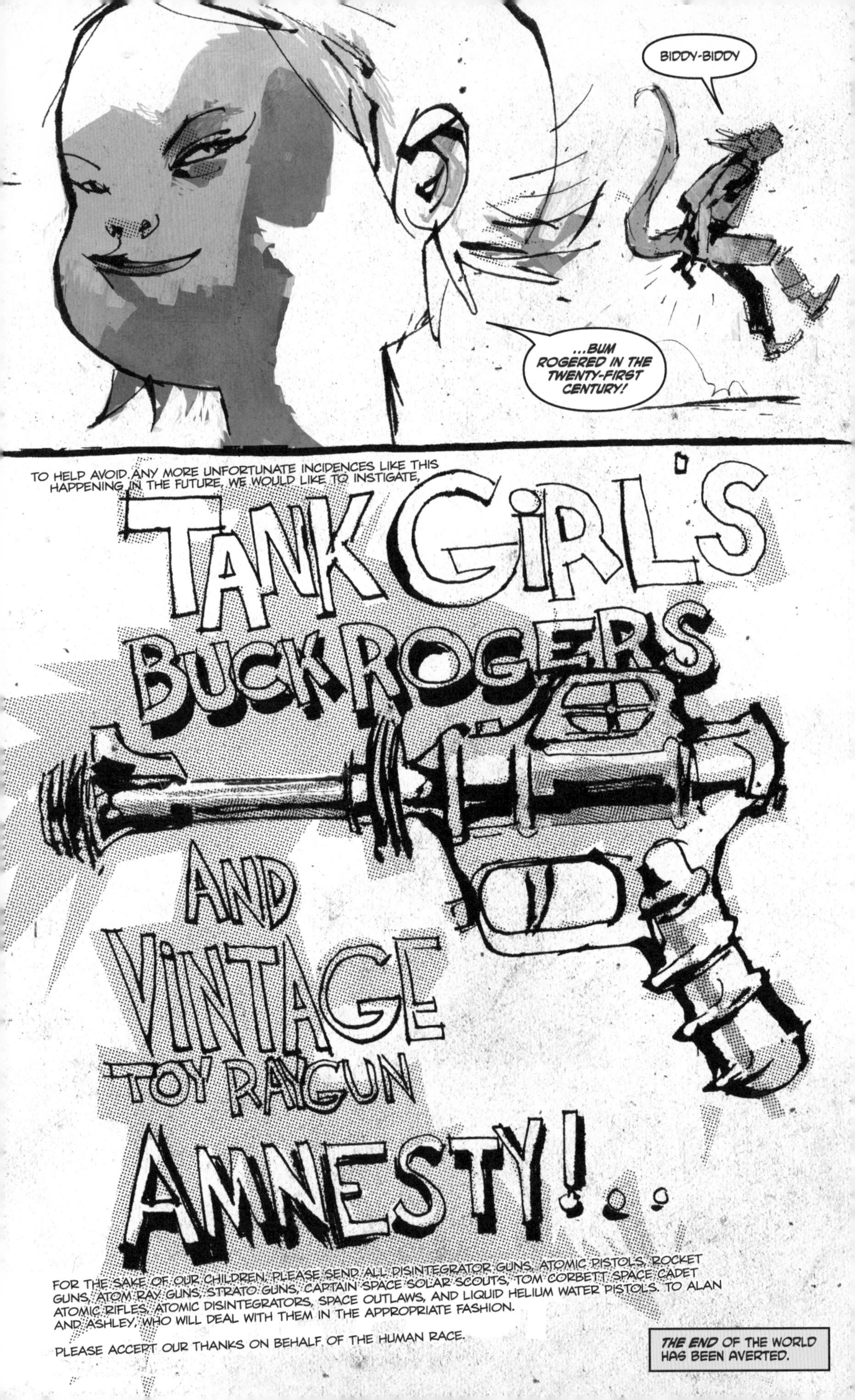
BIDDY-BIDDY
...BUM ROGERED IN THE TWENTY-FIRST CENTURY!
TO HELP AVOID ANY MORE UNFORTUNATE INCIDENCES LIKE THIS HAPPENING IN THE FUTURE, WE WOULD LIKE TO INSTIGATE,
TANK GIRL'S
BUCK ROGERS
AND
VINTAGE
TOY RAYGUN
AMNESTY!..
FOR THE SAKE OF OUR CHILDREN, PLEASE SEND ALL DISINTEGRATOR GUNS, ATOMIC PISTOLS, ROCKET GUNS, ATOM RAY GUNS, STRATO GUNS, CAPTAIN SPACE SOLAR SCOUTS, TOM CORBETT SPACE CADET ATOMIC RIFLES, ATOMIC DISINTEGRATORS, SPACE OUTLAWS, AND LIQUID HELIUM WATER PISTOLS. TO ALAN AND ASHLEY, WHO WILL DEAL WITH THEM IN THE APPROPRIATE FASHION.
PLEASE ACCEPT OUR THANKS ON BEHALF OF THE HUMAN RACE.
THE END OF THE WORLD HAS BEEN AVERTED.

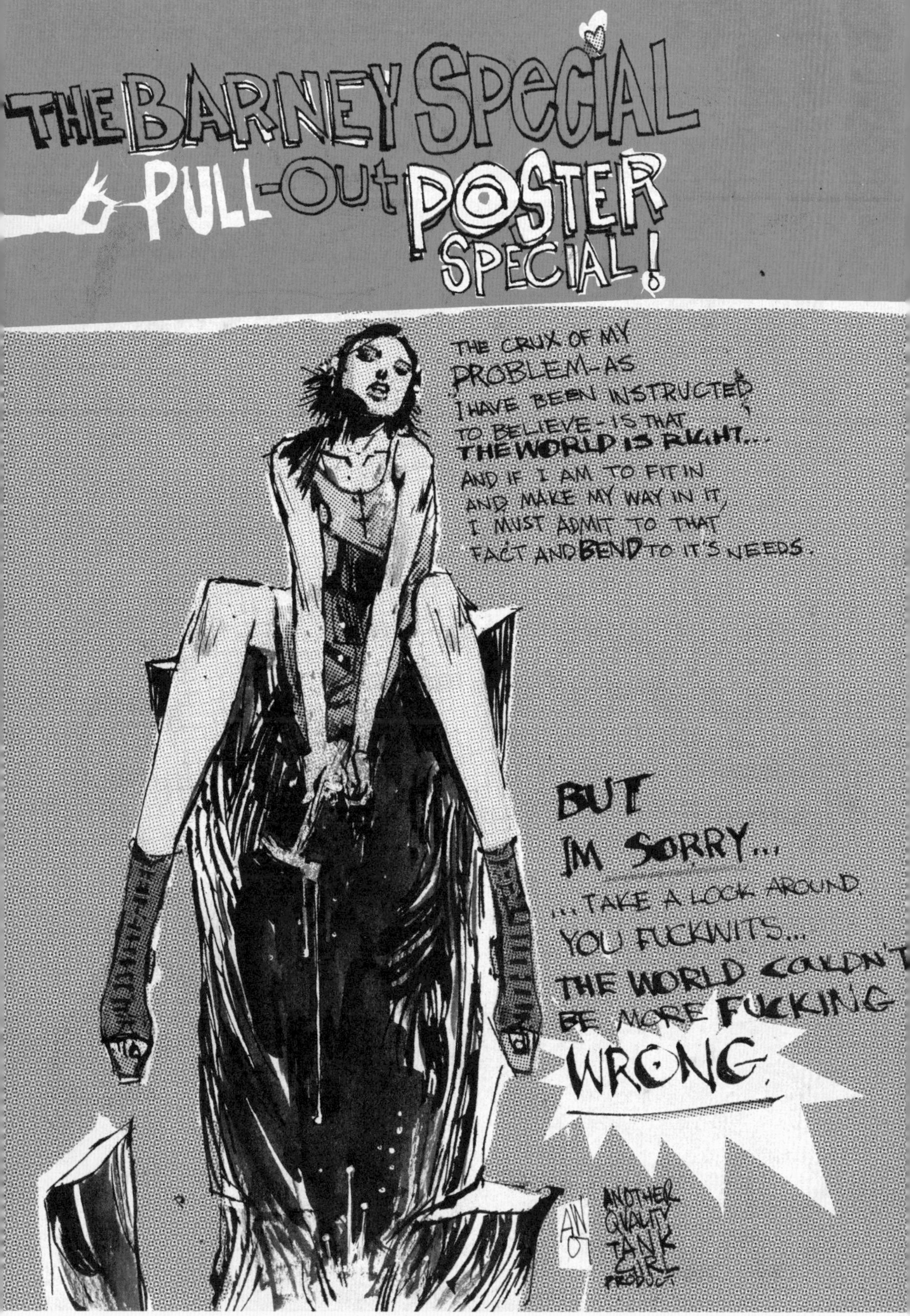
THE BARNEY SPECIAL
PULL-OUT POSTER SPECIAL!
THE CRUX OF MY PROBLEM - AS I HAVE BEEN INSTRUCTED TO BELIEVE - IS THAT THE WORLD IS RIGHT...
AND IF I AM TO FIT IN AND MAKE MY WAY IN IT, I MUST ADMIT TO THAT FACT AND BEND TO IT'S NEEDS.
BUT
I'M SORRY...
...TAKE A LOOK AROUND YOU FUCKWITS...
THE WORLD COULDN'T BE MORE FUCKING
WRONG
ANOTHER QUALITY TANK GIRL PRODUCT

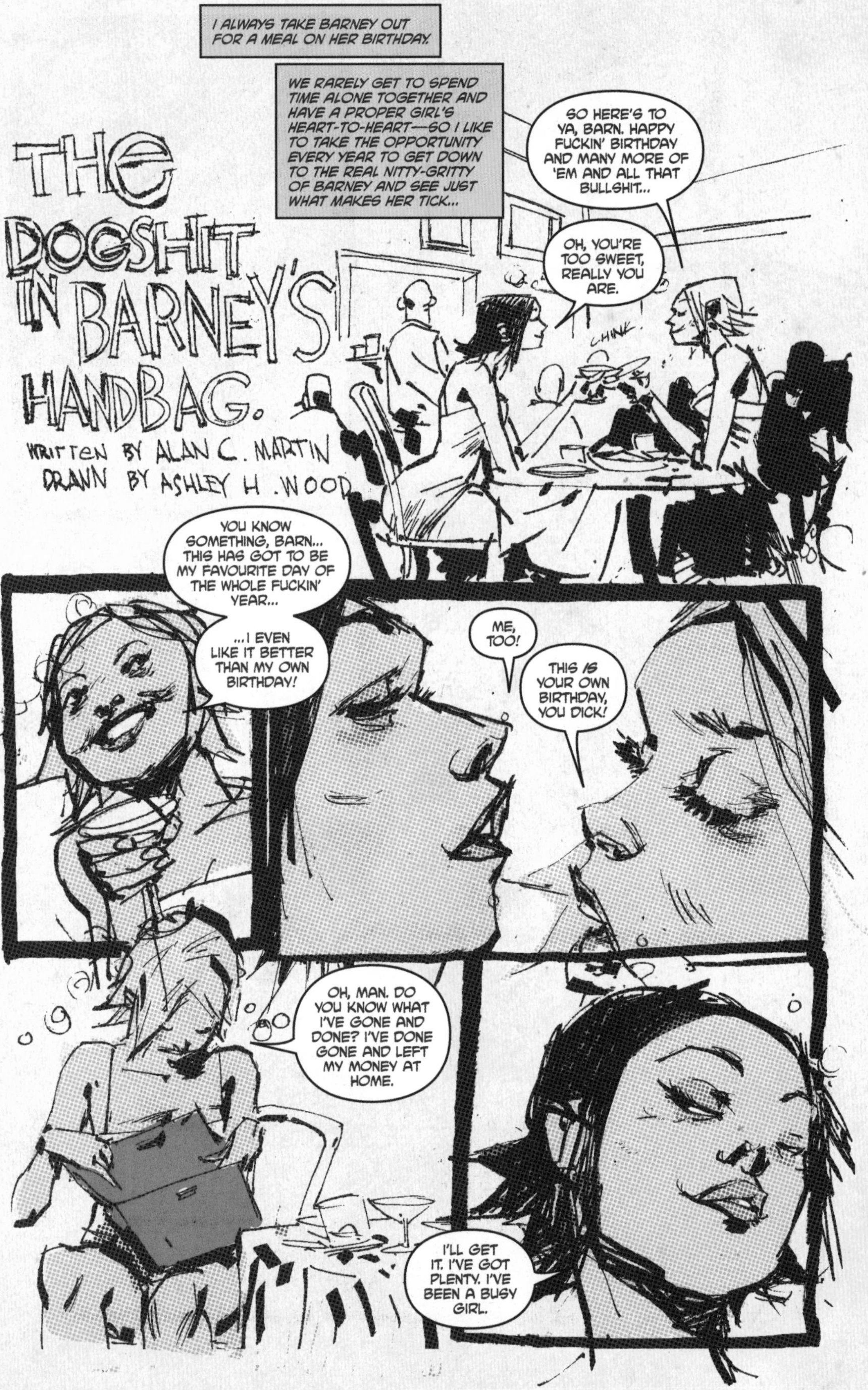
I ALWAYS TAKE BARNEY OUT FOR A MEAL ON HER BIRTHDAY.
WE RARELY GET TO SPEND TIME ALONE TOGETHER AND HAVE A PROPER GIRL'S HEART-TO-HEART—SO I LIKE TO TAKE THE OPPORTUNITY EVERY YEAR TO GET DOWN TO THE REAL NITTY-GRITTY OF BARNEY AND SEE JUST WHAT MAKES HER TICK...
THE DOGSHIT IN BARNEY'S HANDBAG.
WRITTEN BY ALAN C. MARTIN
DRAWN BY ASHLEY H. WOOD
SO HERE'S TO YA, BARN. HAPPY FUCKIN' BIRTHDAY AND MANY MORE OF 'EM AND ALL THAT BULLSHIT...
OH, YOU'RE TOO SWEET, REALLY YOU ARE.
CHINK
YOU KNOW SOMETHING, BARN... THIS HAS GOT TO BE MY FAVOURITE DAY OF THE WHOLE FUCKIN' YEAR...
...I EVEN LIKE IT BETTER THAN MY OWN BIRTHDAY!
ME, TOO!
THIS IS YOUR OWN BIRTHDAY, YOU DICK!
OH, MAN. DO YOU KNOW WHAT I'VE GONE AND DONE? I'VE DONE GONE AND LEFT MY MONEY AT HOME.
I'LL GET IT. I'VE GOT PLENTY. I'VE BEEN A BUSY GIRL.

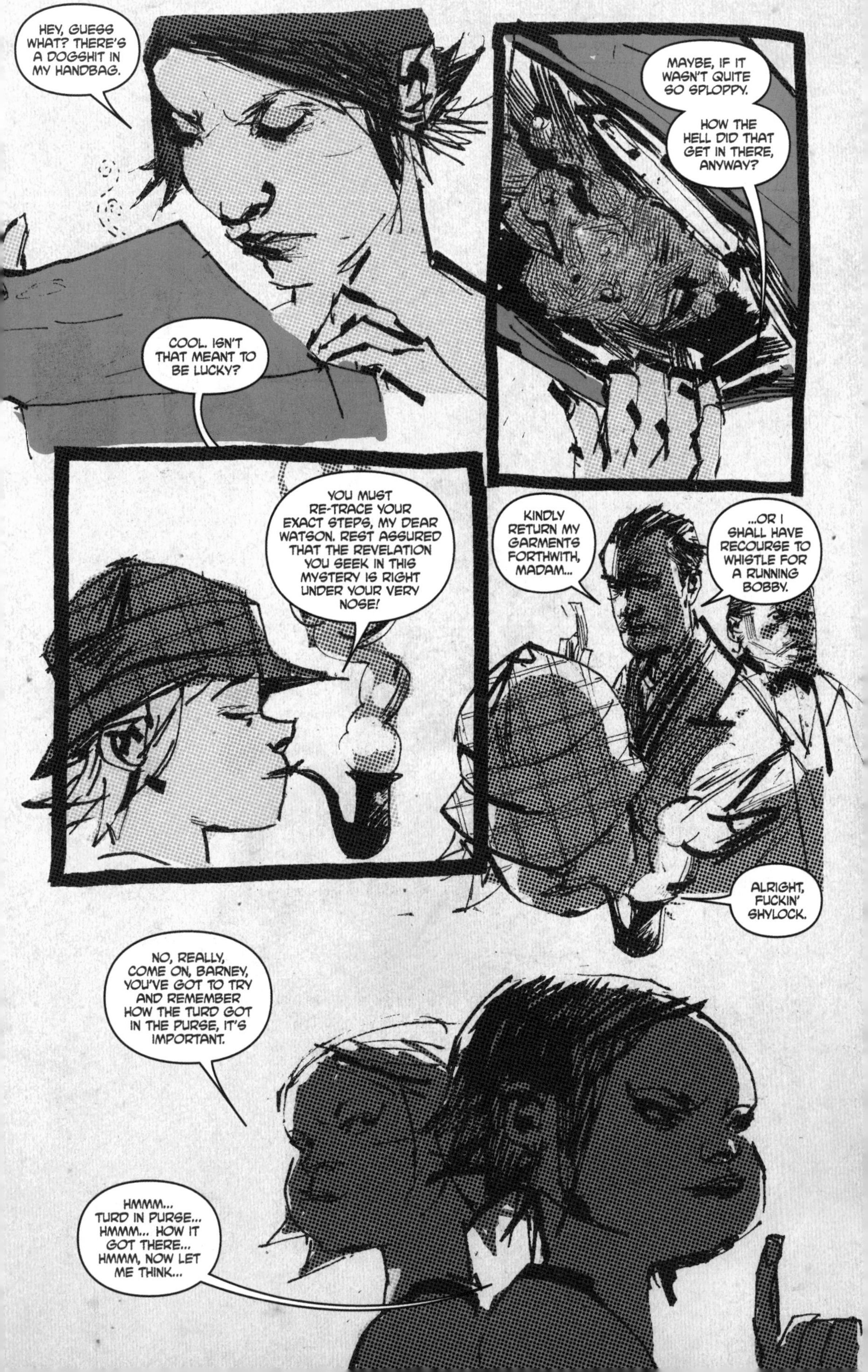
HEY, GUESS WHAT? THERE'S A DOGSHIT IN MY HANDBAG.
COOL. ISN'T THAT MEANT TO BE LUCKY?
MAYBE, IF IT WASN'T QUITE SO SPLOPPY.
HOW THE HELL DID THAT GET IN THERE, ANYWAY?
YOU MUST RE-TRACE YOUR EXACT STEPS, MY DEAR WATSON. REST ASSURED THAT THE REVELATION YOU SEEK IN THIS MYSTERY IS RIGHT UNDER YOUR VERY NOSE!
KINDLY RETURN MY GARMENTS FORTHWITH, MADAM...
...OR I SHALL HAVE RECOURSE TO WHISTLE FOR A RUNNING BOBBY.
ALRIGHT, FUCKIN' SHYLOCK.
NO, REALLY, COME ON, BARNEY, YOU'VE GOT TO TRY AND REMEMBER HOW THE TURD GOT IN THE PURSE, IT'S IMPORTANT.
HMMM... TURD IN PURSE... HMMM... HOW IT GOT THERE... HMMM, NOW LET ME THINK...

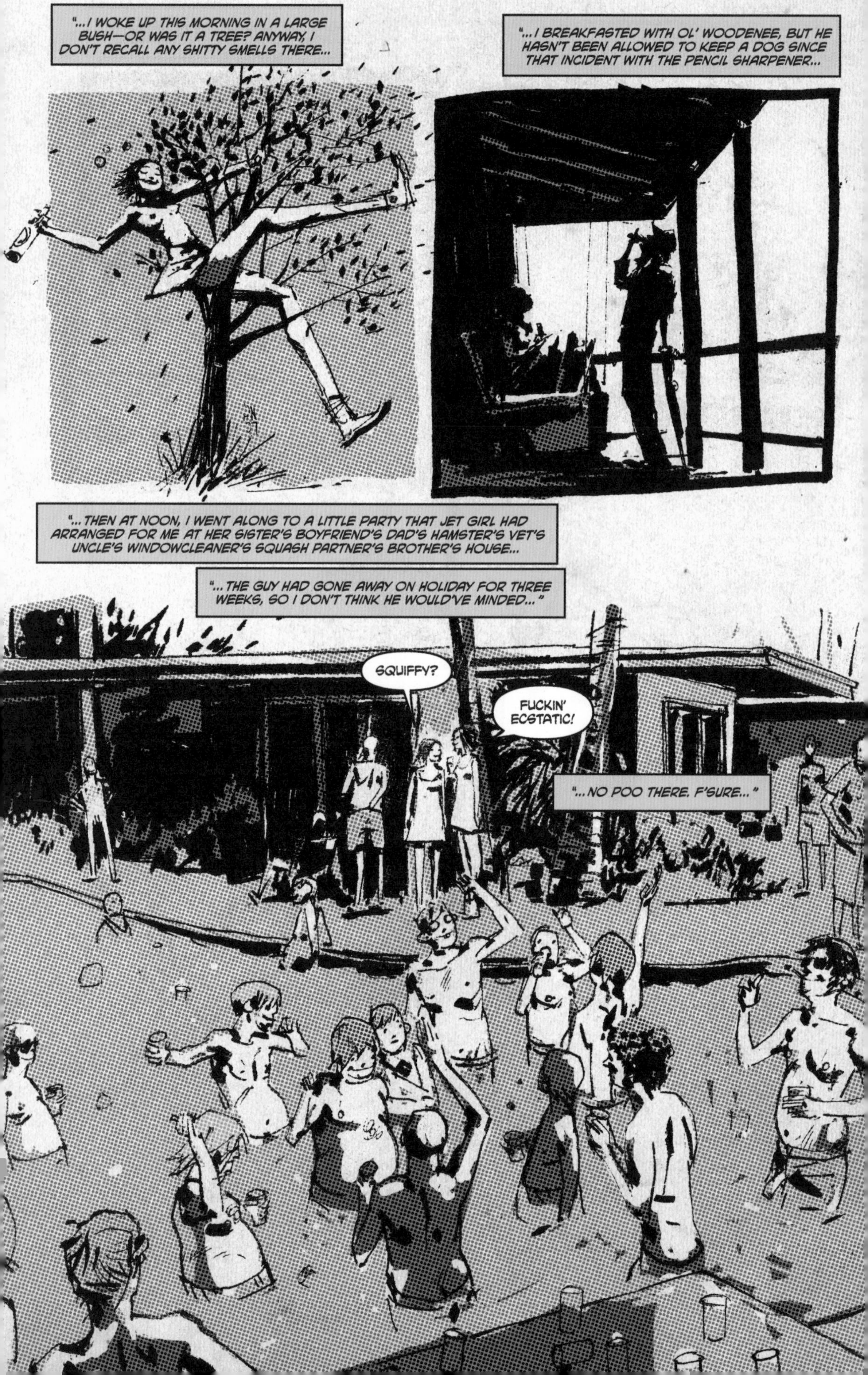
"...I WOKE UP THIS MORNING IN A LARGE BUSH—OR WAS IT A TREE? ANYWAY, I DON'T RECALL ANY SHITTY SMELLS THERE...
"...I BREAKFASTED WITH OL' WOODENEE, BUT HE HASN'T BEEN ALLOWED TO KEEP A DOG SINCE THAT INCIDENT WITH THE PENCIL SHARPENER...
"...THEN AT NOON, I WENT ALONG TO A LITTLE PARTY THAT JET GIRL HAD ARRANGED FOR ME AT HER SISTER'S BOYFRIEND'S DAD'S HAMSTER'S VET'S UNCLE'S WINDOWCLEANER'S SQUASH PARTNER'S BROTHER'S HOUSE...
"...THE GUY HAD GONE AWAY ON HOLIDAY FOR THREE WEEKS, SO I DON'T THINK HE WOULD'VE MINDED..."
SQUIFFY?
FUCKIN' ECSTATIC!
"...NO POO THERE. F'SURE..."

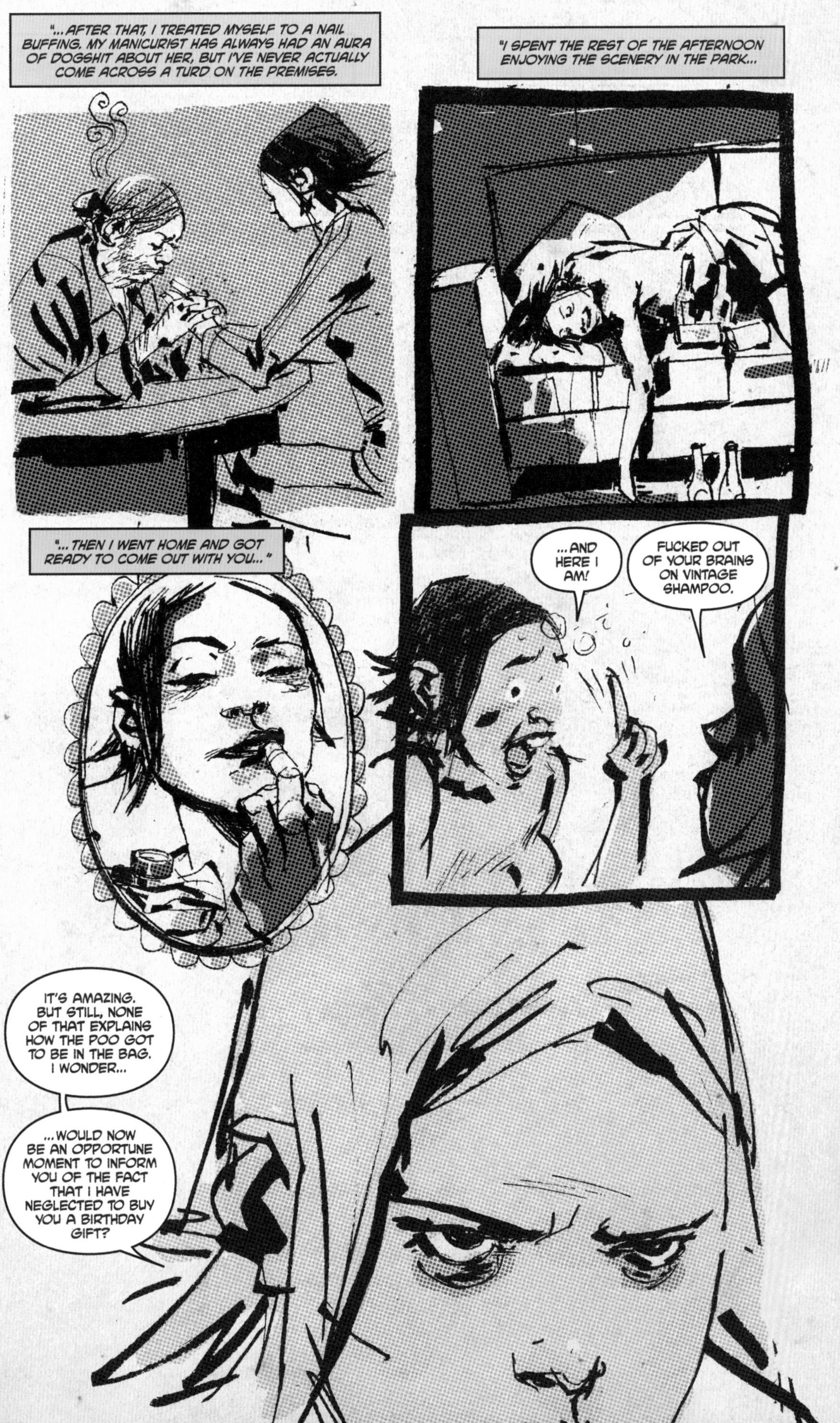
"...AFTER THAT, I TREATED MYSELF TO A NAIL BUFFING. MY MANICURIST HAS ALWAYS HAD AN AURA OF DOGSHIT ABOUT HER, BUT I'VE NEVER ACTUALLY COME ACROSS A TURD ON THE PREMISES.
"I SPENT THE REST OF THE AFTERNOON ENJOYING THE SCENERY IN THE PARK...
"...THEN I WENT HOME AND GOT READY TO COME OUT WITH YOU..."
...AND HERE I AM!
FUCKED OUT OF YOUR BRAINS ON VINTAGE SHAMPOO.
IT'S AMAZING. BUT STILL, NONE OF THAT EXPLAINS HOW THE POO GOT TO BE IN THE BAG. I WONDER...
...WOULD NOW BE AN OPPORTUNE MOMENT TO INFORM YOU OF THE FACT THAT I HAVE NEGLECTED TO BUY YOU A BIRTHDAY GIFT?

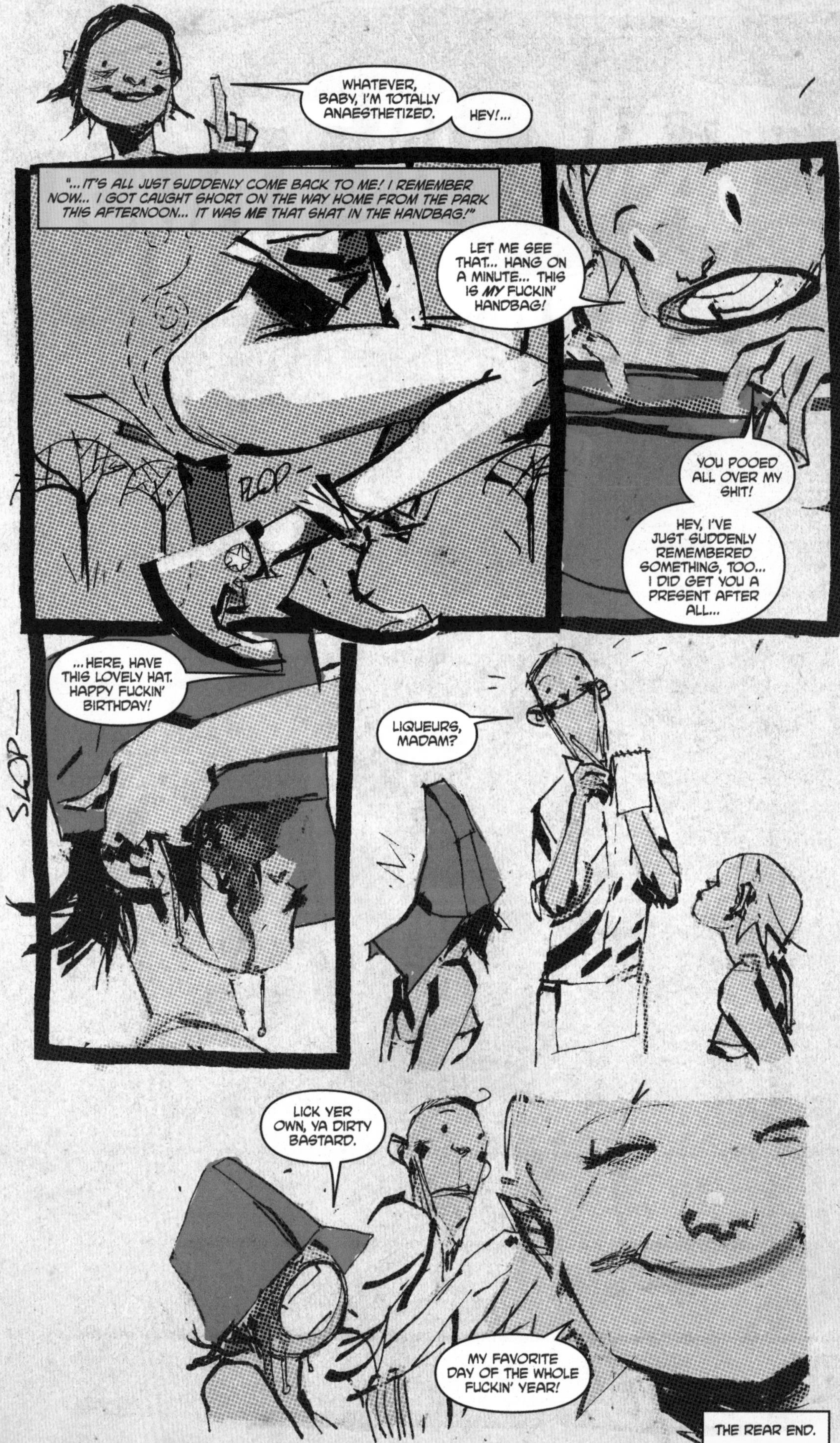
WHATEVER, BABY, I'M TOTALLY ANAESTHETIZED.
HEY!...
"...IT'S ALL JUST SUDDENLY COME BACK TO ME! I REMEMBER NOW... I GOT CAUGHT SHORT ON THE WAY HOME FROM THE PARK THIS AFTERNOON... IT WAS ME THAT SHAT IN THE HANDBAG!"
PLOP
LET ME SEE THAT... HANG ON A MINUTE... THIS IS MY FUCKIN' HANDBAG!
YOU POOED ALL OVER MY SHIT!
HEY, I'VE JUST SUDDENLY REMEMBERED SOMETHING, TOO... I DID GET YOU A PRESENT AFTER ALL...
...HERE, HAVE THIS LOVELY HAT. HAPPY FUCKIN' BIRTHDAY!
SLOP
LIQUEURS, MADAM?
LICK YER OWN, YA DIRTY BASTARD.
MY FAVORITE DAY OF THE WHOLE FUCKIN' YEAR!
THE REAR END.

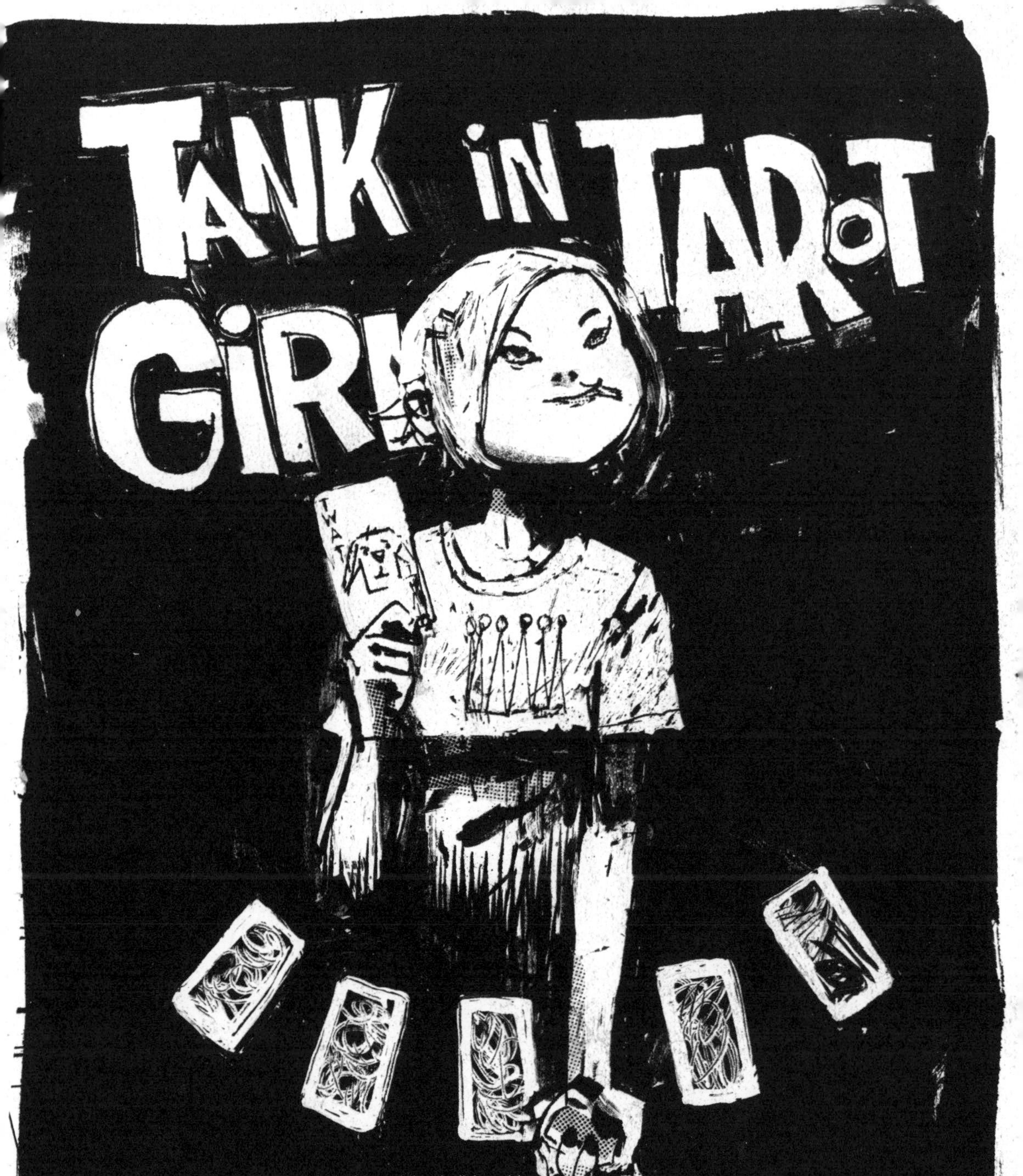
TANK GIRL IN TAROT
TWAT
AW 07

I pulled gently on the knob of the old fashioned doorbell. I could hear a tinkle-tinkle far away, deep in the bowels of the enormous mansion.

I waited.

The sun had already set and a chilly breeze was working its way into my bones. I hunched my shoulders and pulled up the collar of my sheepskin coat. My stomach moaned with hunger, I hadn't eaten for days, ever since some tricky bastard had stolen my packed-lunch. Seagulls wheeled around the sky and yelped their sad songs across the empty bay.

Eventually a funny little butler appeared and greeted me with a snotty leer. "Yes, Madam," he ponced, "what can I do for you?"

"I'm calling for Booga," I replied, a bit taken-a-back by the unfriendliness of my loved one's new housekeeper.

"Mr. Booga is to be found in his library-tower, which can be accessed by the narrow pathway to the south of the house," he instructed, giving me a nod in the right direction and quickly closing the door.

"Huh," I huffed, "charmin'."

I trudged up the muddy track. The library—a beautiful, mock-mediaeval-style turret folly—was tucked away in the woodland, almost invisible from view until you got right up close to it.

The door was open. A warm candlelight glow lit up the rustic, white-walled passage inside.

I went in.

A stone spiral staircase took me to the top floor of the building. Booga was stretched out on a big antique chaise longue, reading an old newspaper, and smoking a long Churchwarden pipe. The room was lavishly decorated in late William Morris with tastefully framed original pre-Raphaelite sketches filling the gaps between the wooden bookshelves.

"Booga?" I enquired.

He lowered the paper and looked up through his half-moon glasses. "Ah, Tank Girl my dear, do come in, I've been expecting you all day."

"Oh, yeah? Exactly why have you been expecting me?" I asked angrily. "You never told me where you were. You just buggered off without a word. It took me ages to trace you here. And anyway... what the fuck do you think you're playing at? Whose place is this?"

"It's mine," he replied proudly.

"No it isn't."

"Yeah, it is. I bought it."

"You bought it?" I questioned, staggering with disbelief.

"Yeah," he replied, "I saved up for it."

"Booga, that is utter bullshit. You've never saved up for a thing in your life. You've never even had a job for fucksake."

"I had a paper-round," he pleaded.

"Yeah," I conceded, "okay, so you had a paper-round. But you couldn't even do that properly. And there's no way you managed to save up for this place by earning three quid a week when you were twelve. This must've cost you fucking millions."

"Well I had a stroke of luck..." he explained.

"Please," I interjected sarcastically, "do go on."

"...well... it happened like this..." he sat up straight to tell his story, re-lighting his pipe and doing up his richly embroidered smoking jacket, "...I was having a crap in the toilets at the church hall..."

I had to butt in straight away, "Booga, what were you doing in the church hall toilets?"

"It was half way through the Sunday service," he answered earnestly, "and they started doing a really boring bit and I really needed to curl one down, so I sneaked out."

"When did you start going to Sunday service?" I asked.

"That was my first time," he replied. "Someone told me that if I went to church and did all of the praying and stuff, then they would give me free wine, because Jesus was really into wine and all that. Fish, too."

That figured.

"Okay," I said, "then what happened?"

"I done a lot into the lav," he explained, "so I needed to use a fair amount of bog-paper. Halfway through the roll I came across this..."

Booga got up and walked over to a shelf of encyclopaedias, carefully taking down the volume marked "X, Y & Z". He opened the book at its end pages and removed a single sheet of expertly pressed white toilet paper. He placed the sheet on the small wine table in front of me.

"Take a look," he offered.

I took a look.

The paper was covered with unrecognisable biro lettering. It was like nothing I'd ever seen before—weird symbols and characters and shit.

"So," I asked Booga, with more than a subtle hint of parody, "what is this? Written in ancient Poo-Poo?"

"It's a cipher," replied Booga. "Here's a translation what I got done."

He handed me another sheet of paper. This time the writing was legible, but still incomprehensible.

It read:

SHEPHERD'S PIE, QUITE TEMPTED, THAT PUSSY, TENNERS, HOLD THE PHONE, PEACE 23. BY THE BUS STOP AND THIS

HORSEMEAT, I COMPLAINED—or DECLINED—TO THIS DEMON STUNT-CYCLIST AT HIGH NOON. CHEESE AND ONION.

"Booga," I complained, "this is complete crap. It doesn't mean anything."

"That's exactly what I thought," he said brightly, "and I was about to wipe my arse with it when the vicar burst in. In my hurry to have a shit, I had neglected to bolt the door properly. He didn't hang around for long, coz of the stink, but the upshot was that I pulled up my trousers pronto and stuffed the bog-paper in my shirt pocket. I didn't think any more of it until I needed to blow my nose, that's when things started to get weird..."

"No kidding," I injected.

"...I took the bit of bog-paper down to the library and the woman there translated it for me," he continued, "she said it was written in sam-script or something."

"You mean Sanskrit?" I asked.

"Yeah, him as well. Anyway, the boff at the library couldn't help me any further so I went and consulted Mandy, my fortune teller."

"Mandy, your fortune teller?" I repeated quizzically, "and what did Mandy have to say?"

"She done my tarot," he explained, "and she said that somehow my destiny had become irrevocably intertwined with that of the universe. She said that I would have to look out for signs, things with hidden meanings, shit like that. And that once the trail had begun, then my future was set and the dice had been cast and stuff."

"And has the trail begun, whatever that means?"

"It has begun and ended already," he replied. "Shortly after my reading, I was walking down the High Street when a feint waft of shepherd's pie hit my sensitive kangaroo nostrils. I thought about going into the café for a portion, but I was distracted by a cat with no tail. Then I found two ten-dollar bills in the gutter and thought I'd give you a call to ask you out for a curry. You couldn't talk coz you were busy doing a jigsaw of The Fonz and you couldn't find the last bit, the twenty-third piece. So I waited for a bus to take me home and this guy started munching into a Mc Farmyards' burger right next to me. So I told him to fuck off and he got on his bike and did a wheelie all the way down the road. When I got in I was starving, so I opened my bag of cheese and onion flavour Potato Fancies."

I'd been following his story through the translation; "CHEESE AND ONION" was where it ended. "And is that it?" I asked. "Where did all of these goodies come from then?"

Booga cleared his throat and prepared to finish his story by licking his lips, "Inside the packet I found a little blue envelope. They were doing a special promotion, giving away cash to lucky eaters. I got the grand prize—two million big ones!"

"You what?!" I screamed. "And you didn't fucking tell me?"

"It was weird," he explained, "I wasn't in control. It was like destiny itself had taken me over and I was flying on auto-pilot."

Just then something dawned on me, "Hold it right there, buster, did you say you had a packet of cheese and onion Potato Fancies?"

"Er... yeah," he answered hesitantly.

"You bastard. It was you that stole my packed-lunch!" then the rest of it dawned on me too, "I was the one who was meant to win the two million quid! And you've fucking spent it! You utter, utter bastard!"

Later that night, as I was using Booga as an ashtray and his butler as a footstool, I contemplated what might have been, had I won all that cash. I daydreamed of living a saintly existence, somewhere near a fountain of healing water in a far-off European mountain village.

"Can I please have a number-two toilet break, ma'am?" Booga asked quietly.

"You can poo in your pants and clean it up with this," I replied sharply, flicking the rolled-up piece of Sanskrit bog-paper at him, "I'll bet that Mandy never predicted this in your reading."

"She did say that the story would end with a nice warm feeling, deep down." **TG**

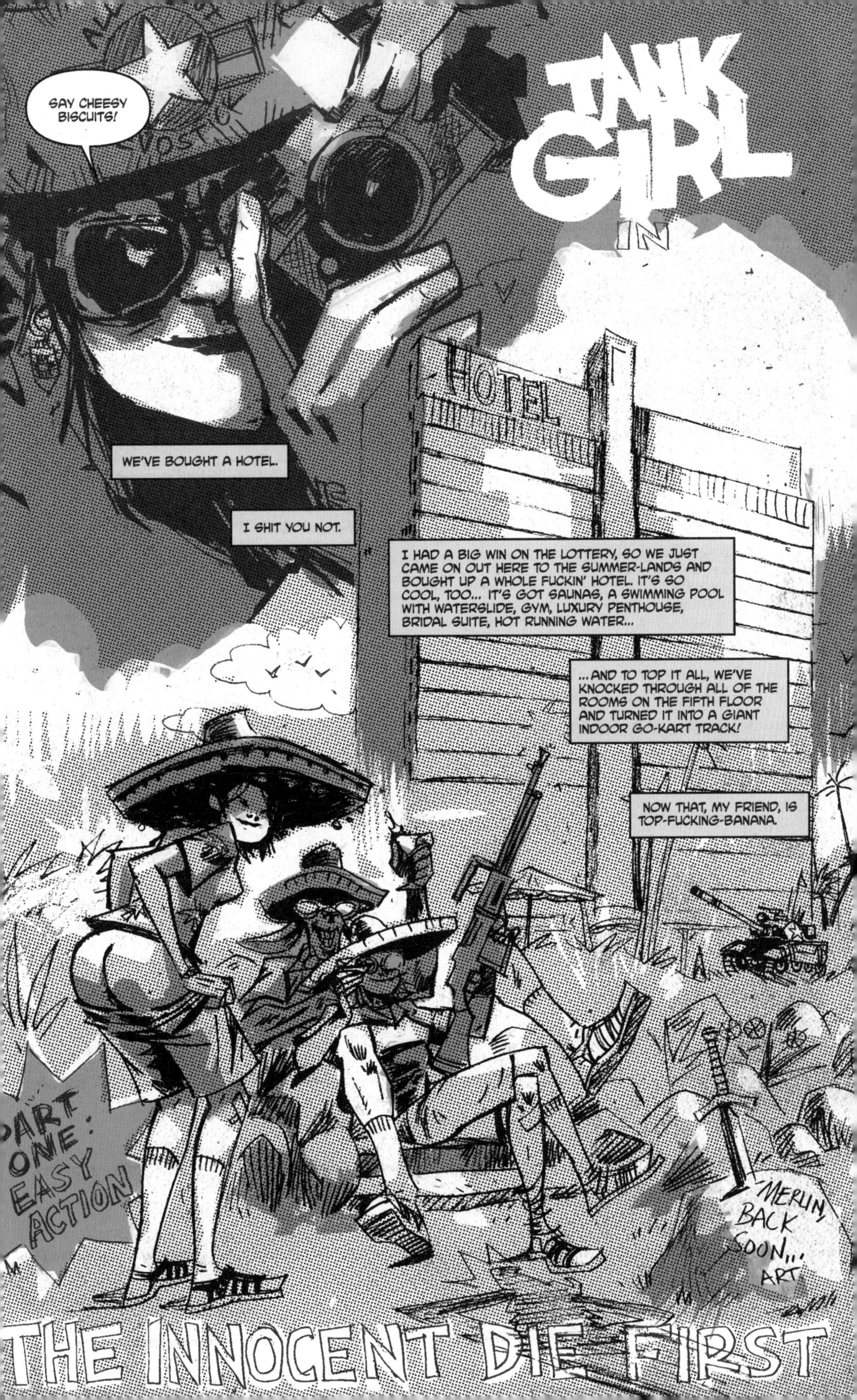
TANK GIRL
IN
SAY CHEESY BISCUITS!
HOTEL
WE'VE BOUGHT A HOTEL.
I SHIT YOU NOT.
I HAD A BIG WIN ON THE LOTTERY, SO WE JUST CAME ON OUT HERE TO THE SUMMER-LANDS AND BOUGHT UP A WHOLE FUCKIN' HOTEL. IT'S SO COOL, TOO... IT'S GOT SAUNAS, A SWIMMING POOL WITH WATERSLIDE, GYM, LUXURY PENTHOUSE, BRIDAL SUITE, HOT RUNNING WATER...
...AND TO TOP IT ALL, WE'VE KNOCKED THROUGH ALL OF THE ROOMS ON THE FIFTH FLOOR AND TURNED IT INTO A GIANT INDOOR GO-KART TRACK!
NOW THAT, MY FRIEND, IS TOP-FUCKING-BANANA.
PART ONE: EASY ACTION
MERLIN, BACK SOON... ART
THE INNOCENT DIE FIRST

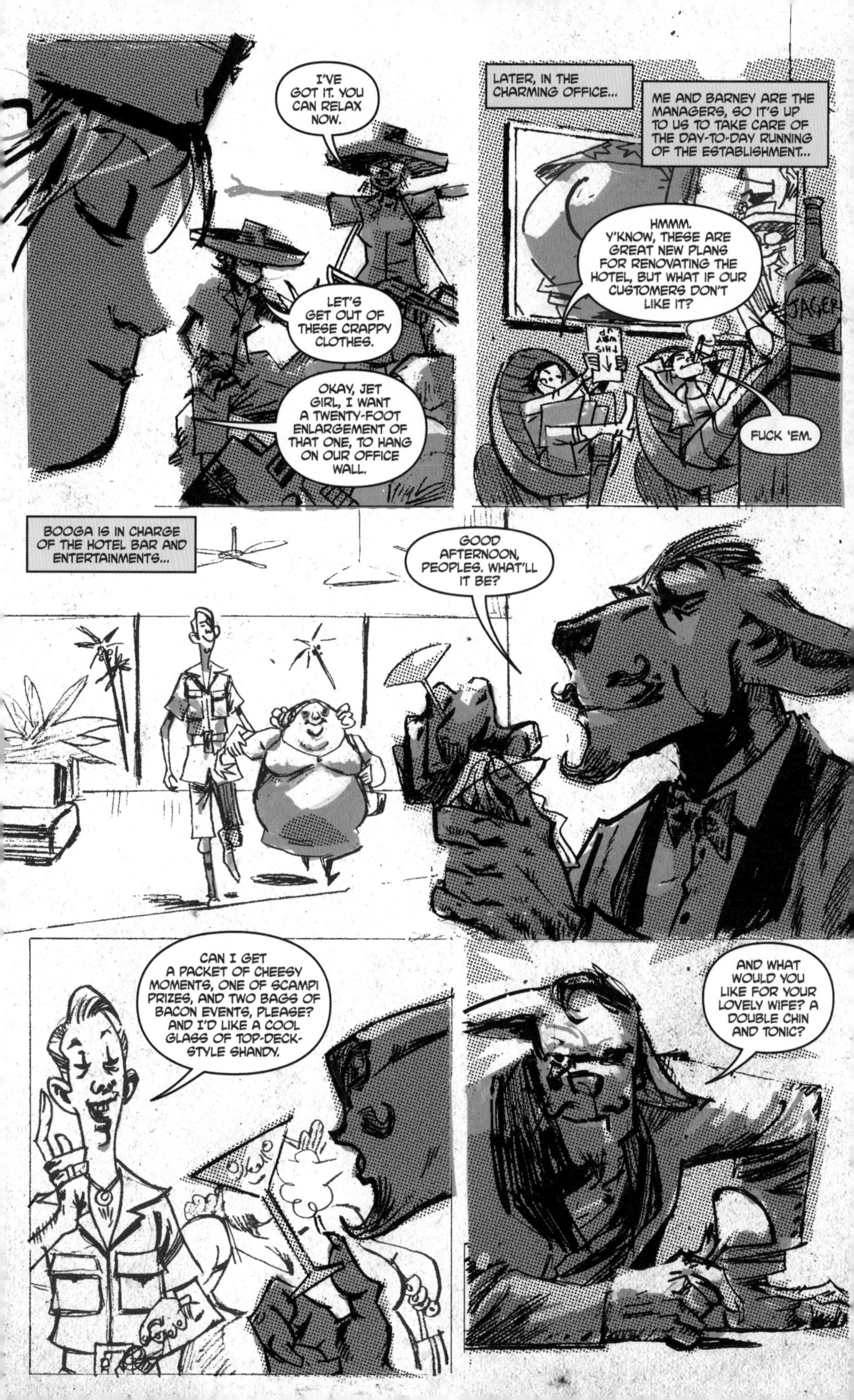
I'VE GOT IT. YOU CAN RELAX NOW.
LET'S GET OUT OF THESE CRAPPY CLOTHES.
OKAY, JET GIRL, I WANT A TWENTY-FOOT ENLARGEMENT OF THAT ONE, TO HANG ON OUR OFFICE WALL.
LATER, IN THE CHARMING OFFICE...
ME AND BARNEY ARE THE MANAGERS, SO IT'S UP TO US TO TAKE CARE OF THE DAY-TO-DAY RUNNING OF THE ESTABLISHMENT...
HMMM. Y'KNOW, THESE ARE GREAT NEW PLANS FOR RENOVATING THE HOTEL, BUT WHAT IF OUR CUSTOMERS DON'T LIKE IT?
FUCK 'EM.
BOOGA IS IN CHARGE OF THE HOTEL BAR AND ENTERTAINMENTS...
GOOD AFTERNOON, PEOPLES. WHAT'LL IT BE?
CAN I GET A PACKET OF CHEESY MOMENTS, ONE OF SCAMPI PRIZES, AND TWO BAGS OF BACON EVENTS, PLEASE? AND I'D LIKE A COOL GLASS OF TOP-DECK-STYLE SHANDY.
AND WHAT WOULD YOU LIKE FOR YOUR LOVELY WIFE? A DOUBLE CHIN AND TONIC?

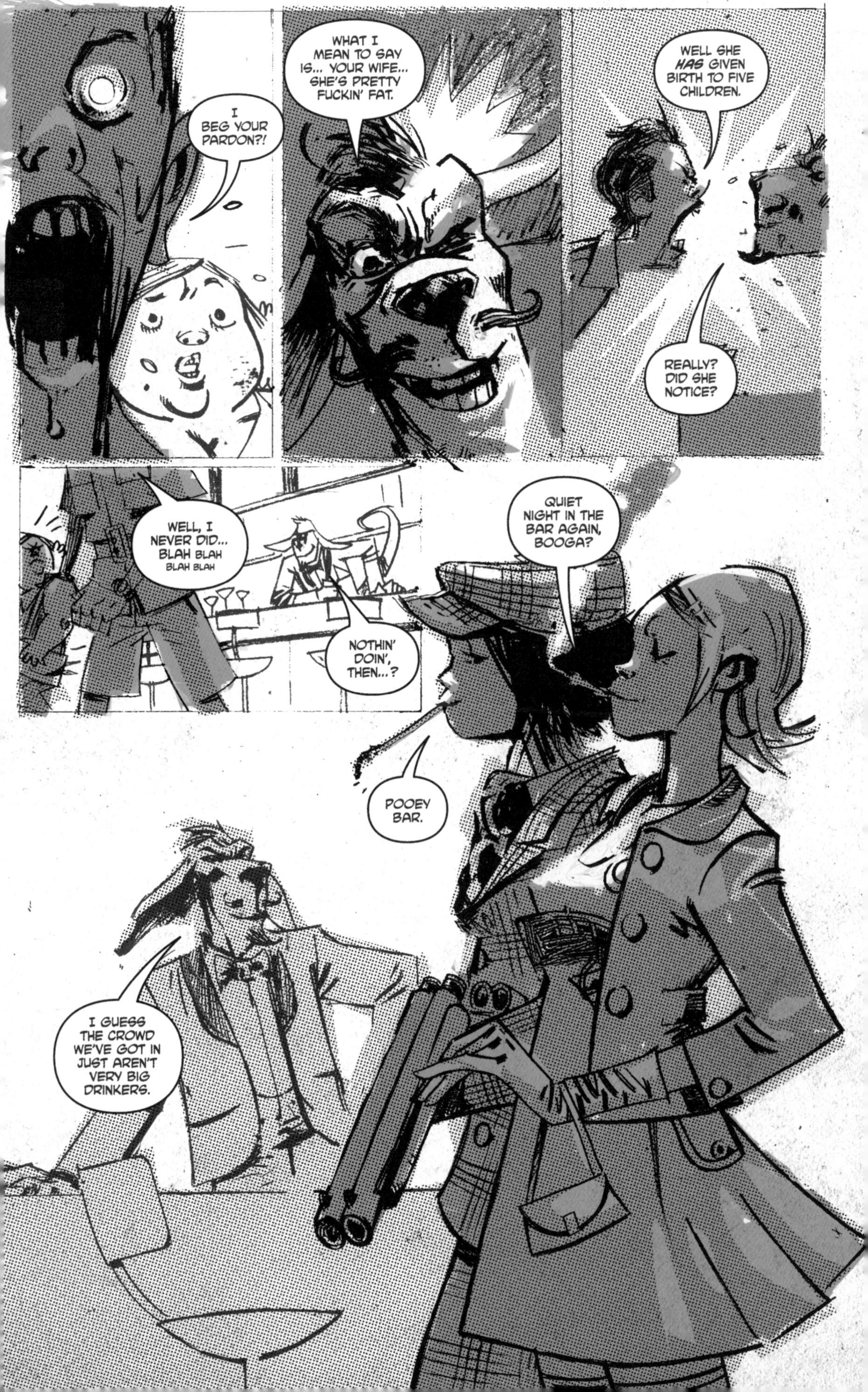
I BEG YOUR PARDON?!
WHAT I MEAN TO SAY IS... YOUR WIFE... SHE'S PRETTY FUCKIN' FAT.
WELL SHE HAS GIVEN BIRTH TO FIVE CHILDREN.
REALLY? DID SHE NOTICE?
WELL, I NEVER DID... BLAH BLAH BLAH BLAH
NOTHIN' DOIN', THEN...?
QUIET NIGHT IN THE BAR AGAIN, BOOGA?
POOEY BAR.
I GUESS THE CROWD WE'VE GOT IN JUST AREN'T VERY BIG DRINKERS.

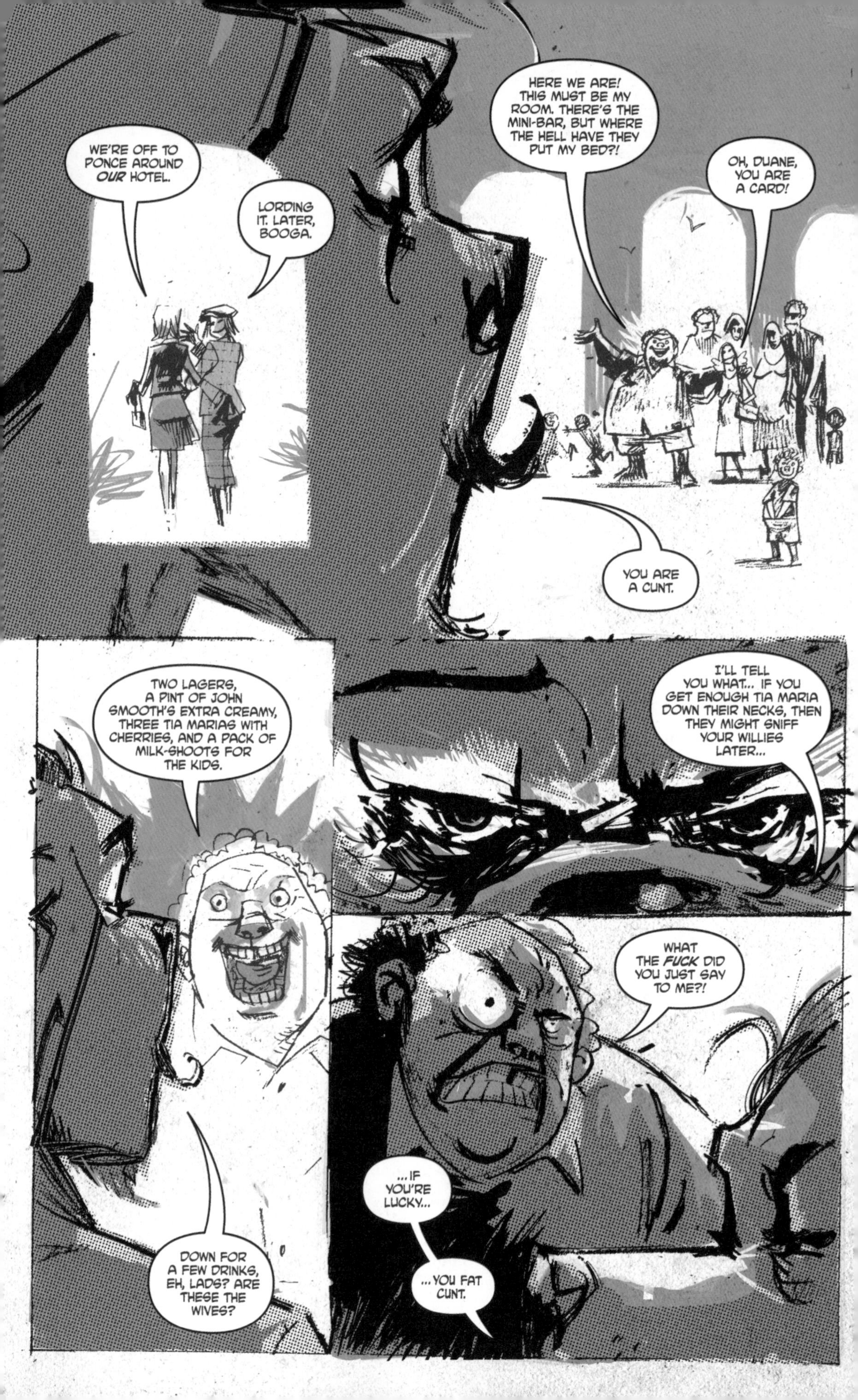
WE'RE OFF TO PONCE AROUND *OUR* HOTEL.
LORDING IT. LATER, BOOGA.
HERE WE ARE! THIS MUST BE MY ROOM. THERE'S THE MINI-BAR, BUT WHERE THE HELL HAVE THEY PUT MY BED?!
OH, DUANE, YOU ARE A CARD!
YOU ARE A CUNT.
TWO LAGERS, A PINT OF JOHN SMOOTH'S EXTRA CREAMY, THREE TIA MARIAS WITH CHERRIES, AND A PACK OF MILK-SHOOTS FOR THE KIDS.
DOWN FOR A FEW DRINKS, EH, LADS? ARE THESE THE WIVES?
I'LL TELL YOU WHAT... IF YOU GET ENOUGH TIA MARIA DOWN THEIR NECKS, THEN THEY MIGHT SNIFF YOUR WILLIES LATER...
...IF YOU'RE LUCKY...
...YOU FAT CUNT.
WHAT THE *FUCK* DID YOU JUST SAY TO ME?!

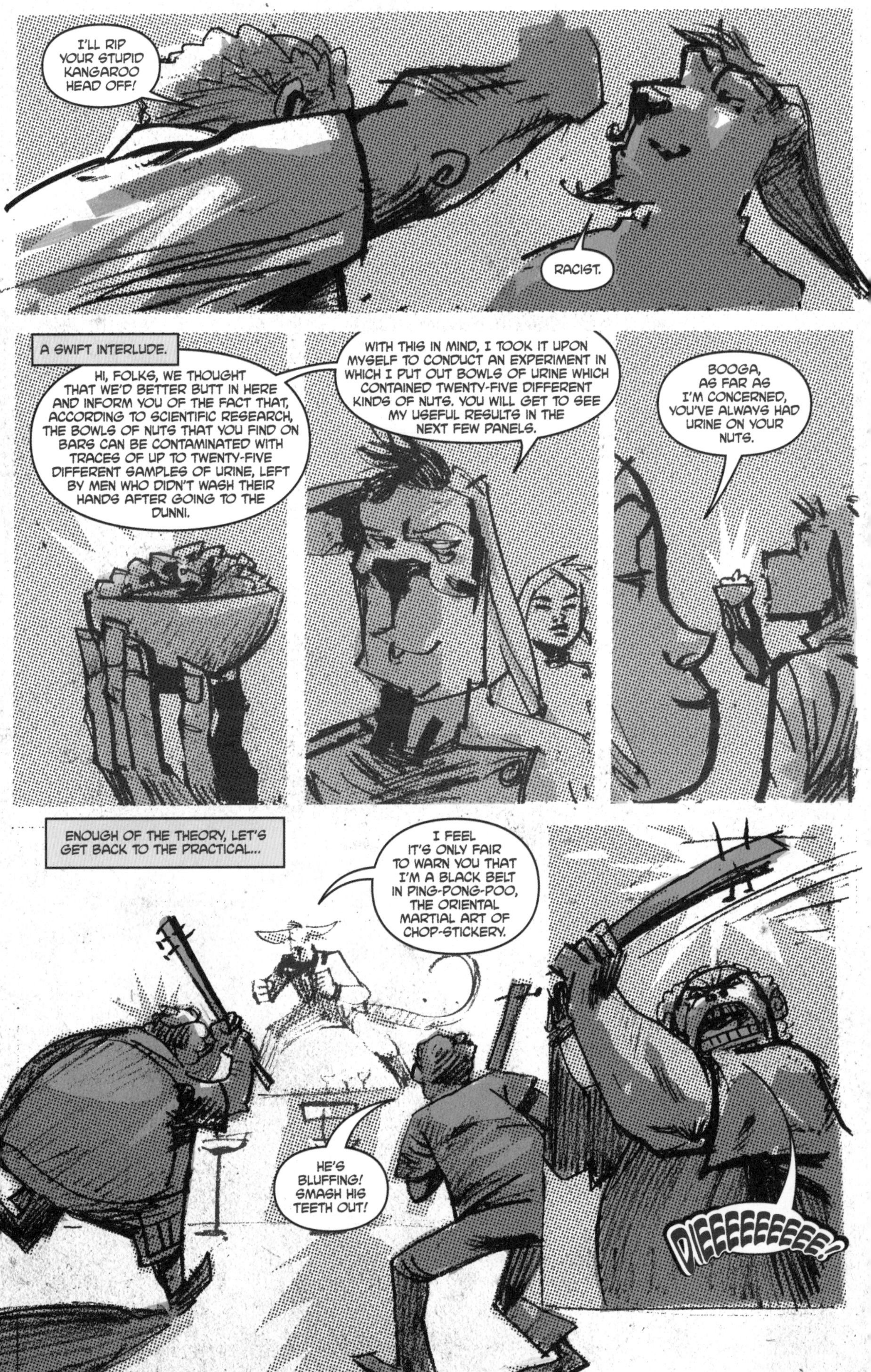
I'LL RIP YOUR STUPID KANGAROO HEAD OFF!
RACIST.
A SWIFT INTERLUDE.
HI, FOLKS, WE THOUGHT THAT WE'D BETTER BUTT IN HERE AND INFORM YOU OF THE FACT THAT, ACCORDING TO SCIENTIFIC RESEARCH, THE BOWLS OF NUTS THAT YOU FIND ON BARS CAN BE CONTAMINATED WITH TRACES OF UP TO TWENTY-FIVE DIFFERENT SAMPLES OF URINE, LEFT BY MEN WHO DIDN'T WASH THEIR HANDS AFTER GOING TO THE DUNNI.
WITH THIS IN MIND, I TOOK IT UPON MYSELF TO CONDUCT AN EXPERIMENT IN WHICH I PUT OUT BOWLS OF URINE WHICH CONTAINED TWENTY-FIVE DIFFERENT KINDS OF NUTS. YOU WILL GET TO SEE MY USEFUL RESULTS IN THE NEXT FEW PANELS.
BOOGA, AS FAR AS I'M CONCERNED, YOU'VE ALWAYS HAD URINE ON YOUR NUTS.
ENOUGH OF THE THEORY, LET'S GET BACK TO THE PRACTICAL...
I FEEL IT'S ONLY FAIR TO WARN YOU THAT I'M A BLACK BELT IN PING-PONG-POO, THE ORIENTAL MARTIAL ART OF CHOP-STICKERY.
HE'S BLUFFING! SMASH HIS TEETH OUT!
DIEEEEEEEEEE!

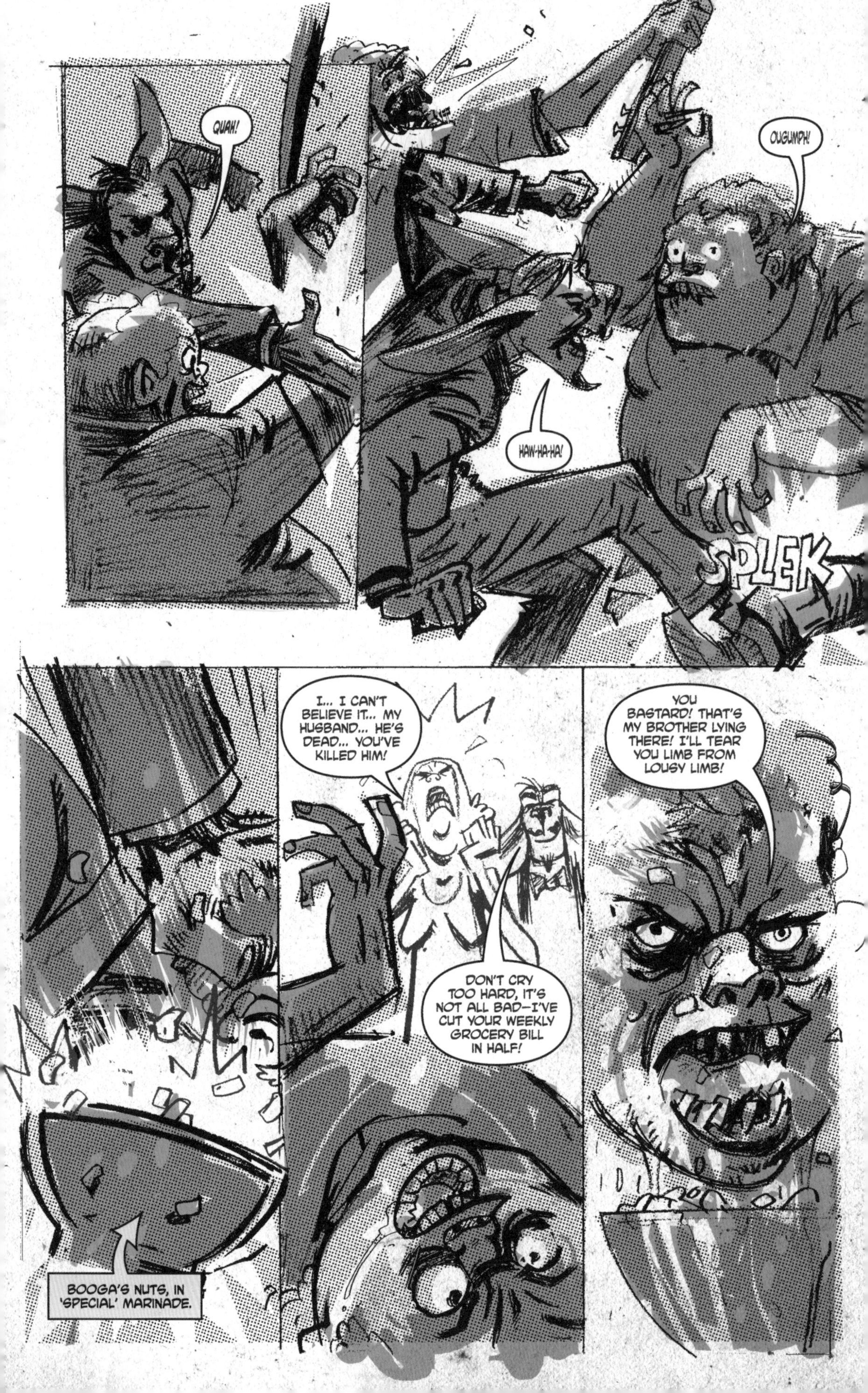
QUAH!
OUGUMPH!
HAW-HA-HA!
SPLEK
BOOGA'S NUTS, IN 'SPECIAL' MARINADE.
I... I CAN'T BELIEVE IT... MY HUSBAND... HE'S DEAD... YOU'VE KILLED HIM!
DON'T CRY TOO HARD, IT'S NOT ALL BAD–I'VE CUT YOUR WEEKLY GROCERY BILL IN HALF!
YOU BASTARD! THAT'S MY BROTHER LYING THERE! I'LL TEAR YOU LIMB FROM LOUSY LIMB!

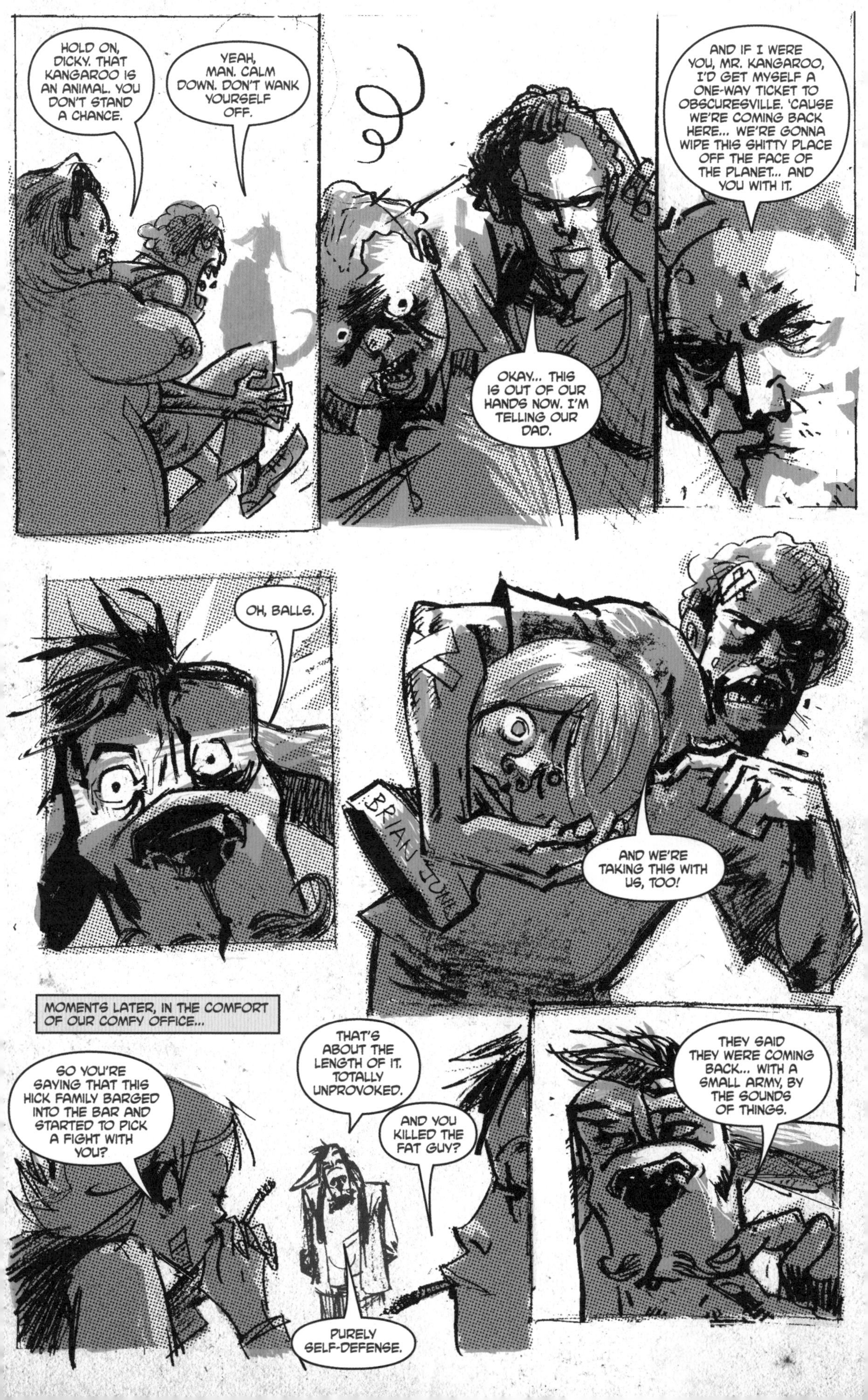
HOLD ON, DICKY. THAT KANGAROO IS AN ANIMAL. YOU DON'T STAND A CHANCE.
YEAH, MAN. CALM DOWN. DON'T WANK YOURSELF OFF.
OKAY... THIS IS OUT OF OUR HANDS NOW. I'M TELLING OUR DAD.
AND IF I WERE YOU, MR. KANGAROO, I'D GET MYSELF A ONE-WAY TICKET TO OBSCURESVILLE. 'CAUSE WE'RE COMING BACK HERE... WE'RE GONNA WIPE THIS SHITTY PLACE OFF THE FACE OF THE PLANET... AND YOU WITH IT.
OH, BALLS.
BRIAN JONES
AND WE'RE TAKING THIS WITH US, TOO!
MOMENTS LATER, IN THE COMFORT OF OUR COMFY OFFICE...
SO YOU'RE SAYING THAT THIS HICK FAMILY BARGED INTO THE BAR AND STARTED TO PICK A FIGHT WITH YOU?
THAT'S ABOUT THE LENGTH OF IT. TOTALLY UNPROVOKED.
AND YOU KILLED THE FAT GUY?
PURELY SELF-DEFENSE.
THEY SAID THEY WERE COMING BACK... WITH A SMALL ARMY, BY THE SOUNDS OF THINGS.

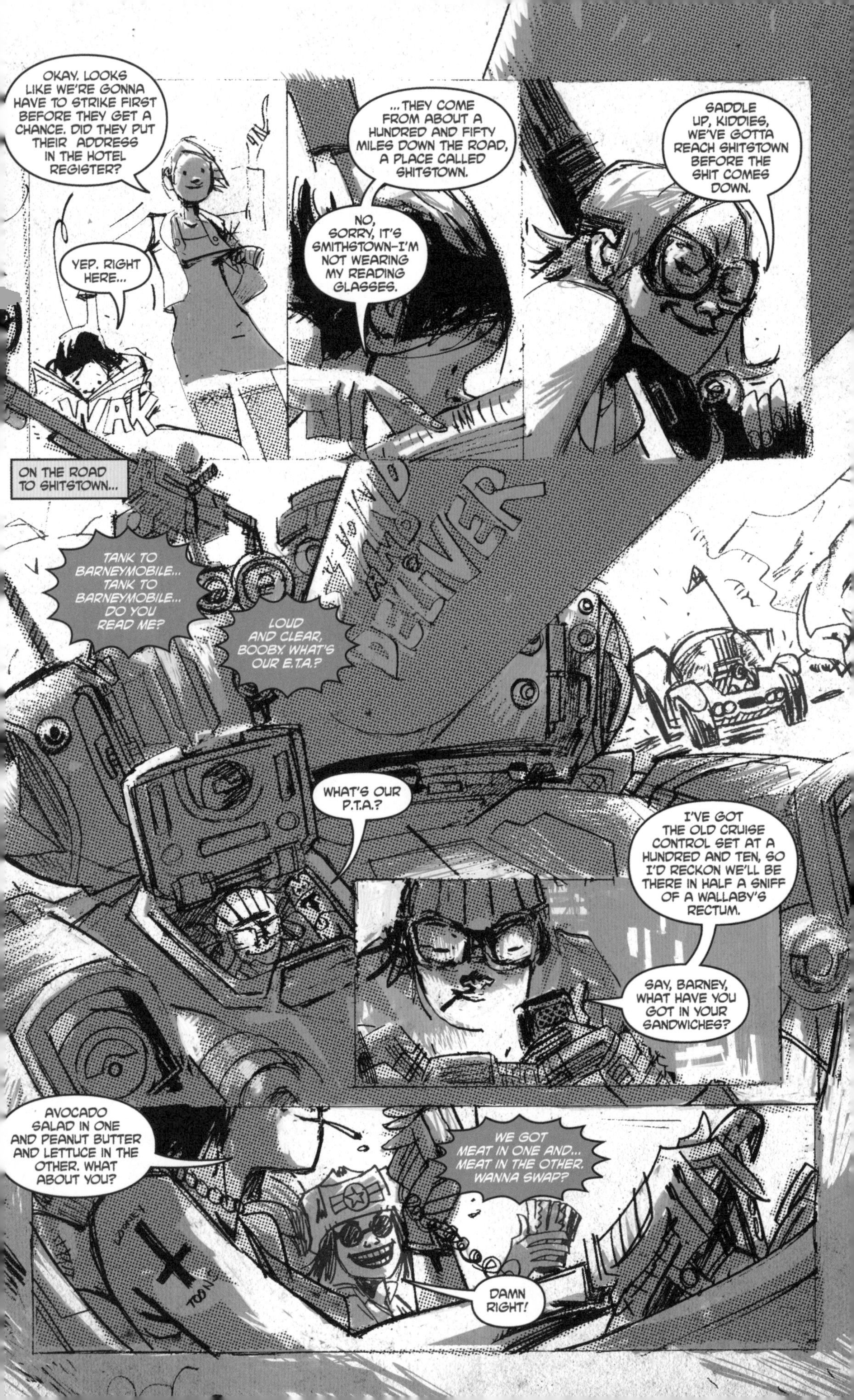
OKAY. LOOKS LIKE WE'RE GONNA HAVE TO STRIKE FIRST BEFORE THEY GET A CHANCE. DID THEY PUT THEIR ADDRESS IN THE HOTEL REGISTER?
YEP. RIGHT HERE...
WAK
...THEY COME FROM ABOUT A HUNDRED AND FIFTY MILES DOWN THE ROAD, A PLACE CALLED SHITSTOWN.
NO, SORRY, IT'S SMITHSTOWN–I'M NOT WEARING MY READING GLASSES.
SADDLE UP, KIDDIES, WE'VE GOTTA REACH SHITSTOWN BEFORE THE SHIT COMES DOWN.
ON THE ROAD TO SHITSTOWN...
DELIVER
TANK TO BARNEYMOBILE... TANK TO BARNEYMOBILE... DO YOU READ ME?
LOUD AND CLEAR, BOOBY. WHAT'S OUR E.T.A.?
WHAT'S OUR P.T.A.?
I'VE GOT THE OLD CRUISE CONTROL SET AT A HUNDRED AND TEN, SO I'D RECKON WE'LL BE THERE IN HALF A SNIFF OF A WALLABY'S RECTUM.
SAY, BARNEY, WHAT HAVE YOU GOT IN YOUR SANDWICHES?
AVOCADO SALAD IN ONE AND PEANUT BUTTER AND LETTUCE IN THE OTHER. WHAT ABOUT YOU?
WE GOT MEAT IN ONE AND... MEAT IN THE OTHER. WANNA SWAP?
DAMN RIGHT!

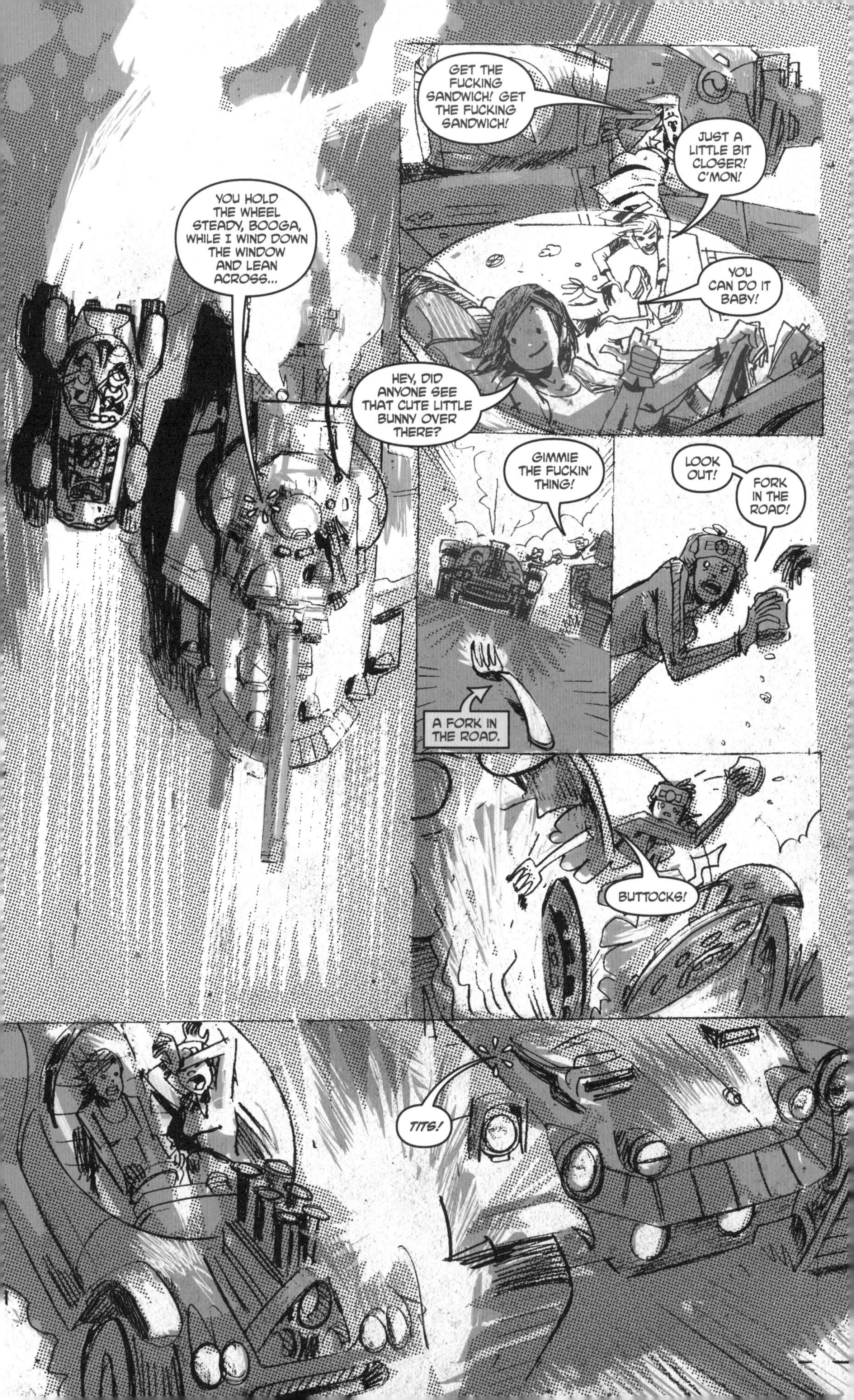
YOU HOLD THE WHEEL STEADY, BOOGA, WHILE I WIND DOWN THE WINDOW AND LEAN ACROSS...
GET THE FUCKING SANDWICH! GET THE FUCKING SANDWICH!
JUST A LITTLE BIT CLOSER! C'MON!
YOU CAN DO IT BABY!
HEY, DID ANYONE SEE THAT CUTE LITTLE BUNNY OVER THERE?
GIMMIE THE FUCKIN' THING!
A FORK IN THE ROAD.
LOOK OUT!
FORK IN THE ROAD!
BUTTOCKS!
TITS!

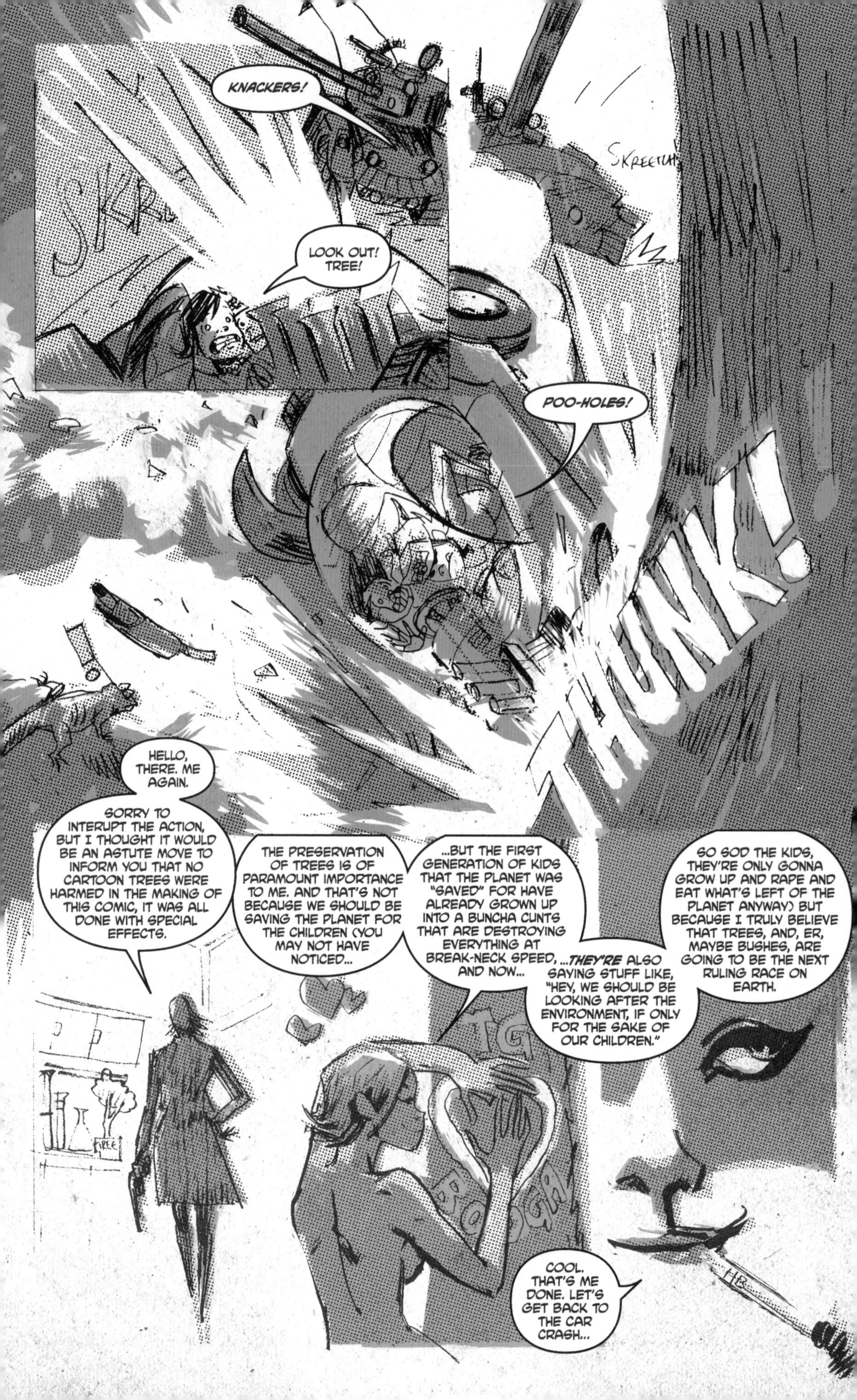

KNACKERS!
SKREETCH
LOOK OUT! TREE!
POO-HOLES!
THUNK!
HELLO, THERE. ME AGAIN.
SORRY TO INTERUPT THE ACTION, BUT I THOUGHT IT WOULD BE AN ASTUTE MOVE TO INFORM YOU THAT NO CARTOON TREES WERE HARMED IN THE MAKING OF THIS COMIC, IT WAS ALL DONE WITH SPECIAL EFFECTS.
THE PRESERVATION OF TREES IS OF PARAMOUNT IMPORTANCE TO ME. AND THAT'S NOT BECAUSE WE SHOULD BE SAVING THE PLANET FOR THE CHILDREN (YOU MAY NOT HAVE NOTICED...
...BUT THE FIRST GENERATION OF KIDS THAT THE PLANET WAS "SAVED" FOR HAVE ALREADY GROWN UP INTO A BUNCHA CUNTS THAT ARE DESTROYING EVERYTHING AT BREAK-NECK SPEED, AND NOW...
...*THEY'RE* ALSO SAYING STUFF LIKE, "HEY, WE SHOULD BE LOOKING AFTER THE ENVIRONMENT, IF ONLY FOR THE SAKE OF OUR CHILDREN."
SO SOD THE KIDS, THEY'RE ONLY GONNA GROW UP AND RAPE AND EAT WHAT'S LEFT OF THE PLANET ANYWAY) BUT BECAUSE I TRULY BELIEVE THAT TREES, AND, ER, MAYBE BUSHES, ARE GOING TO BE THE NEXT RULING RACE ON EARTH.
COOL. THAT'S ME DONE. LET'S GET BACK TO THE CAR CRASH...

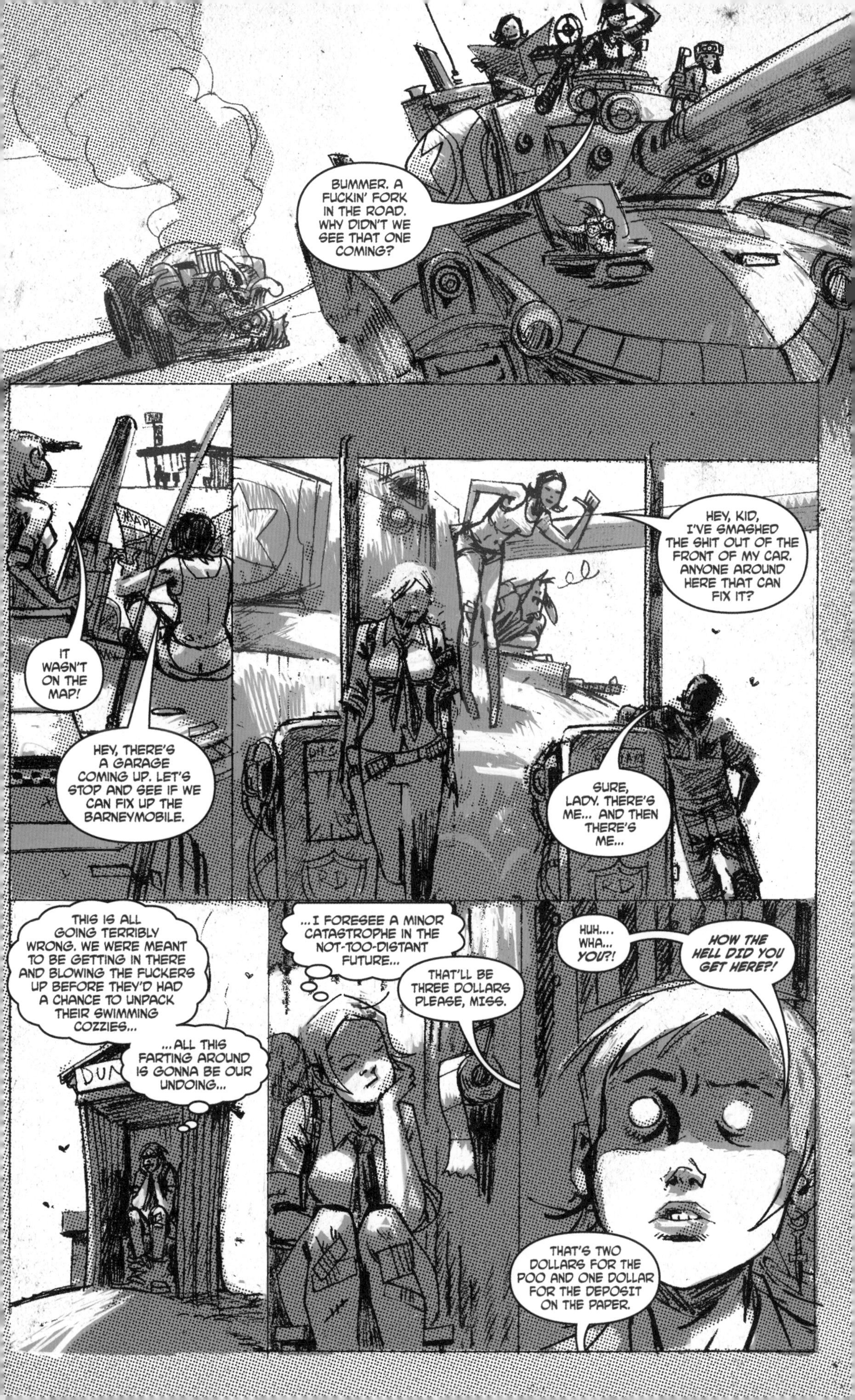
BUMMER. A FUCKIN' FORK IN THE ROAD. WHY DIDN'T WE SEE THAT ONE COMING?
IT WASN'T ON THE MAP!
MAP
HEY, THERE'S A GARAGE COMING UP. LET'S STOP AND SEE IF WE CAN FIX UP THE BARNEYMOBILE.
HEY, KID, I'VE SMASHED THE SHIT OUT OF THE FRONT OF MY CAR. ANYONE AROUND HERE THAT CAN FIX IT?
SURE, LADY. THERE'S ME... AND THEN THERE'S ME...
THIS IS ALL GOING TERRIBLY WRONG. WE WERE MEANT TO BE GETTING IN THERE AND BLOWING THE FUCKERS UP BEFORE THEY'D HAD A CHANCE TO UNPACK THEIR SWIMMING COZZIES...
...ALL THIS FARTING AROUND IS GONNA BE OUR UNDOING...
DUN
...I FORESEE A MINOR CATASTROPHE IN THE NOT-TOO-DISTANT FUTURE...
THAT'LL BE THREE DOLLARS PLEASE, MISS.
HUH.... WHA... YOU?!
HOW THE HELL DID YOU GET HERE?!
THAT'S TWO DOLLARS FOR THE POO AND ONE DOLLAR FOR THE DEPOSIT ON THE PAPER.

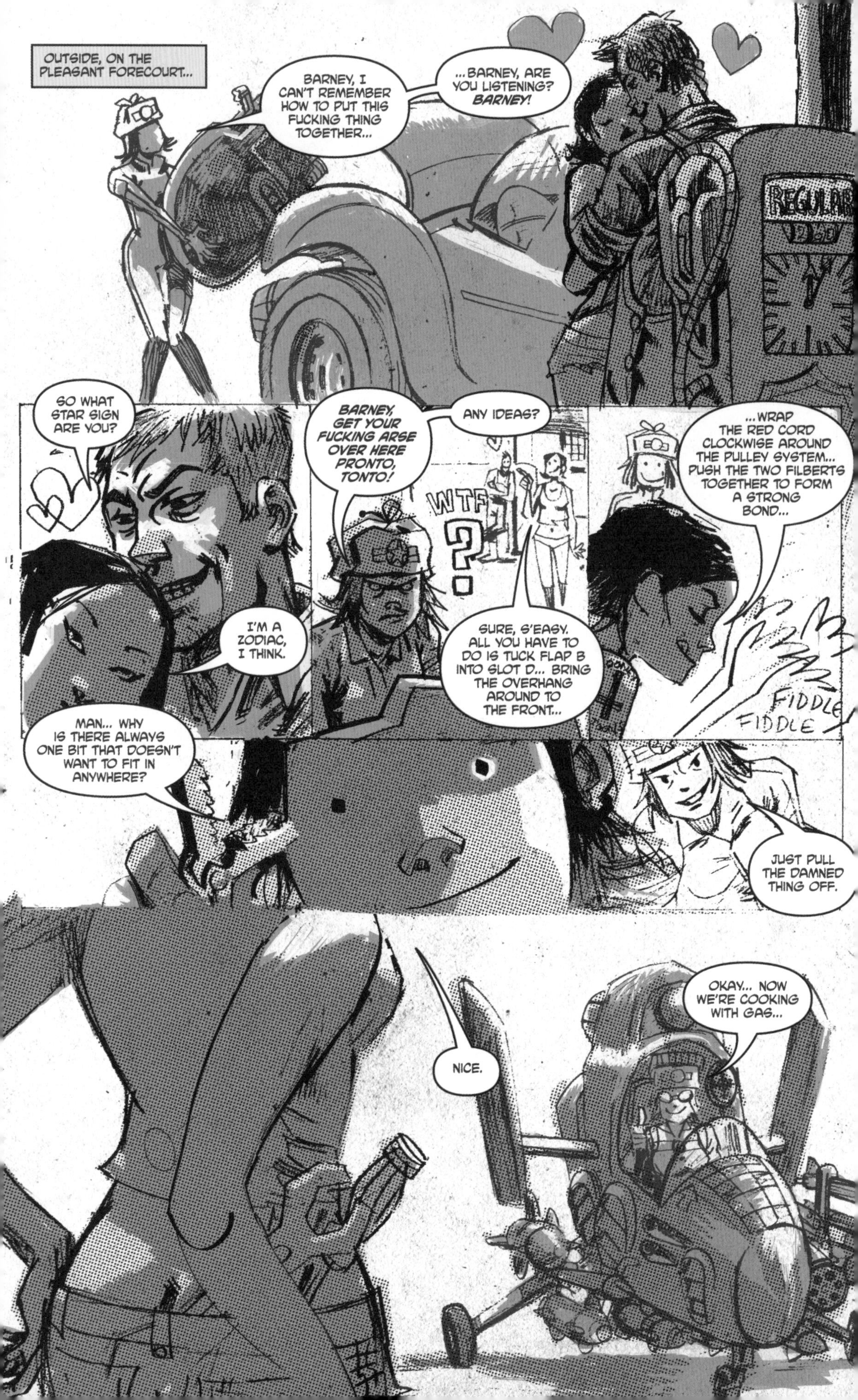
OUTSIDE, ON THE PLEASANT FORECOURT...
BARNEY, I CAN'T REMEMBER HOW TO PUT THIS FUCKING THING TOGETHER...
...BARNEY, ARE YOU LISTENING? BARNEY!
REGULAR
SO WHAT STAR SIGN ARE YOU?
I'M A ZODIAC, I THINK.
BARNEY, GET YOUR FUCKING ARSE OVER HERE PRONTO, TONTO!
ANY IDEAS?
WTF ?
SURE, S'EASY. ALL YOU HAVE TO DO IS TUCK FLAP B INTO SLOT D... BRING THE OVERHANG AROUND TO THE FRONT...
...WRAP THE RED CORD CLOCKWISE AROUND THE PULLEY SYSTEM... PUSH THE TWO FILBERTS TOGETHER TO FORM A STRONG BOND...
FIDDLE FIDDLE
MAN... WHY IS THERE ALWAYS ONE BIT THAT DOESN'T WANT TO FIT IN ANYWHERE?
JUST PULL THE DAMNED THING OFF.
NICE.
OKAY... NOW WE'RE COOKING WITH GAS...

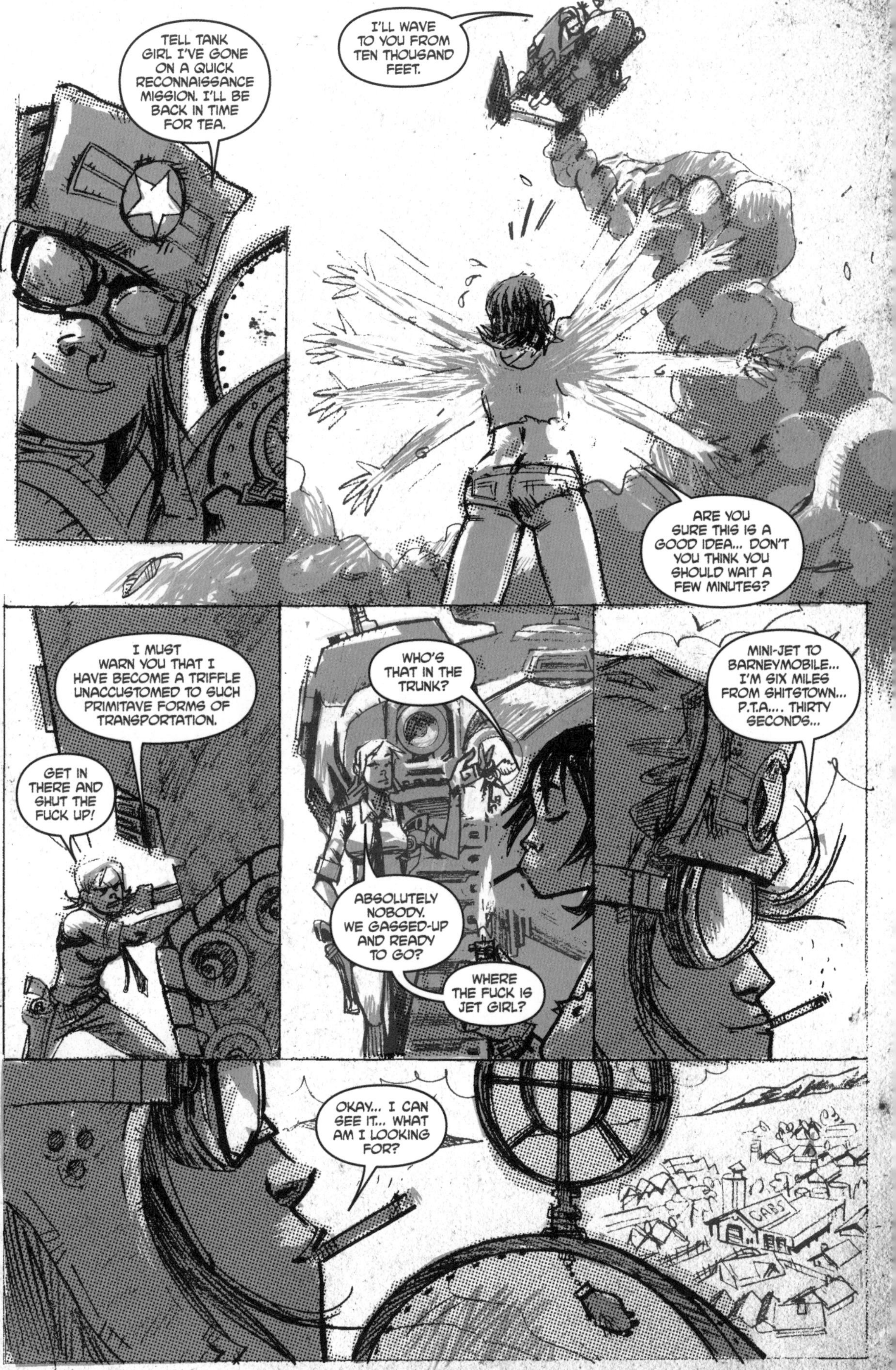

TELL TANK GIRL I'VE GONE ON A QUICK RECONNAISSANCE MISSION. I'LL BE BACK IN TIME FOR TEA.
I'LL WAVE TO YOU FROM TEN THOUSAND FEET.
ARE YOU SURE THIS IS A GOOD IDEA... DON'T YOU THINK YOU SHOULD WAIT A FEW MINUTES?
I MUST WARN YOU THAT I HAVE BECOME A TRIFFLE UNACCUSTOMED TO SUCH PRIMITAVE FORMS OF TRANSPORTATION.
GET IN THERE AND SHUT THE FUCK UP!
WHO'S THAT IN THE TRUNK?
ABSOLUTELY NOBODY. WE GASSED-UP AND READY TO GO?
WHERE THE FUCK IS JET GIRL?
MINI-JET TO BARNEYMOBILE... I'M SIX MILES FROM SHITSTOWN... P.T.A.... THIRTY SECONDS...
OKAY... I CAN SEE IT... WHAT AM I LOOKING FOR?
GABS

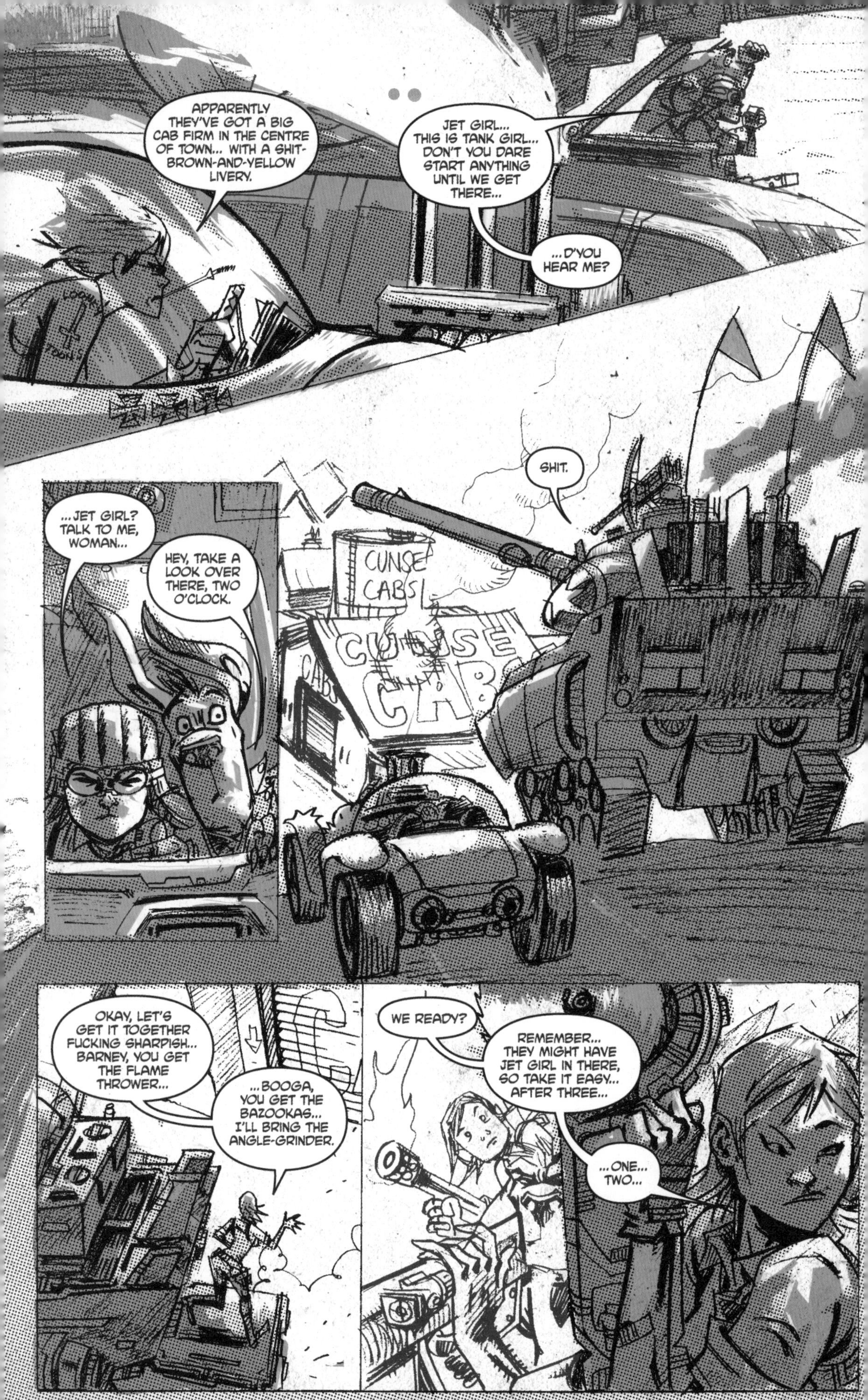
APPARENTLY THEY'VE GOT A BIG CAB FIRM IN THE CENTRE OF TOWN... WITH A SHIT-BROWN-AND-YELLOW LIVERY.
JET GIRL... THIS IS TANK GIRL... DON'T YOU DARE START ANYTHING UNTIL WE GET THERE...
...D'YOU HEAR ME?
...JET GIRL? TALK TO ME, WOMAN...
HEY, TAKE A LOOK OVER THERE, TWO O'CLOCK.
SHIT.
CUNSE CABS
CUNSE CABS
OKAY, LET'S GET IT TOGETHER FUCKING SHARPISH... BARNEY, YOU GET THE FLAME THROWER...
...BOOGA, YOU GET THE BAZOOKAS... I'LL BRING THE ANGLE-GRINDER.
WE READY?
REMEMBER... THEY MIGHT HAVE JET GIRL IN THERE, SO TAKE IT EASY... AFTER THREE...
...ONE... TWO...

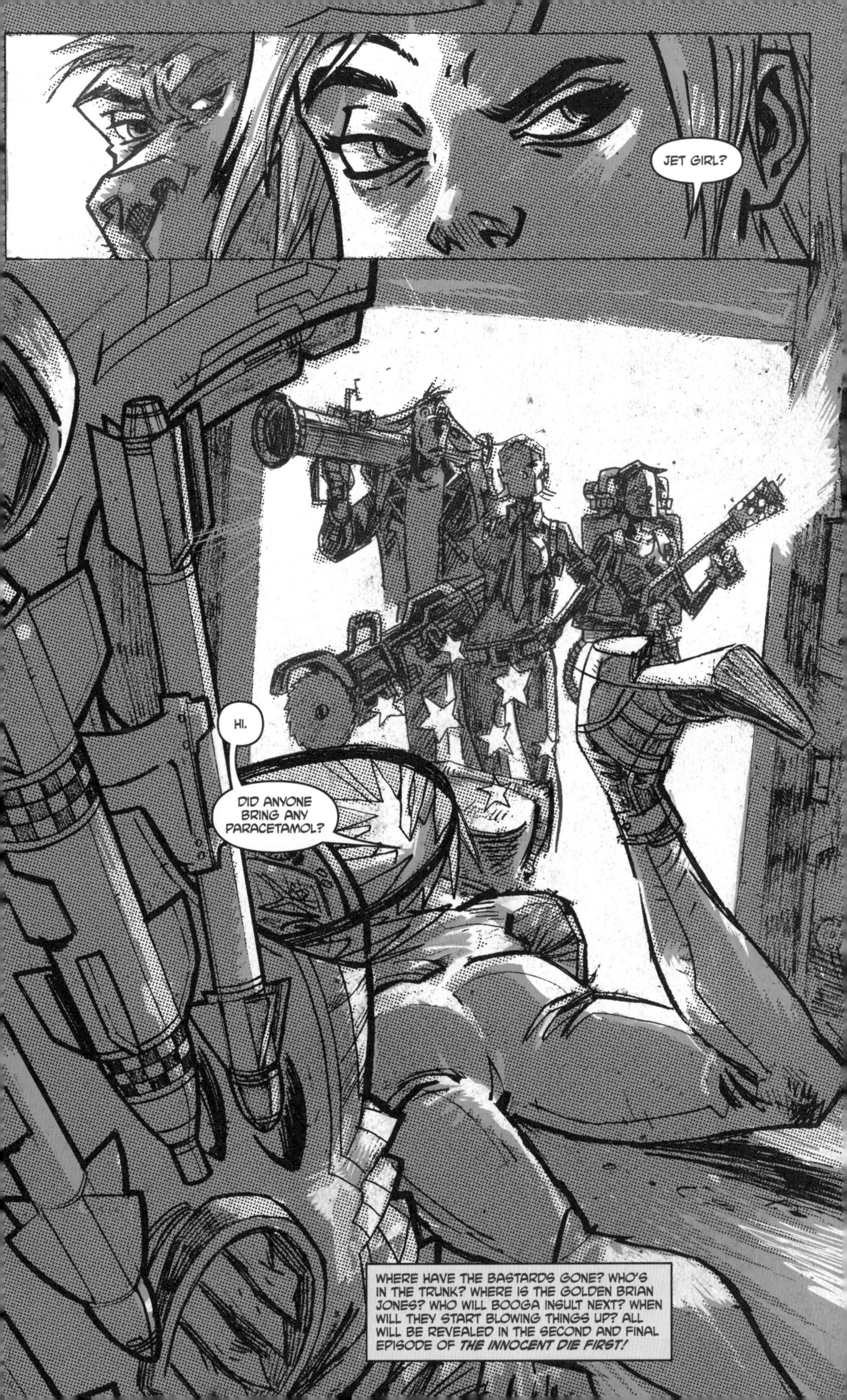
JET GIRL?
HI.
DID ANYONE BRING ANY PARACETAMOL?
WHERE HAVE THE BASTARDS GONE? WHO'S IN THE TRUNK? WHERE IS THE GOLDEN BRIAN JONES? WHO WILL BOOGA INSULT NEXT? WHEN WILL THEY START BLOWING THINGS UP? ALL WILL BE REVEALED IN THE SECOND AND FINAL EPISODE OF *THE INNOCENT DIE FIRST!*

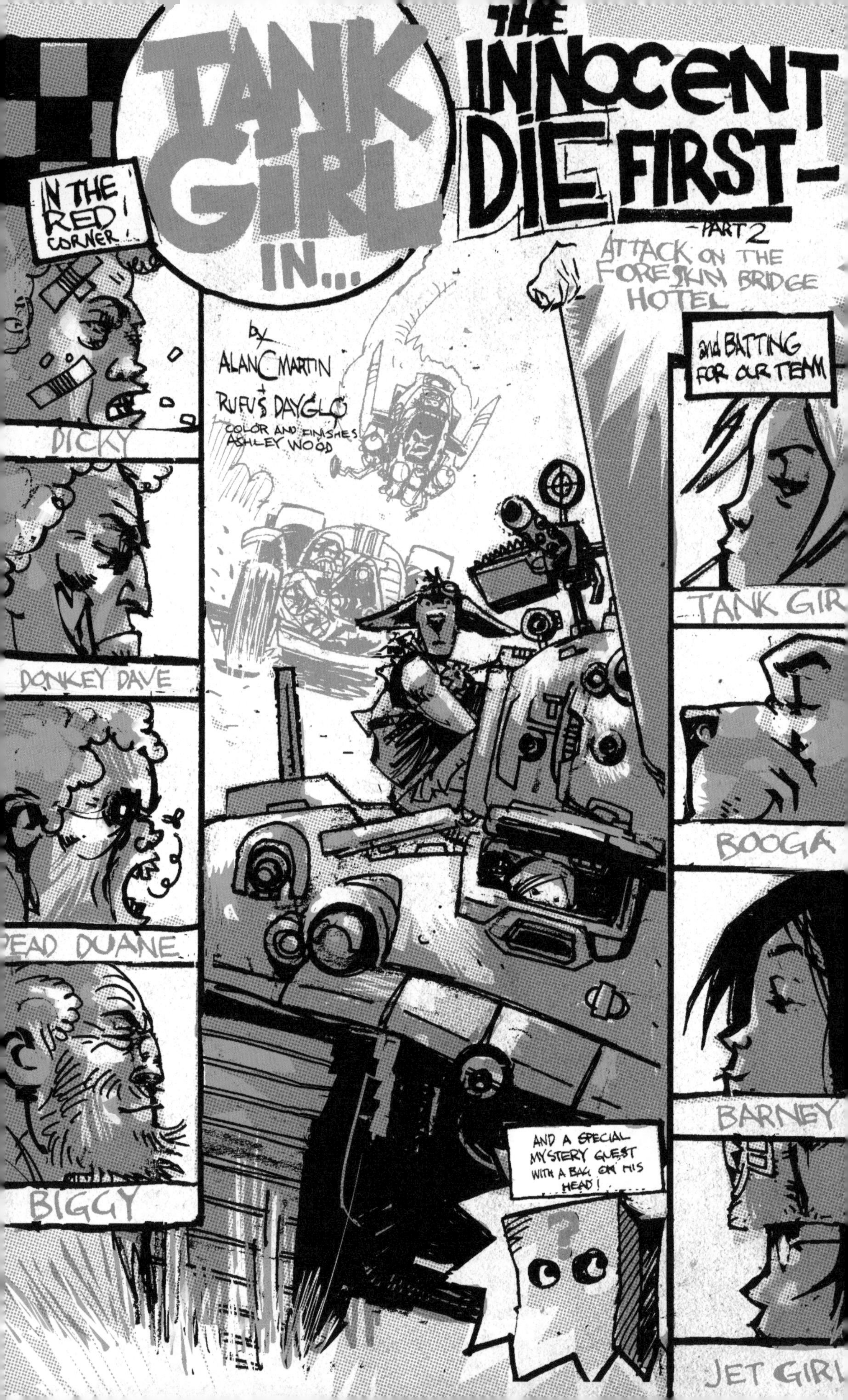
TANK GIRL IN...
IN THE RED CORNER
THE INNOCENT DIE FIRST -
- PART 2
ATTACK ON THE FORESKIN BRIDGE HOTEL
BY ALAN C MARTIN + RUFUS DAYGLO
COLOR AND FINISHES ASHLEY WOOD
and BATTING FOR OUR TEAM
DICKY
DONKEY DAVE
EAD DUANE
BIGGY
TANK GIR
BOOGA
BARNEY
AND A SPECIAL MYSTERY GUEST WITH A BAG ON HIS HEAD!
JET GIRL

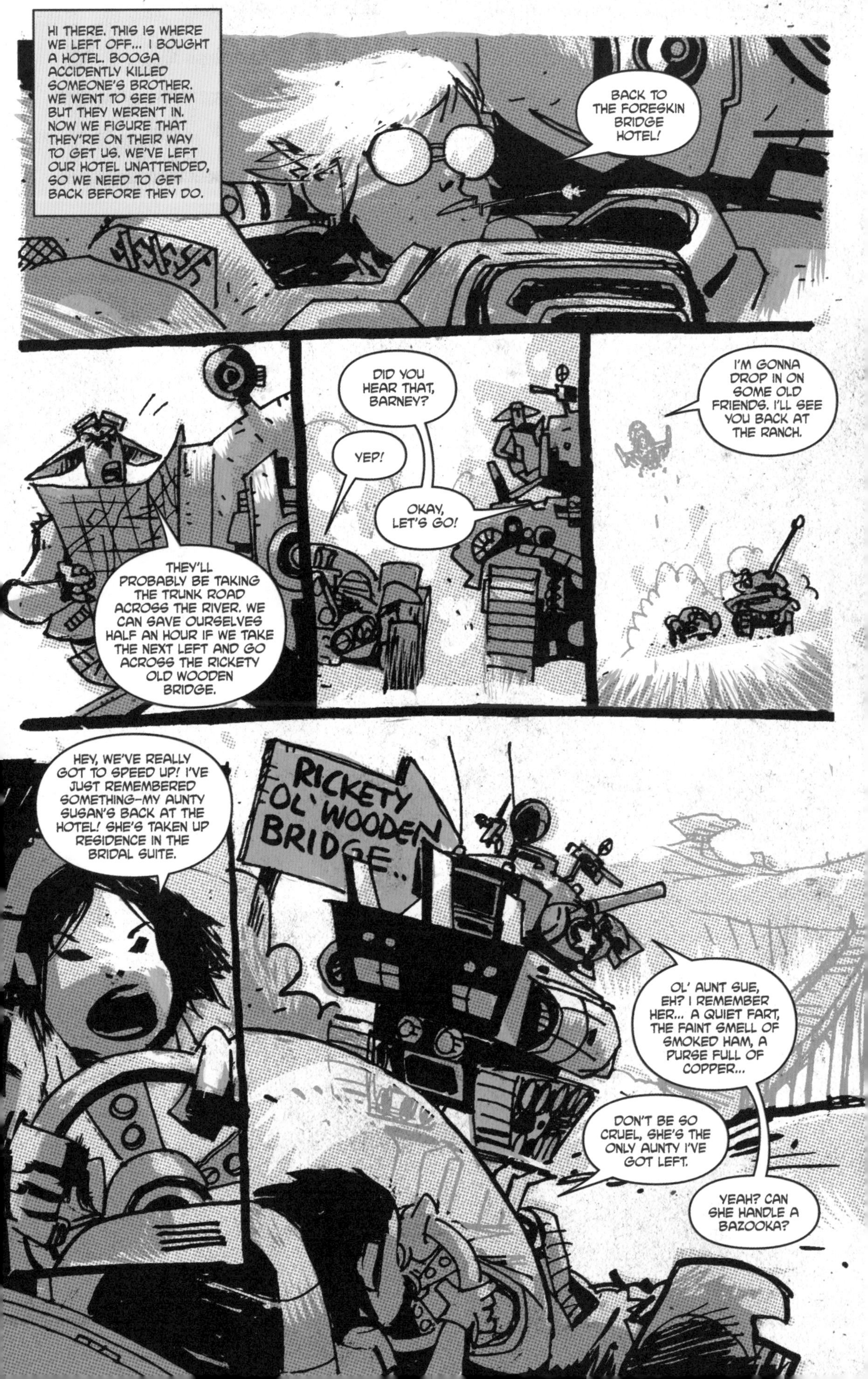
HI THERE. THIS IS WHERE WE LEFT OFF... I BOUGHT A HOTEL. BOOGA ACCIDENTLY KILLED SOMEONE'S BROTHER. WE WENT TO SEE THEM BUT THEY WEREN'T IN. NOW WE FIGURE THAT THEY'RE ON THEIR WAY TO GET US. WE'VE LEFT OUR HOTEL UNATTENDED, SO WE NEED TO GET BACK BEFORE THEY DO.
BACK TO THE FORESKIN BRIDGE HOTEL!
THEY'LL PROBABLY BE TAKING THE TRUNK ROAD ACROSS THE RIVER. WE CAN SAVE OURSELVES HALF AN HOUR IF WE TAKE THE NEXT LEFT AND GO ACROSS THE RICKETY OLD WOODEN BRIDGE.
DID YOU HEAR THAT, BARNEY?
YEP!
OKAY, LET'S GO!
I'M GONNA DROP IN ON SOME OLD FRIENDS. I'LL SEE YOU BACK AT THE RANCH.
HEY, WE'VE REALLY GOT TO SPEED UP! I'VE JUST REMEMBERED SOMETHING–MY AUNTY SUSAN'S BACK AT THE HOTEL! SHE'S TAKEN UP RESIDENCE IN THE BRIDAL SUITE.
RICKETY OL' WOODEN BRIDGE..
OL' AUNT SUE, EH? I REMEMBER HER... A QUIET FART, THE FAINT SMELL OF SMOKED HAM, A PURSE FULL OF COPPER...
DON'T BE SO CRUEL, SHE'S THE ONLY AUNTY I'VE GOT LEFT.
YEAH? CAN SHE HANDLE A BAZOOKA?

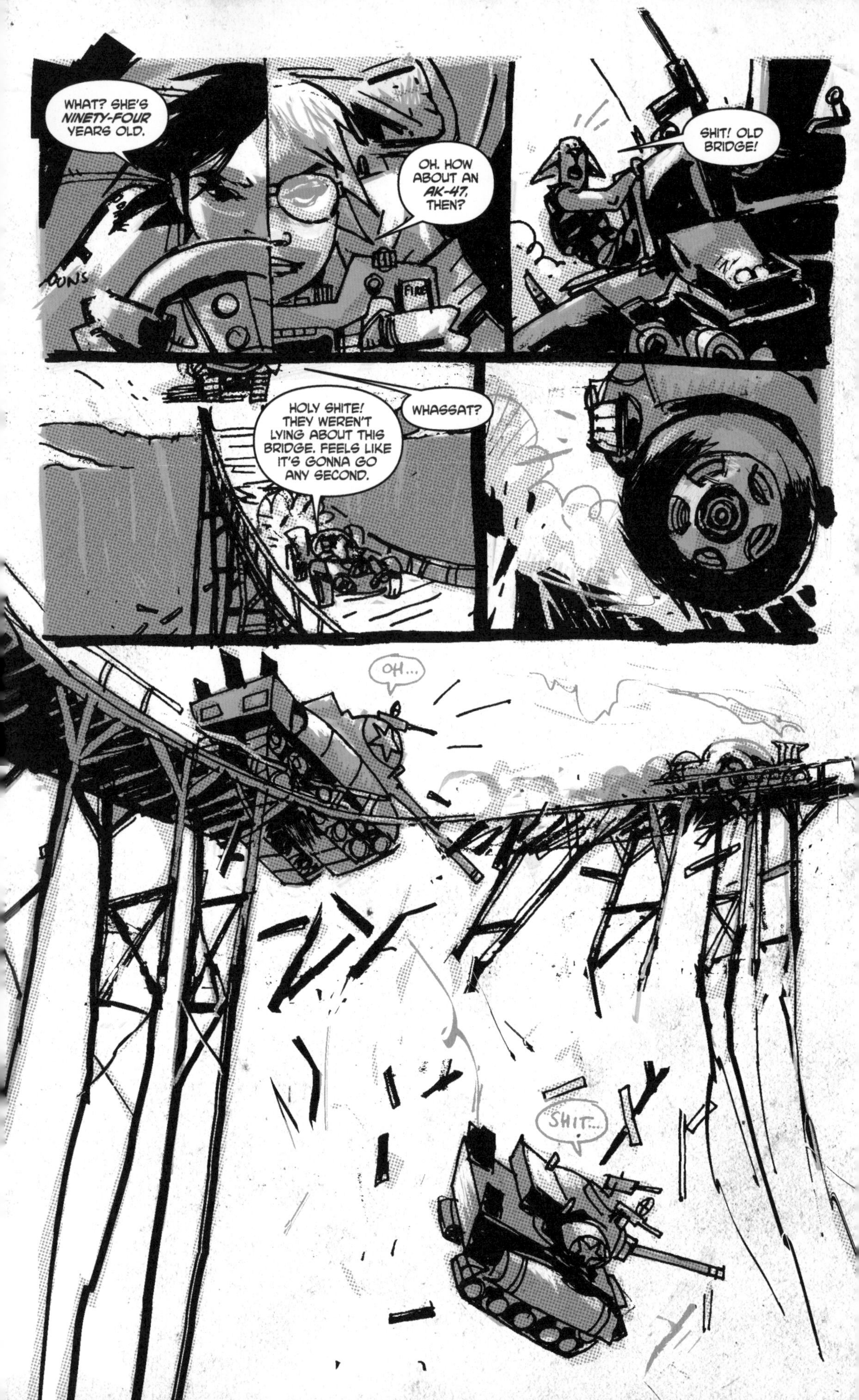
WHAT? SHE'S *NINETY-FOUR* YEARS OLD.
OH. HOW ABOUT AN *AK-47,* THEN?
SHIT! OLD BRIDGE!
HOLY SHITE! THEY WEREN'T LYING ABOUT THIS BRIDGE. FEELS LIKE IT'S GONNA GO ANY SECOND.
WHASSAT?
OH...
SHIT...

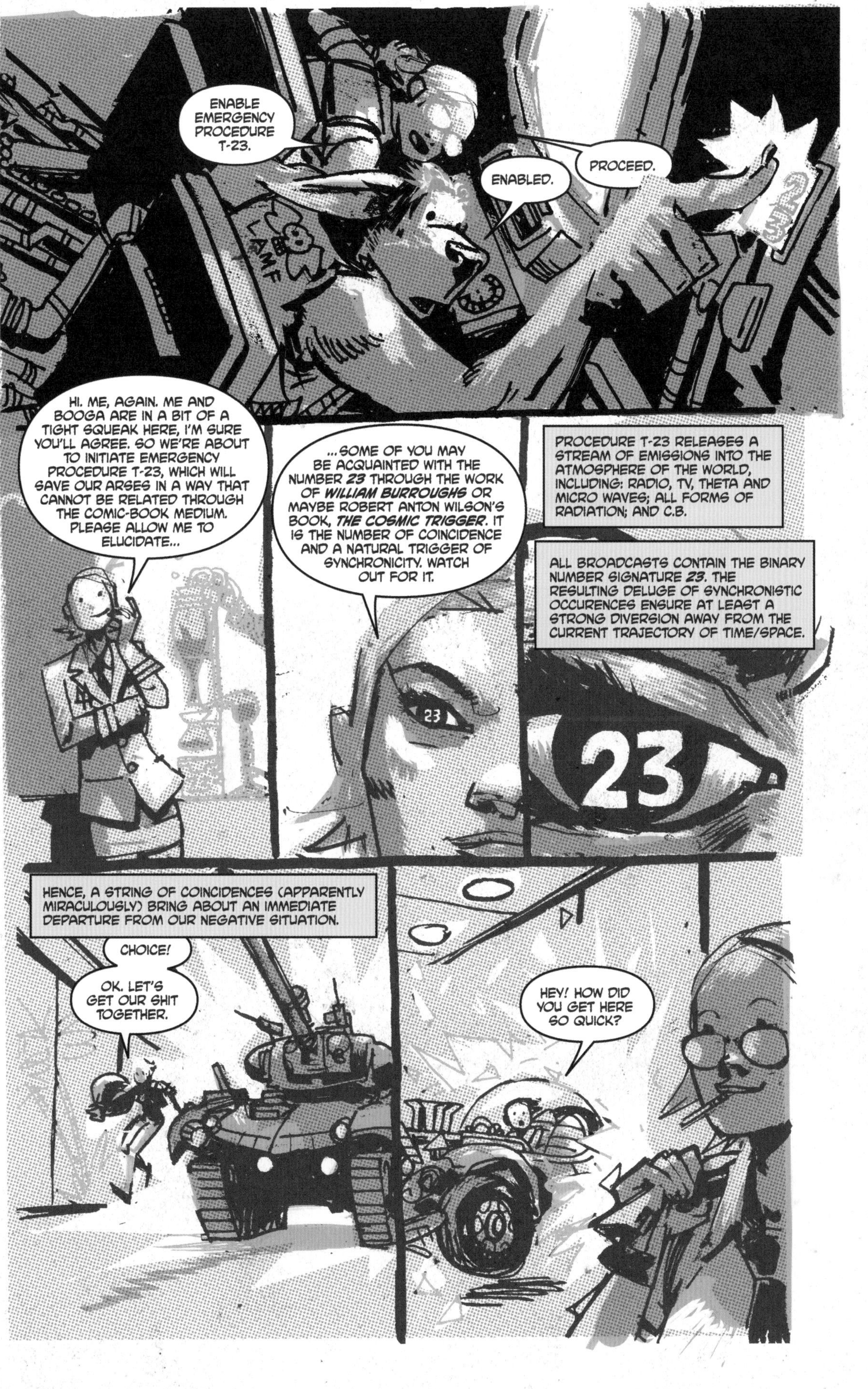

ENABLE EMERGENCY PROCEDURE T-23.
ENABLED.
PROCEED.
HI. ME, AGAIN. ME AND BOOGA ARE IN A BIT OF A TIGHT SQUEAK HERE, I'M SURE YOU'LL AGREE. SO WE'RE ABOUT TO INITIATE EMERGENCY PROCEDURE T-23, WHICH WILL SAVE OUR ARSES IN A WAY THAT CANNOT BE RELATED THROUGH THE COMIC-BOOK MEDIUM. PLEASE ALLOW ME TO ELUCIDATE...
...SOME OF YOU MAY BE ACQUAINTED WITH THE NUMBER *23* THROUGH THE WORK OF ***WILLIAM BURROUGHS*** OR MAYBE ROBERT ANTON WILSON'S BOOK, ***THE COSMIC TRIGGER***. IT IS THE NUMBER OF COINCIDENCE AND A NATURAL TRIGGER OF SYNCHRONICITY. WATCH OUT FOR IT.
PROCEDURE T-23 RELEASES A STREAM OF EMISSIONS INTO THE ATMOSPHERE OF THE WORLD, INCLUDING: RADIO, TV, THETA AND MICRO WAVES; ALL FORMS OF RADIATION; AND C.B.
ALL BROADCASTS CONTAIN THE BINARY NUMBER SIGNATURE *23*. THE RESULTING DELUGE OF SYNCHRONISTIC OCCURENCES ENSURE AT LEAST A STRONG DIVERSION AWAY FROM THE CURRENT TRAJECTORY OF TIME/SPACE.
23
23
HENCE, A STRING OF COINCIDENCES (APPARENTLY MIRACULOUSLY) BRING ABOUT AN IMMEDIATE DEPARTURE FROM OUR NEGATIVE SITUATION.
CHOICE!
OK. LET'S GET OUR SHIT TOGETHER.
HEY! HOW DID YOU GET HERE SO QUICK?

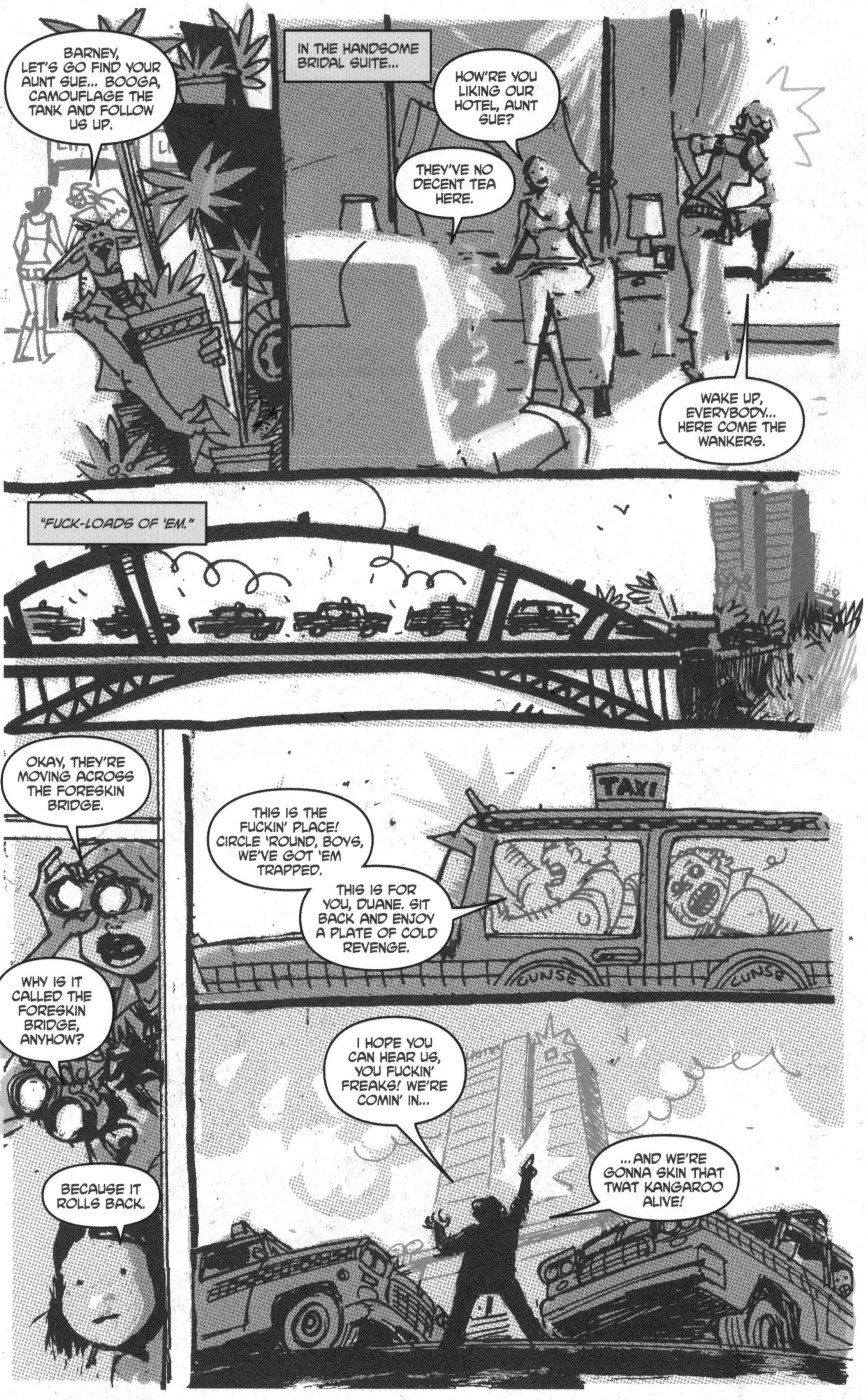
BARNEY, LET'S GO FIND YOUR AUNT SUE... BOOGA, CAMOUFLAGE THE TANK AND FOLLOW US UP.
IN THE HANDSOME BRIDAL SUITE...
HOW'RE YOU LIKING OUR HOTEL, AUNT SUE?
THEY'VE NO DECENT TEA HERE.
WAKE UP, EVERYBODY... HERE COME THE WANKERS.
"FUCK-LOADS OF 'EM."
OKAY, THEY'RE MOVING ACROSS THE FORESKIN BRIDGE.
WHY IS IT CALLED THE FORESKIN BRIDGE, ANYHOW?
BECAUSE IT ROLLS BACK.
TAXI
THIS IS THE FUCKIN' PLACE! CIRCLE 'ROUND, BOYS, WE'VE GOT 'EM TRAPPED.
THIS IS FOR YOU, DUANE. SIT BACK AND ENJOY A PLATE OF COLD REVENGE.
I HOPE YOU CAN HEAR US, YOU FUCKIN' FREAKS! WE'RE COMIN' IN...
...AND WE'RE GONNA SKIN THAT TWAT KANGAROO ALIVE!

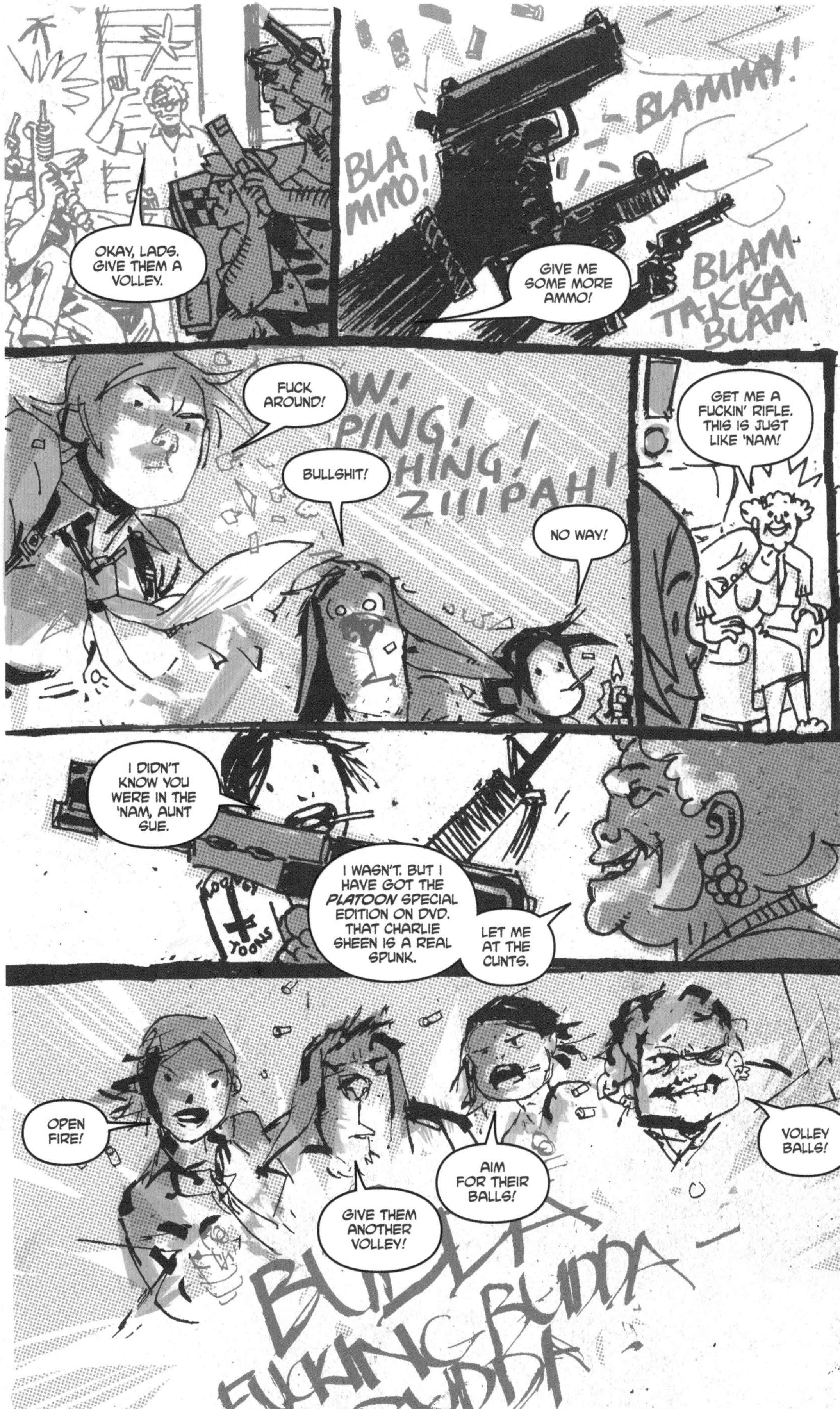
OKAY, LADS. GIVE THEM A VOLLEY.
BLA MMO!
BLAMMM!
GIVE ME SOME MORE AMMO!
BLAM TAKKA BLAM
FUCK AROUND!
PING! HING! ZIIIPAH!
BULLSHIT!
NO WAY!
GET ME A FUCKIN' RIFLE. THIS IS JUST LIKE 'NAM!
I DIDN'T KNOW YOU WERE IN THE 'NAM, AUNT SUE.
I WASN'T. BUT I HAVE GOT THE *PLATOON* SPECIAL EDITION ON DVD. THAT CHARLIE SHEEN IS A REAL SPUNK.
LET ME AT THE CUNTS.
OPEN FIRE!
GIVE THEM ANOTHER VOLLEY!
AIM FOR THEIR BALLS!
VOLLEY BALLS!
BUDDA FUCKING BUDDA BUDDA

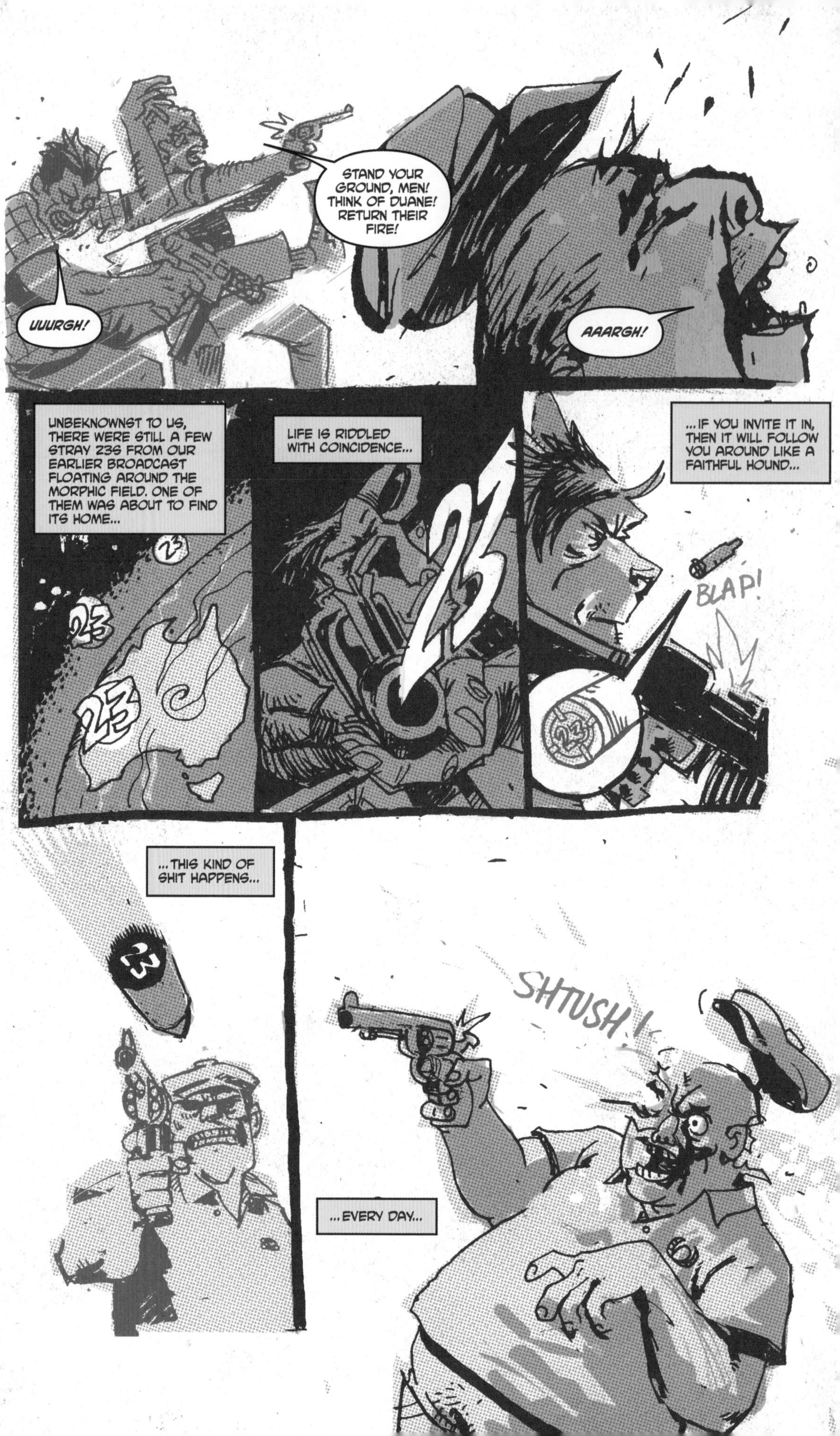
STAND YOUR GROUND, MEN! THINK OF DUANE! RETURN THEIR FIRE!
UUURGH!
AAARGH!
UNBEKNOWNST TO US, THERE WERE STILL A FEW STRAY 23S FROM OUR EARLIER BROADCAST FLOATING AROUND THE MORPHIC FIELD. ONE OF THEM WAS ABOUT TO FIND ITS HOME...
LIFE IS RIDDLED WITH COINCIDENCE...
...IF YOU INVITE IT IN, THEN IT WILL FOLLOW YOU AROUND LIKE A FAITHFUL HOUND...
BLAP!
...THIS KIND OF SHIT HAPPENS...
SHTUSH!
...EVERY DAY...

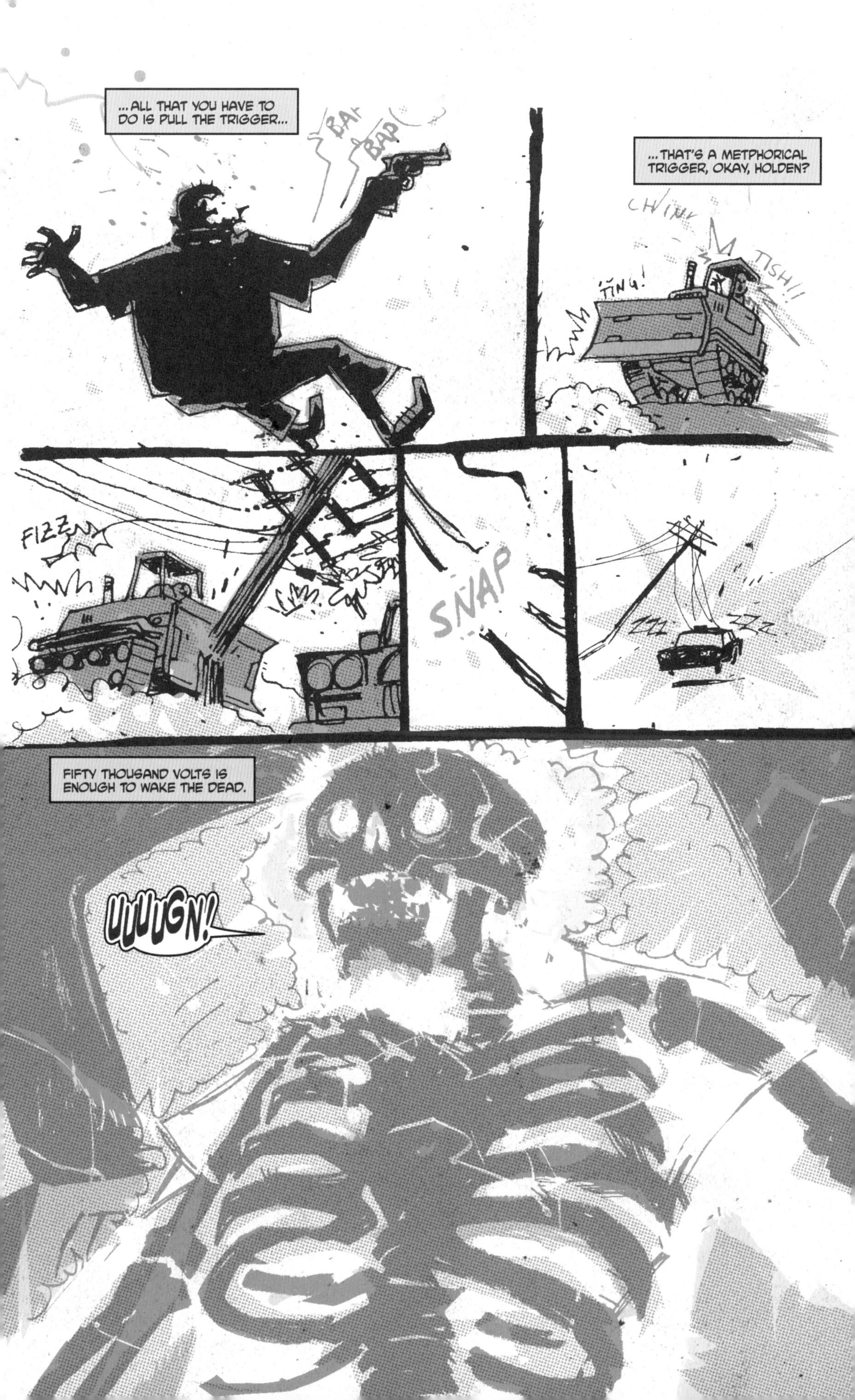
...ALL THAT YOU HAVE TO DO IS PULL THE TRIGGER...
BAP
BAP
...THAT'S A METPHORICAL TRIGGER, OKAY, HOLDEN?
TING!
TISH!!
FIZZ
SNAP
FIFTY THOUSAND VOLTS IS ENOUGH TO WAKE THE DEAD.
UUUUGN!

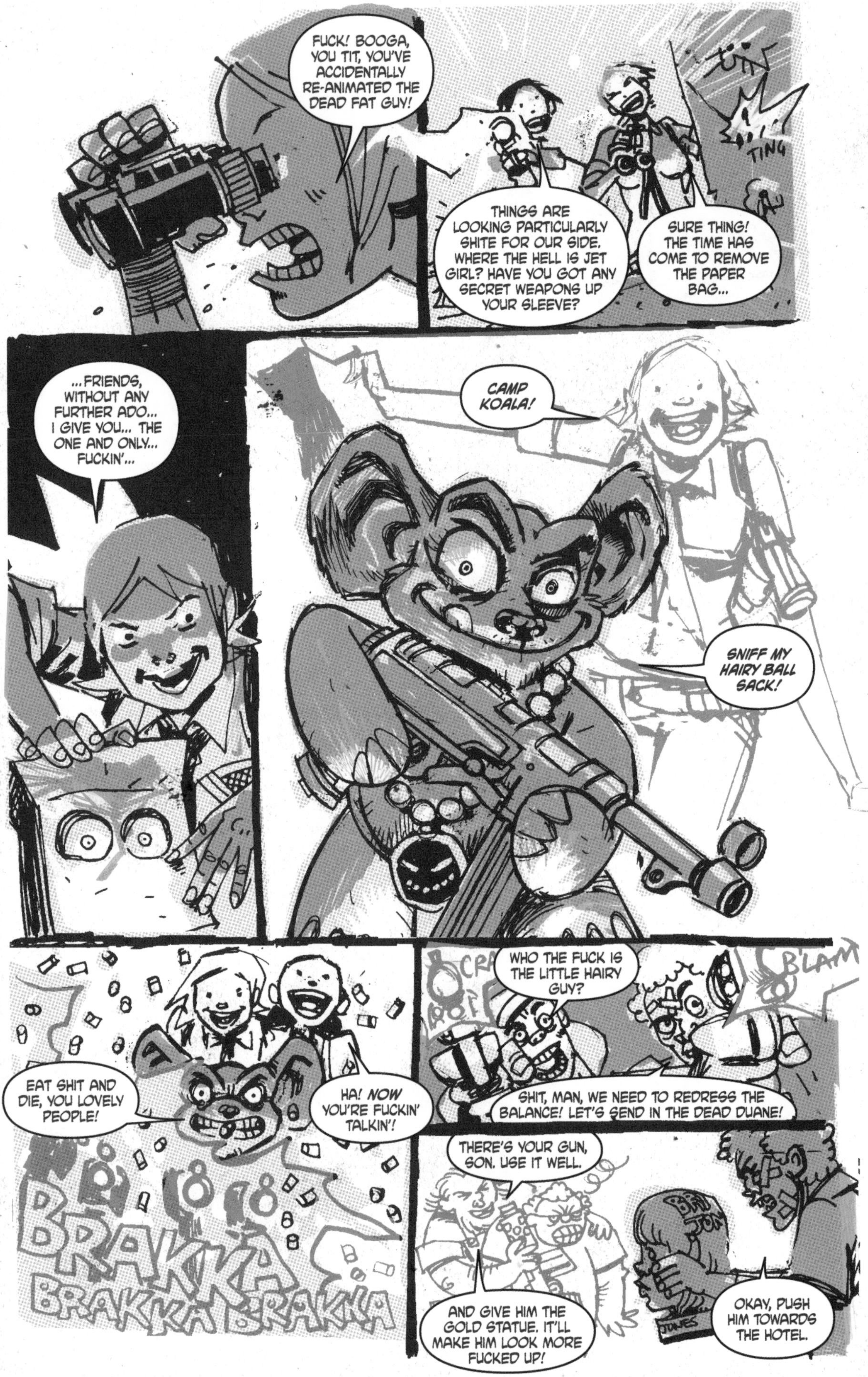
FUCK! BOOGA, YOU TIT, YOU'VE ACCIDENTALLY RE-ANIMATED THE DEAD FAT GUY!
TING
THINGS ARE LOOKING PARTICULARLY SHITE FOR OUR SIDE. WHERE THE HELL IS JET GIRL? HAVE YOU GOT ANY SECRET WEAPONS UP YOUR SLEEVE?
SURE THING! THE TIME HAS COME TO REMOVE THE PAPER BAG...
...FRIENDS, WITHOUT ANY FURTHER ADO... I GIVE YOU... THE ONE AND ONLY... FUCKIN'...
CAMP KOALA!
SNIFF MY HAIRY BALL SACK!
EAT SHIT AND DIE, YOU LOVELY PEOPLE!
HA! NOW YOU'RE FUCKIN' TALKIN'!
BRAKKA
BRAKKA BRAKKA
WHO THE FUCK IS THE LITTLE HAIRY GUY?
B'LAM
SHIT, MAN, WE NEED TO REDRESS THE BALANCE! LET'S SEND IN THE DEAD DUANE!
THERE'S YOUR GUN, SON. USE IT WELL.
AND GIVE HIM THE GOLD STATUE. IT'LL MAKE HIM LOOK MORE FUCKED UP!
OKAY, PUSH HIM TOWARDS THE HOTEL.
JONES

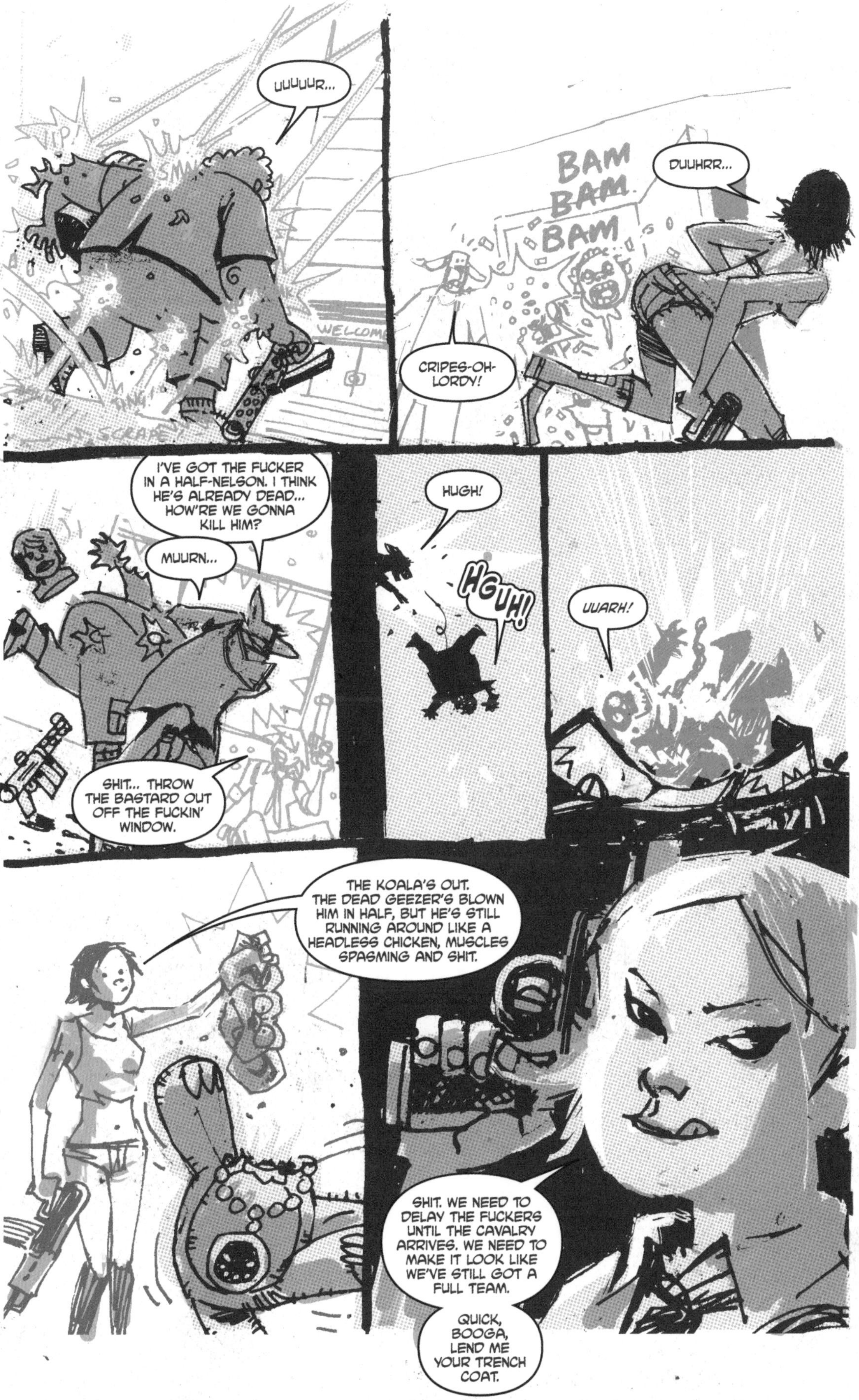
UUUUUR...
DUUHRR...
BAM
BAM
BAM
CRIPES-OH-LORDY!
WELCOM
I'VE GOT THE FUCKER IN A HALF-NELSON. I THINK HE'S ALREADY DEAD... HOW'RE WE GONNA KILL HIM?
MUURN...
SHIT... THROW THE BASTARD OUT OFF THE FUCKIN' WINDOW.
HUGH!
HGUH!
UUARH!
THE KOALA'S OUT. THE DEAD GEEZER'S BLOWN HIM IN HALF, BUT HE'S STILL RUNNING AROUND LIKE A HEADLESS CHICKEN, MUSCLES SPASMING AND SHIT.
SHIT. WE NEED TO DELAY THE FUCKERS UNTIL THE CAVALRY ARRIVES. WE NEED TO MAKE IT LOOK LIKE WE'VE STILL GOT A FULL TEAM.
QUICK, BOOGA, LEND ME YOUR TRENCH COAT.

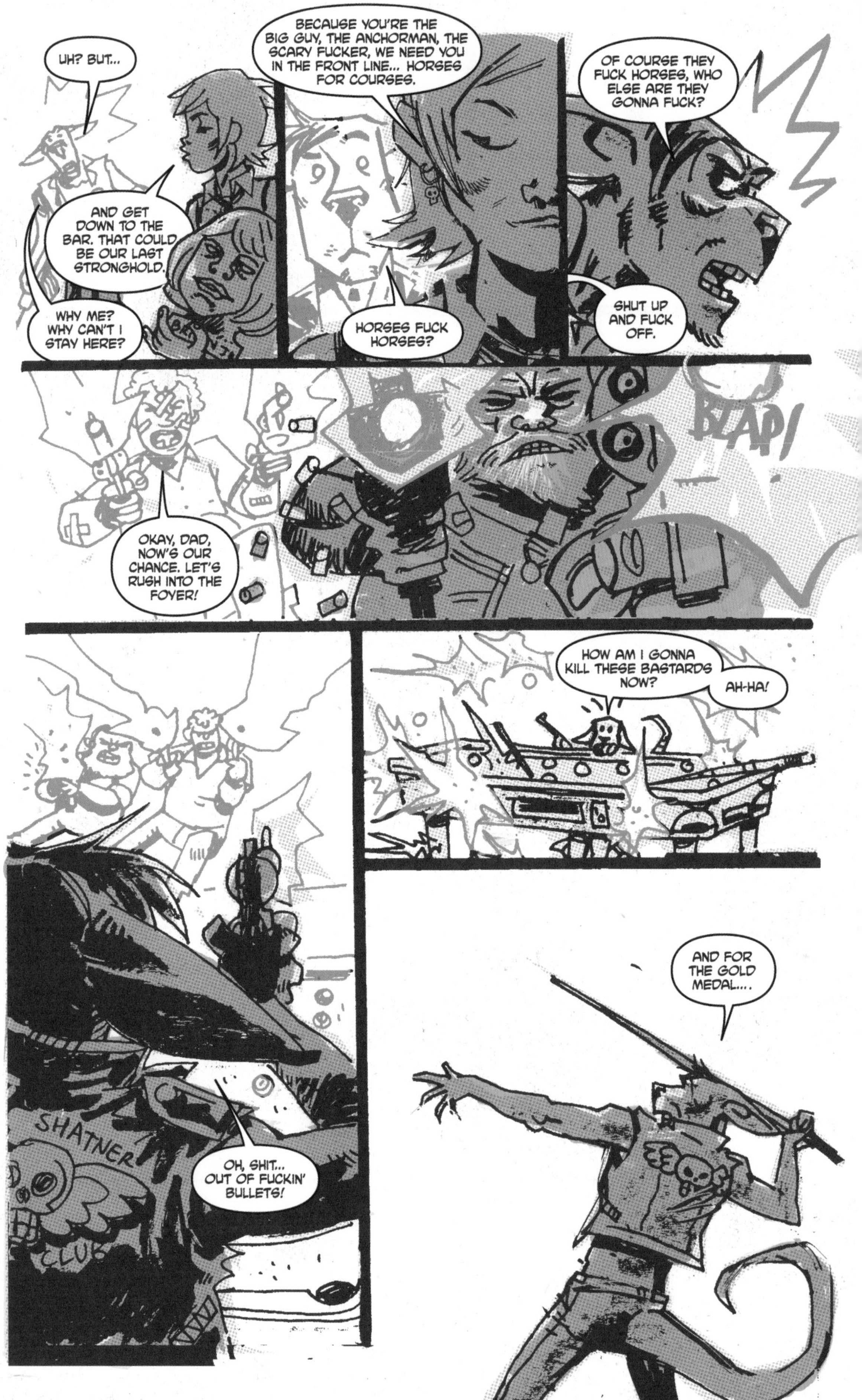
UH? BUT...
AND GET DOWN TO THE BAR. THAT COULD BE OUR LAST STRONGHOLD.
WHY ME? WHY CAN'T I STAY HERE?
BECAUSE YOU'RE THE BIG GUY, THE ANCHORMAN, THE SCARY FUCKER, WE NEED YOU IN THE FRONT LINE... HORSES FOR COURSES.
HORSES FUCK HORSES?
OF COURSE THEY FUCK HORSES, WHO ELSE ARE THEY GONNA FUCK?
SHUT UP AND FUCK OFF.
BLAP!
OKAY, DAD, NOW'S OUR CHANCE. LET'S RUSH INTO THE FOYER!
HOW AM I GONNA KILL THESE BASTARDS NOW?
AH-HA!
SHATNER
OH, SHIT... OUT OF FUCKIN' BULLETS!
AND FOR THE GOLD MEDAL....

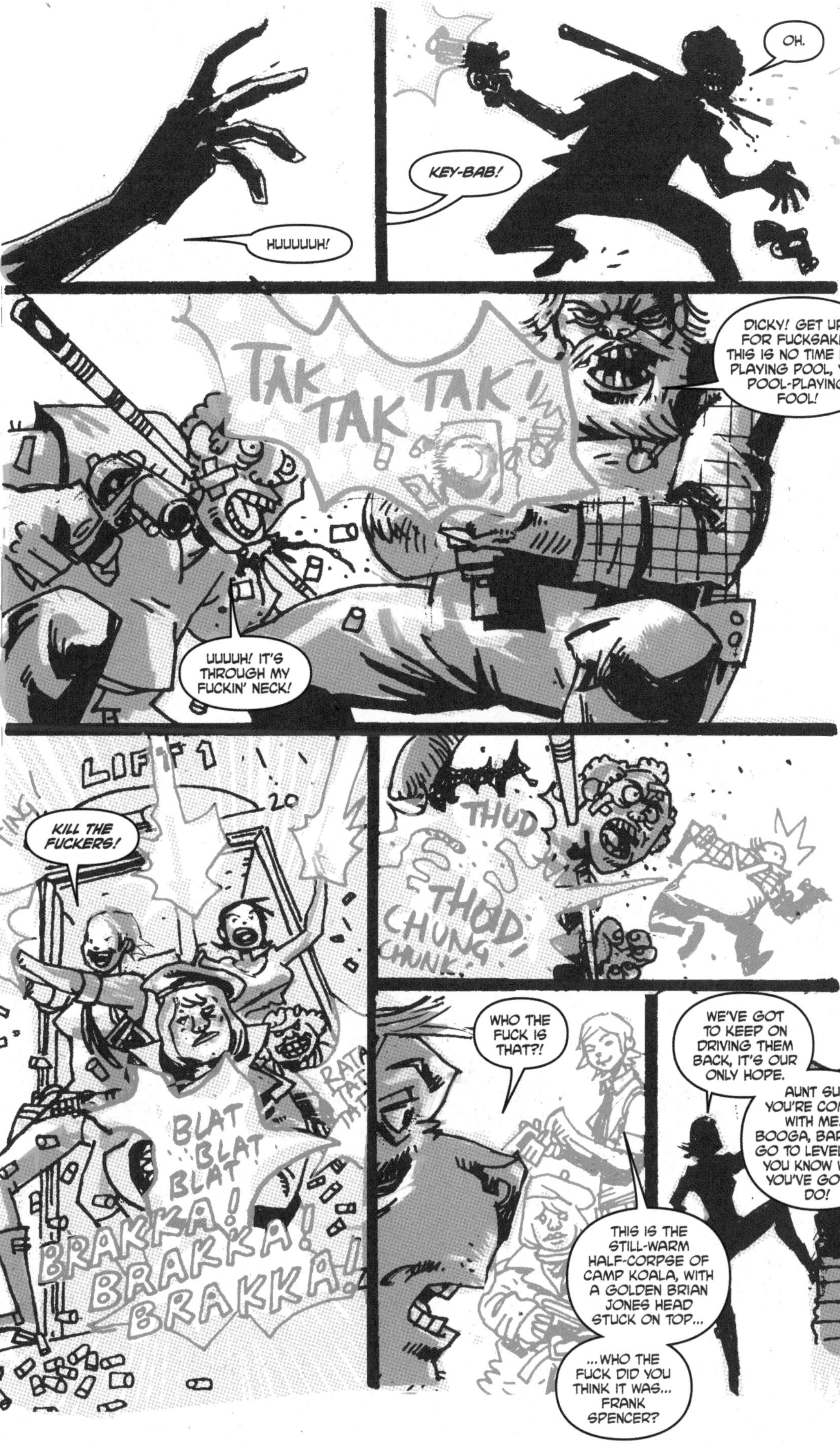
HUUUUUH!
KEY-BAB!
OH.
TAK TAK TAK!
DICKY! GET UP! FOR FUCKSAKE! THIS IS NO TIME FOR PLAYING POOL, YOU POOL-PLAYING FOOL!
UUUUH! IT'S THROUGH MY FUCKIN' NECK!
LIFT 1
TING!
KILL THE FUCKERS!
RATA TAT TAT
BLAT BLAT BLAT
BRAKKA! BRAKKA! BRAKKA!
THUD
THUD!
CHUNG CHUNK!
WHO THE FUCK IS THAT?!
THIS IS THE STILL-WARM HALF-CORPSE OF CAMP KOALA, WITH A GOLDEN BRIAN JONES HEAD STUCK ON TOP...
...WHO THE FUCK DID YOU THINK IT WAS... FRANK SPENCER?
WE'VE GOT TO KEEP ON DRIVING THEM BACK, IT'S OUR ONLY HOPE.
AUNT SUE, YOU'RE COMING WITH ME... BOOGA, BARNEY... GO TO LEVEL FIVE. YOU KNOW WHAT YOU'VE GOT TO DO!

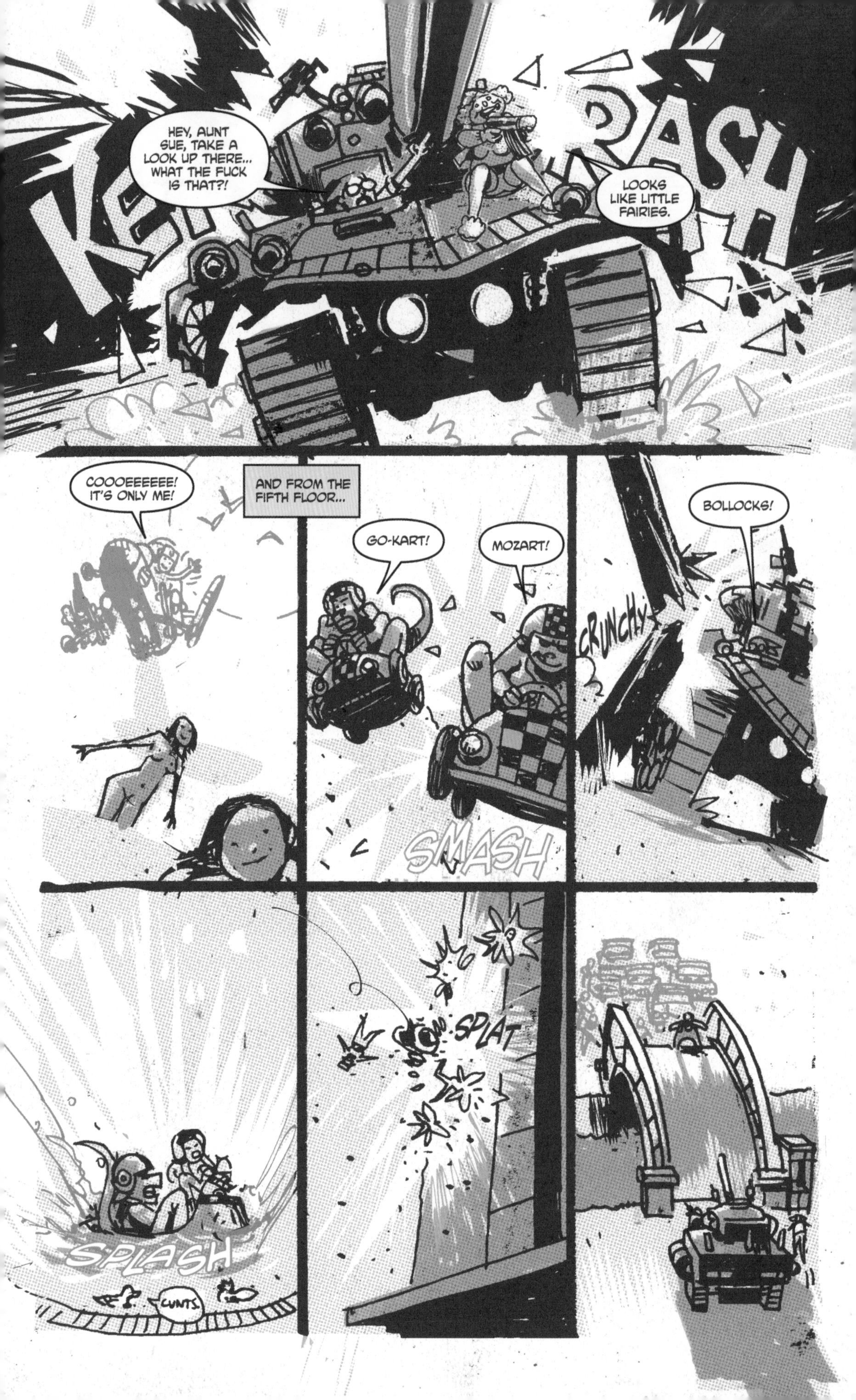
RASH
HEY, AUNT SUE, TAKE A LOOK UP THERE... WHAT THE FUCK IS THAT?!
LOOKS LIKE LITTLE FAIRIES.
COOOEEEEEE! IT'S ONLY ME!
AND FROM THE FIFTH FLOOR...
GO-KART!
MOZART!
SMASH
BOLLOCKS!
CRUNCHY
SPLASH
CUNTS.
SPLAT

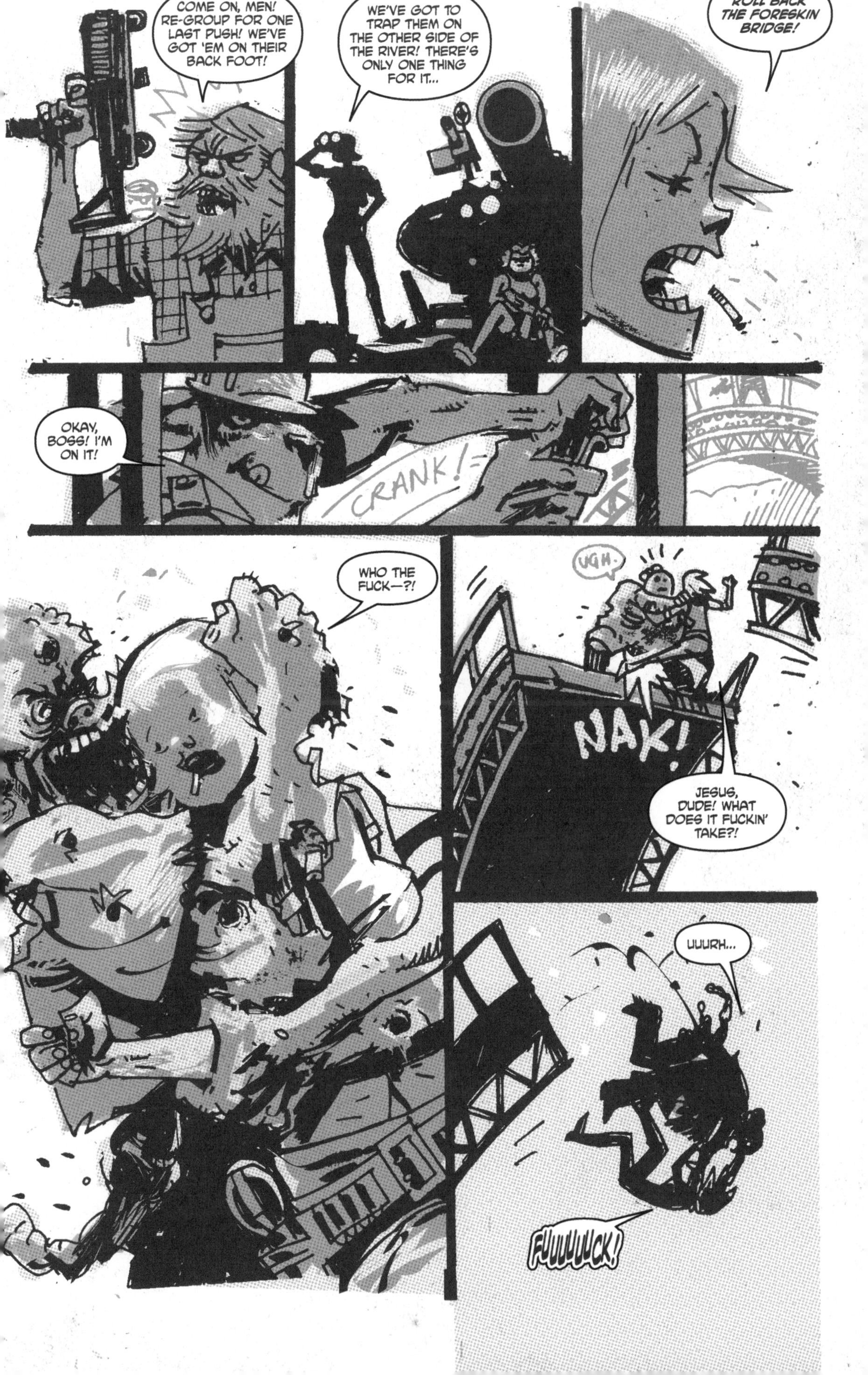
COME ON, MEN! RE-GROUP FOR ONE LAST PUSH! WE'VE GOT 'EM ON THEIR BACK FOOT!
WE'VE GOT TO TRAP THEM ON THE OTHER SIDE OF THE RIVER! THERE'S ONLY ONE THING FOR IT...
ROLL BACK THE FORESKIN BRIDGE!
OKAY, BOSS! I'M ON IT!
CRANK!
WHO THE FUCK—?!
UGH.
NAK!
JESUS, DUDE! WHAT DOES IT FUCKIN' TAKE?!
UUURH...
FUUUUUCK!

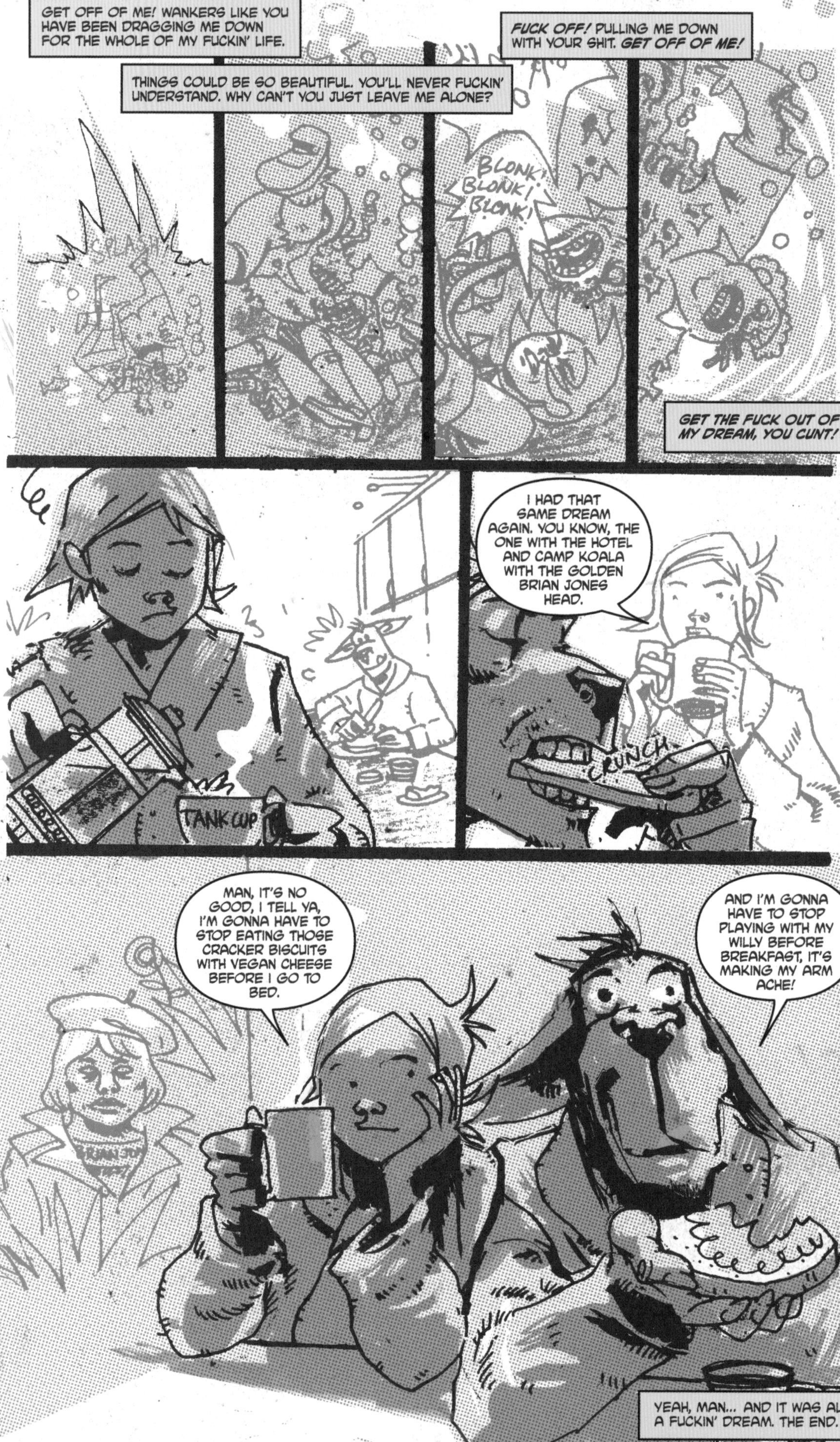
GET OFF OF ME! WANKERS LIKE YOU HAVE BEEN DRAGGING ME DOWN FOR THE WHOLE OF MY FUCKIN' LIFE.
THINGS COULD BE SO BEAUTIFUL. YOU'LL NEVER FUCKIN' UNDERSTAND. WHY CAN'T YOU JUST LEAVE ME ALONE?
FUCK OFF! PULLING ME DOWN WITH YOUR SHIT. GET OFF OF ME!
BLONK! BLONK! BLONK!
GET THE FUCK OUT OF MY DREAM, YOU CUNT!
TANK CUP
I HAD THAT SAME DREAM AGAIN. YOU KNOW, THE ONE WITH THE HOTEL AND CAMP KOALA WITH THE GOLDEN BRIAN JONES HEAD.
CRUNCH
MAN, IT'S NO GOOD, I TELL YA, I'M GONNA HAVE TO STOP EATING THOSE CRACKER BISCUITS WITH VEGAN CHEESE BEFORE I GO TO BED.
AND I'M GONNA HAVE TO STOP PLAYING WITH MY WILLY BEFORE BREAKFAST, IT'S MAKING MY ARM ACHE!
YEAH, MAN... AND IT WAS ALL A FUCKIN' DREAM. THE END.

THE MILKING

The making

The styling

The faking

The smiling

The meeting

The sifting

The rogering

The gifting

The hoping

The praying

The leaving

The staying

The waiting

The lying

The sighing

The crying

The wishing

The dreaming

The fishing

The creaming

The milking

The milking

The milking

Tank Girl

The milking

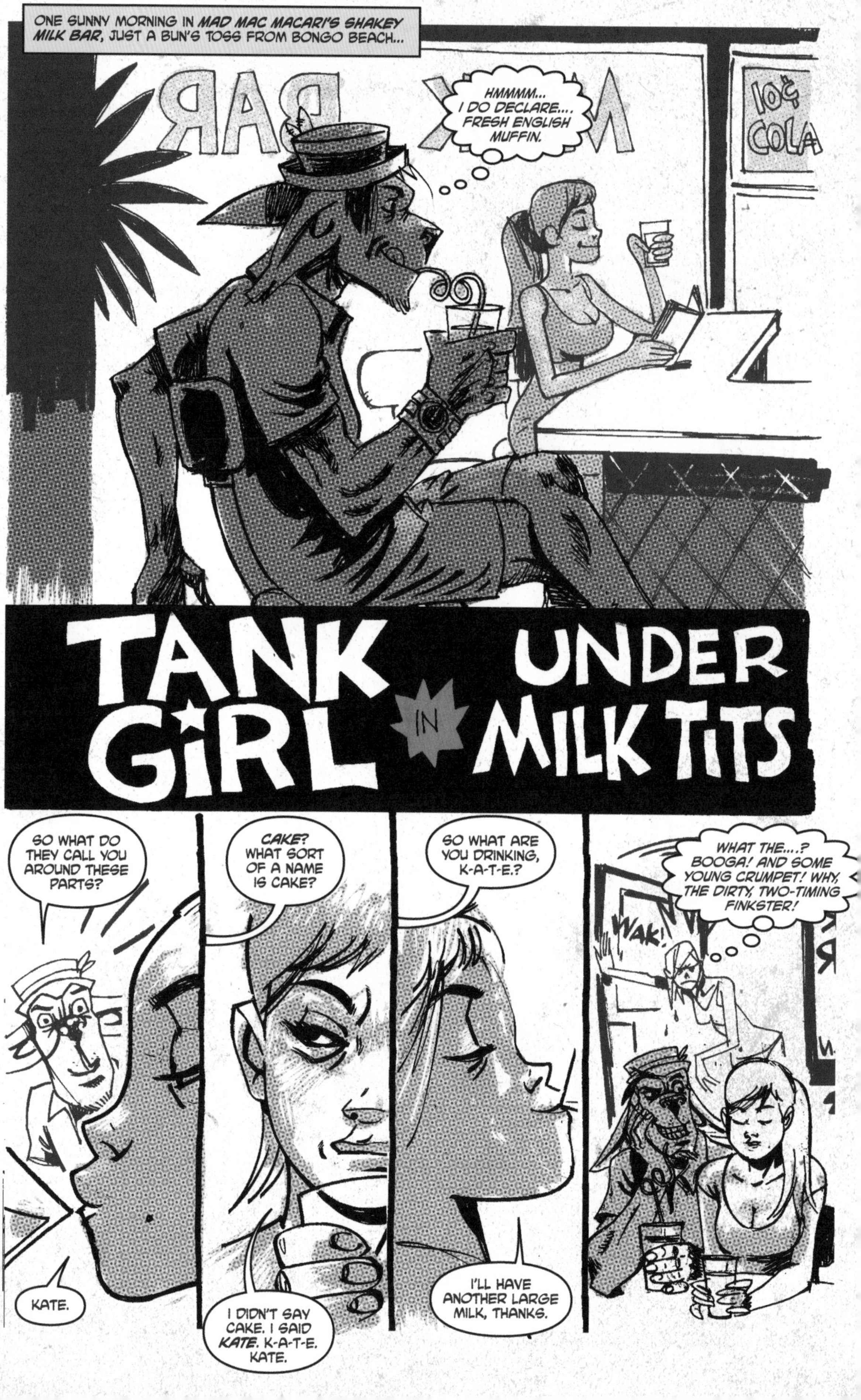
ONE SUNNY MORNING IN MAD MAC MACARI'S SHAKEY MILK BAR, JUST A BUN'S TOSS FROM BONGO BEACH...
BAR
10¢ COLA
HMMMM... I DO DECLARE.... FRESH ENGLISH MUFFIN.
TANK GIRL IN UNDER MILK TITS
SO WHAT DO THEY CALL YOU AROUND THESE PARTS?
KATE.
CAKE? WHAT SORT OF A NAME IS CAKE?
I DIDN'T SAY CAKE. I SAID KATE. K-A-T-E. KATE.
SO WHAT ARE YOU DRINKING, K-A-T-E.?
I'LL HAVE ANOTHER LARGE MILK, THANKS.
WHAT THE....? BOOGA! AND SOME YOUNG CRUMPET! WHY, THE DIRTY, TWO-TIMING FINKSTER!
WAK!

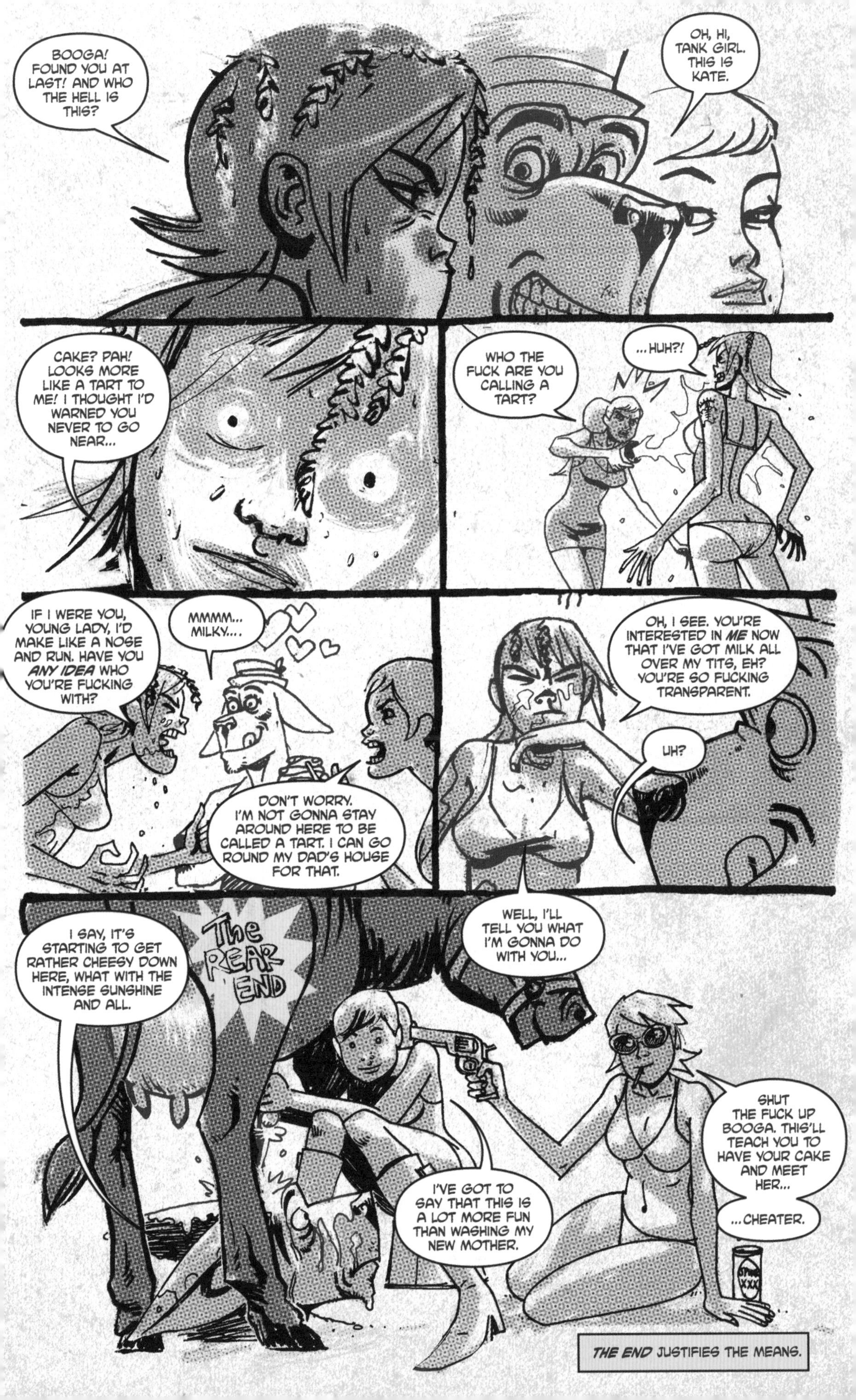

BOOGA! FOUND YOU AT LAST! AND WHO THE HELL IS THIS?
OH, HI, TANK GIRL. THIS IS KATE.
CAKE? PAH! LOOKS MORE LIKE A TART TO ME! I THOUGHT I'D WARNED YOU NEVER TO GO NEAR...
WHO THE FUCK ARE YOU CALLING A TART?
...HUH?!
IF I WERE YOU, YOUNG LADY, I'D MAKE LIKE A NOSE AND RUN. HAVE YOU ANY IDEA WHO YOU'RE FUCKING WITH?
MMMM... MILKY....
DON'T WORRY. I'M NOT GONNA STAY AROUND HERE TO BE CALLED A TART. I CAN GO ROUND MY DAD'S HOUSE FOR THAT.
OH, I SEE. YOU'RE INTERESTED IN ME NOW THAT I'VE GOT MILK ALL OVER MY TITS, EH? YOU'RE SO FUCKING TRANSPARENT.
UH?
WELL, I'LL TELL YOU WHAT I'M GONNA DO WITH YOU...
The REAR END
I SAY, IT'S STARTING TO GET RATHER CHEESY DOWN HERE, WHAT WITH THE INTENSE SUNSHINE AND ALL.
I'VE GOT TO SAY THAT THIS IS A LOT MORE FUN THAN WASHING MY NEW MOTHER.
SHUT THE FUCK UP BOOGA. THIS'LL TEACH YOU TO HAVE YOUR CAKE AND MEET HER...
...CHEATER.
THE END JUSTIFIES THE MEANS.

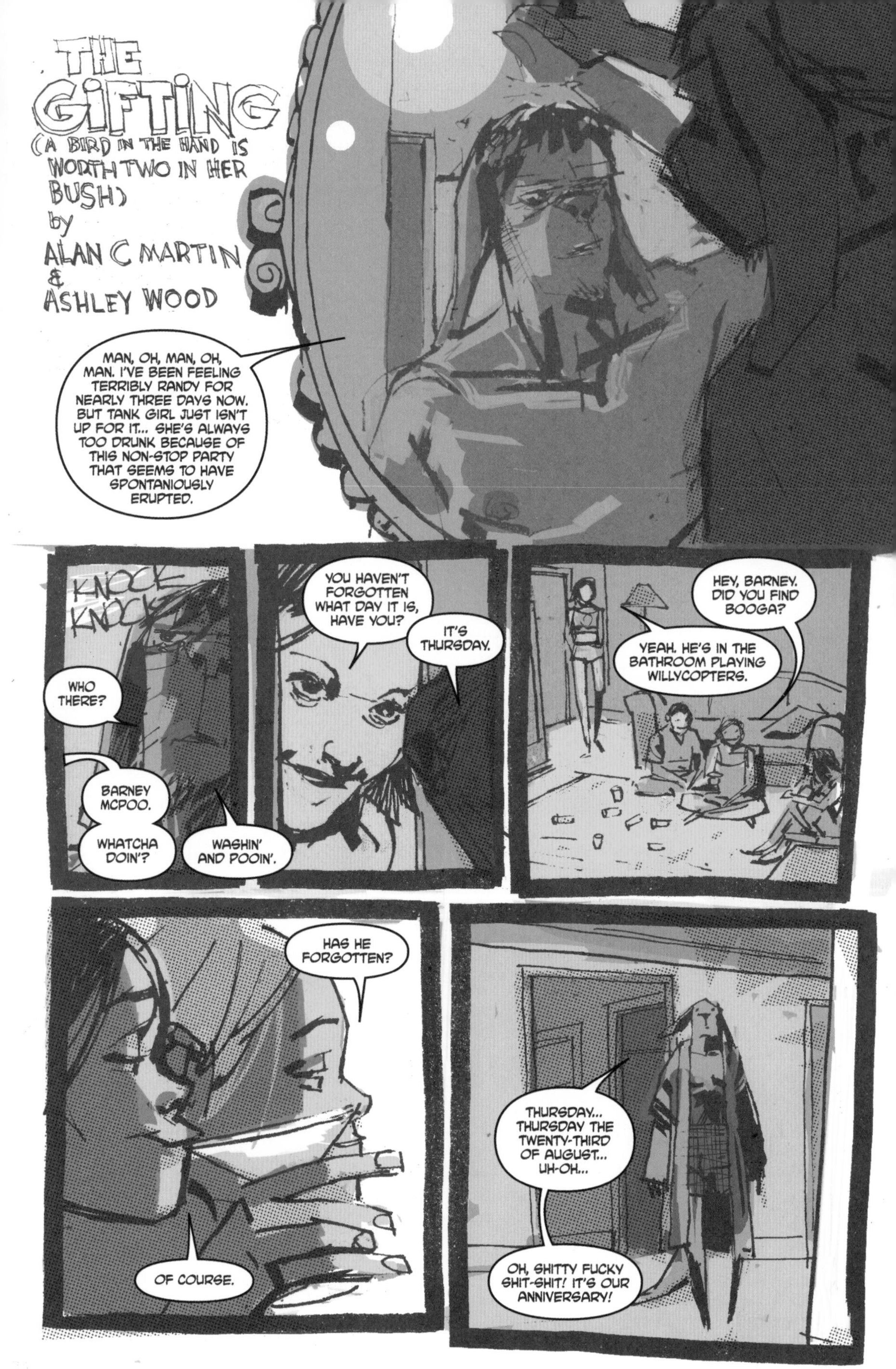
THE GIFTING
(A BIRD IN THE HAND IS WORTH TWO IN HER BUSH)
by
ALAN C MARTIN
&
ASHLEY WOOD
MAN, OH, MAN, OH, MAN. I'VE BEEN FEELING TERRIBLY RANDY FOR NEARLY THREE DAYS NOW. BUT TANK GIRL JUST ISN'T UP FOR IT... SHE'S ALWAYS TOO DRUNK BECAUSE OF THIS NON-STOP PARTY THAT SEEMS TO HAVE SPONTANIOUSLY ERUPTED.
KNOCK KNOCK
WHO THERE?
BARNEY MCPOO.
WHATCHA DOIN'?
WASHIN' AND POOIN'.
YOU HAVEN'T FORGOTTEN WHAT DAY IT IS, HAVE YOU?
IT'S THURSDAY.
HEY, BARNEY. DID YOU FIND BOOGA?
YEAH. HE'S IN THE BATHROOM PLAYING WILLYCOPTERS.
HAS HE FORGOTTEN?
OF COURSE.
THURSDAY... THURSDAY THE TWENTY-THIRD OF AUGUST... UH-OH...
OH, SHITTY FUCKY SHIT-SHIT! IT'S OUR ANNIVERSARY!

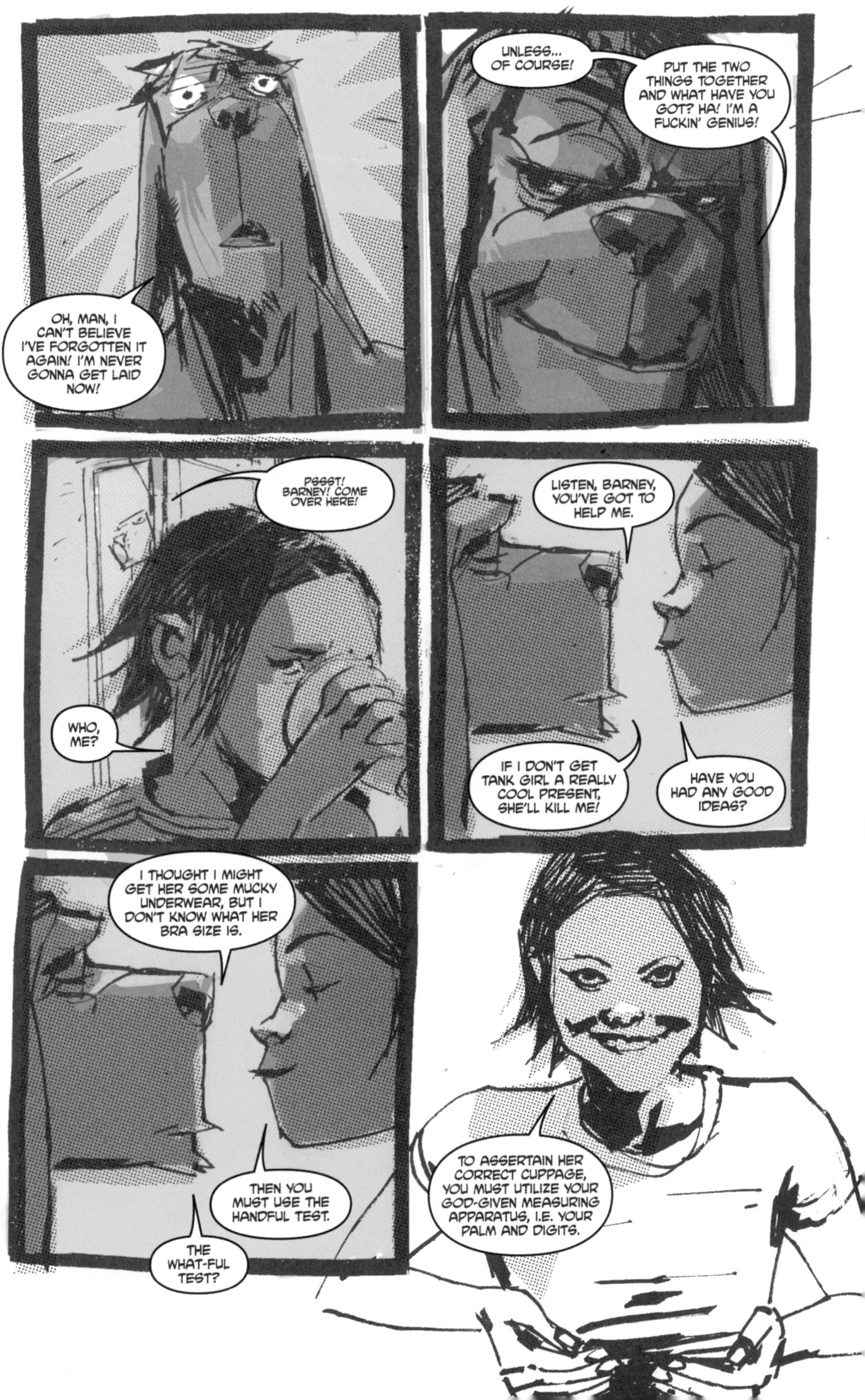
OH, MAN, I CAN'T BELIEVE I'VE FORGOTTEN IT AGAIN! I'M NEVER GONNA GET LAID NOW!
UNLESS... OF COURSE!
PUT THE TWO THINGS TOGETHER AND WHAT HAVE YOU GOT? HA! I'M A FUCKIN' GENIUS!
PSSST! BARNEY! COME OVER HERE!
WHO, ME?
LISTEN, BARNEY, YOU'VE GOT TO HELP ME.
IF I DON'T GET TANK GIRL A REALLY COOL PRESENT, SHE'LL KILL ME!
HAVE YOU HAD ANY GOOD IDEAS?
I THOUGHT I MIGHT GET HER SOME MUCKY UNDERWEAR, BUT I DON'T KNOW WHAT HER BRA SIZE IS.
THEN YOU MUST USE THE HANDFUL TEST.
THE WHAT-FUL TEST?
TO ASSERTAIN HER CORRECT CUPPAGE, YOU MUST UTILIZE YOUR GOD-GIVEN MEASURING APPARATUS, I.E. YOUR PALM AND DIGITS.

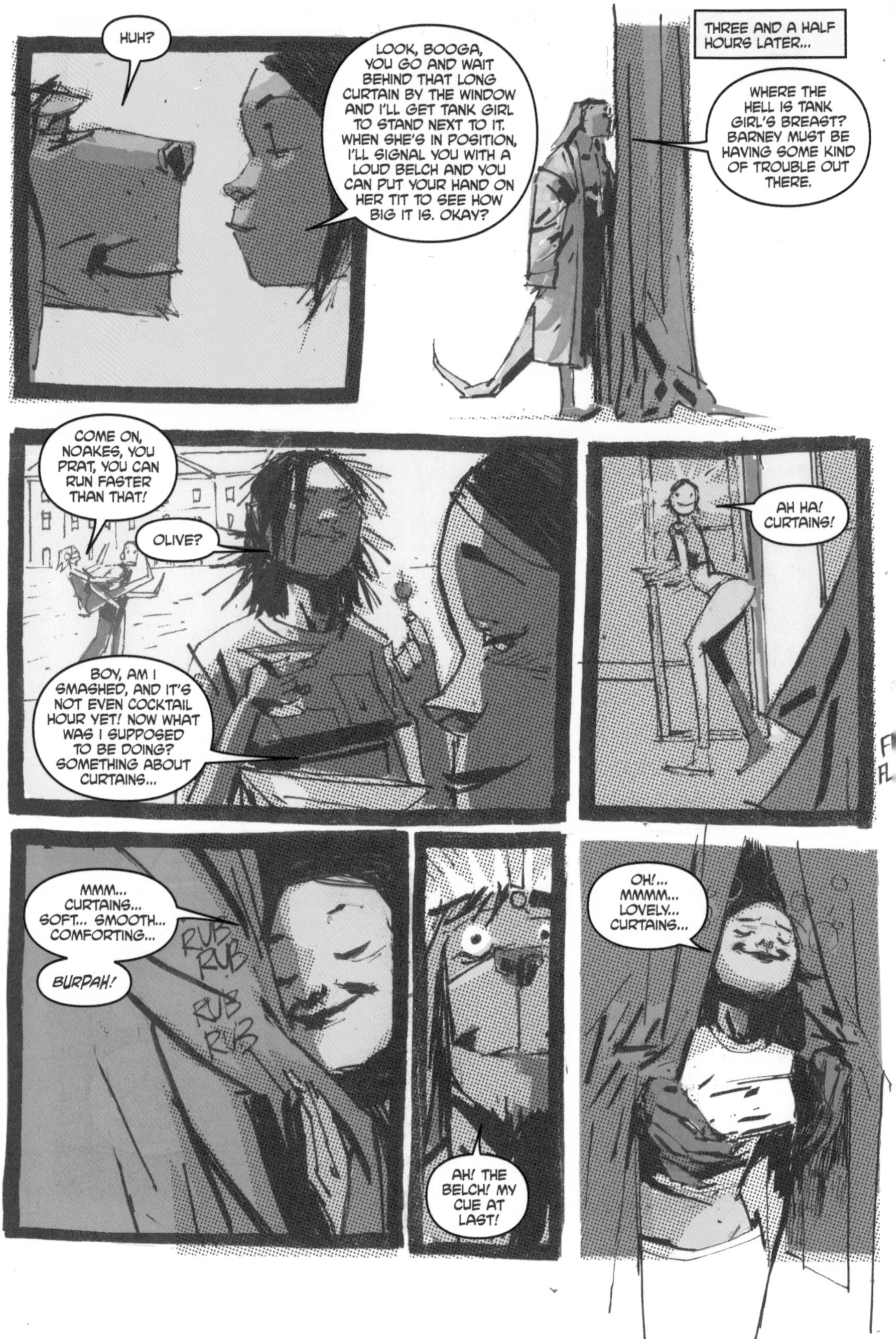
HUH?
LOOK, BOOGA, YOU GO AND WAIT BEHIND THAT LONG CURTAIN BY THE WINDOW AND I'LL GET TANK GIRL TO STAND NEXT TO IT. WHEN SHE'S IN POSITION, I'LL SIGNAL YOU WITH A LOUD BELCH AND YOU CAN PUT YOUR HAND ON HER TIT TO SEE HOW BIG IT IS. OKAY?
THREE AND A HALF HOURS LATER...
WHERE THE HELL IS TANK GIRL'S BREAST? BARNEY MUST BE HAVING SOME KIND OF TROUBLE OUT THERE.
COME ON, NOAKES, YOU PRAT, YOU CAN RUN FASTER THAN THAT!
OLIVE?
BOY, AM I SMASHED, AND IT'S NOT EVEN COCKTAIL HOUR YET! NOW WHAT WAS I SUPPOSED TO BE DOING? SOMETHING ABOUT CURTAINS...
AH HA! CURTAINS!
MMM... CURTAINS... SOFT... SMOOTH... COMFORTING...
RUB RUB
RUB RUB
BURPAH!
AH! THE BELCH! MY CUE AT LAST!
OH!... MMMM... LOVELY... CURTAINS...

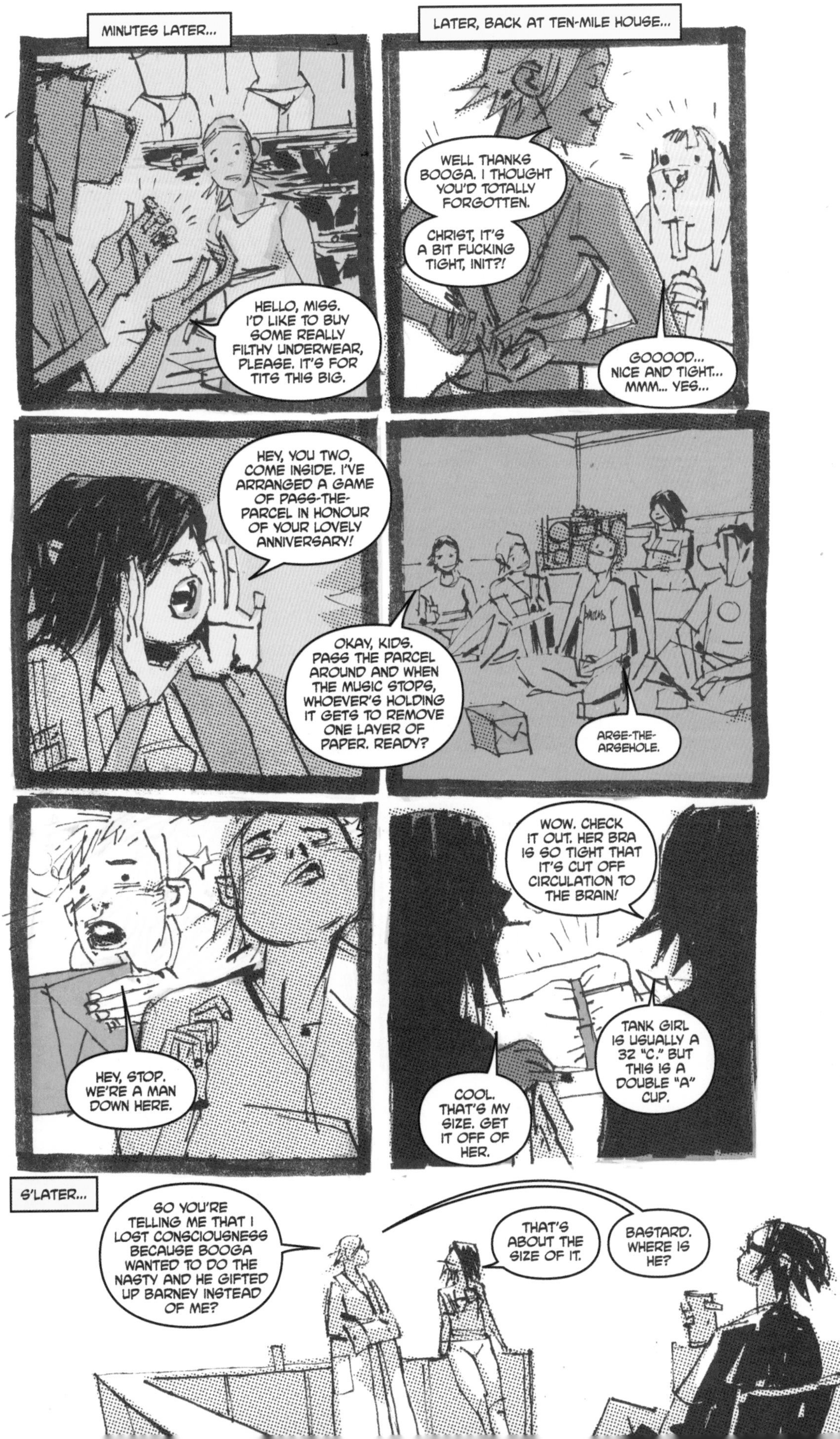

MINUTES LATER...
HELLO, MISS. I'D LIKE TO BUY SOME REALLY FILTHY UNDERWEAR, PLEASE. IT'S FOR TITS THIS BIG.
LATER, BACK AT TEN-MILE HOUSE...
WELL THANKS BOOGA. I THOUGHT YOU'D TOTALLY FORGOTTEN.
CHRIST, IT'S A BIT FUCKING TIGHT, INIT?!
GOOOOD... NICE AND TIGHT... MMM... YES...
HEY, YOU TWO, COME INSIDE. I'VE ARRANGED A GAME OF PASS-THE-PARCEL IN HONOUR OF YOUR LOVELY ANNIVERSARY!
OKAY, KIDS. PASS THE PARCEL AROUND AND WHEN THE MUSIC STOPS, WHOEVER'S HOLDING IT GETS TO REMOVE ONE LAYER OF PAPER. READY?
ARSE-THE-ARSEHOLE.
HEY, STOP. WE'RE A MAN DOWN HERE.
WOW. CHECK IT OUT. HER BRA IS SO TIGHT THAT IT'S CUT OFF CIRCULATION TO THE BRAIN!
TANK GIRL IS USUALLY A 32 "C." BUT THIS IS A DOUBLE "A" CUP.
COOL. THAT'S MY SIZE. GET IT OFF OF HER.
S'LATER...
SO YOU'RE TELLING ME THAT I LOST CONSCIOUSNESS BECAUSE BOOGA WANTED TO DO THE NASTY AND HE GIFTED UP BARNEY INSTEAD OF ME?
THAT'S ABOUT THE SIZE OF IT.
BASTARD. WHERE IS HE?

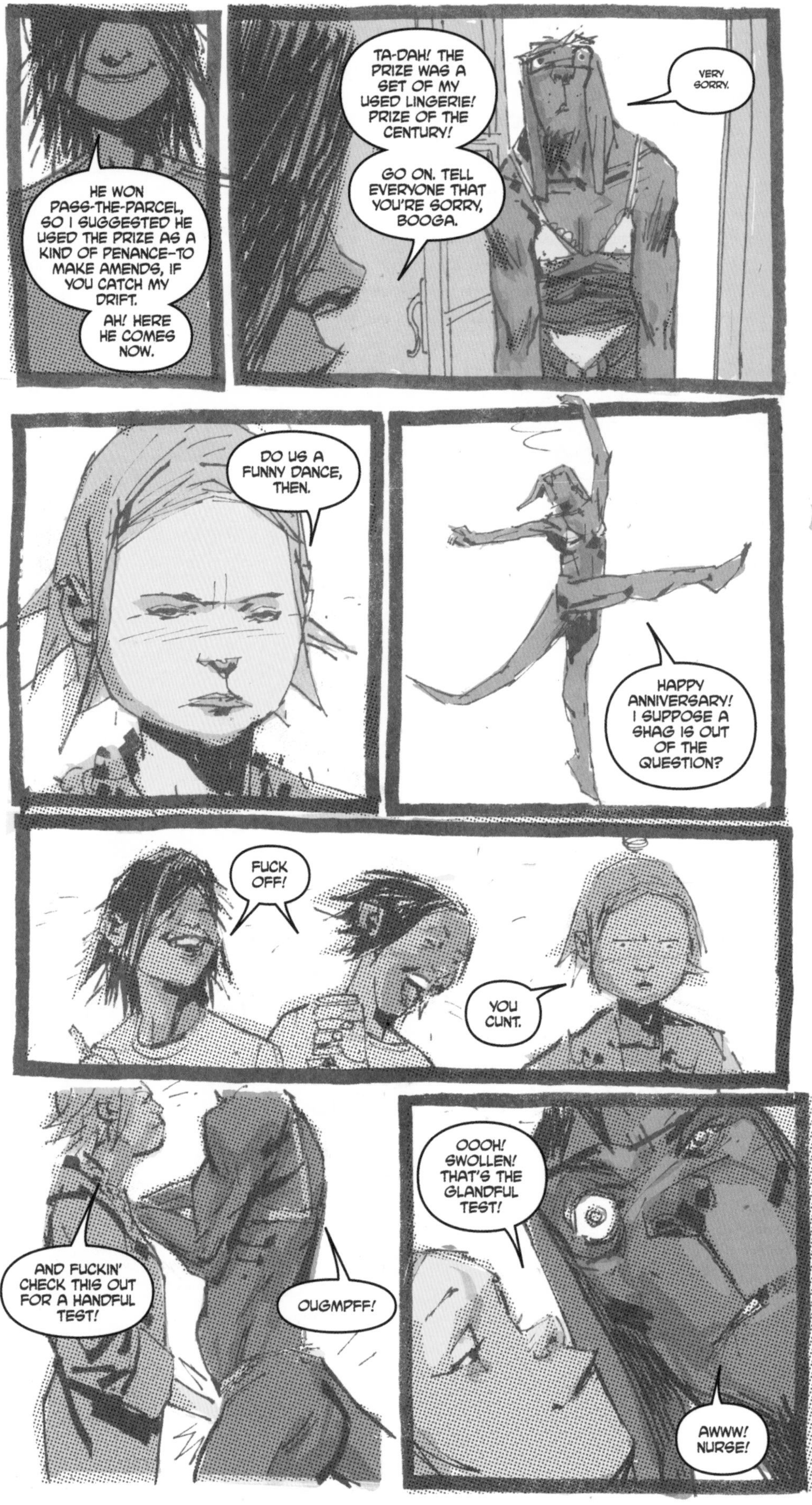
HE WON PASS-THE-PARCEL, SO I SUGGESTED HE USED THE PRIZE AS A KIND OF PENANCE--TO MAKE AMENDS, IF YOU CATCH MY DRIFT.
AH! HERE HE COMES NOW.
TA-DAH! THE PRIZE WAS A SET OF MY USED LINGERIE! PRIZE OF THE CENTURY!
GO ON. TELL EVERYONE THAT YOU'RE SORRY, BOOGA.
VERY SORRY.
DO US A FUNNY DANCE, THEN.
HAPPY ANNIVERSARY! I SUPPOSE A SHAG IS OUT OF THE QUESTION?
FUCK OFF!
YOU CUNT.
AND FUCKIN' CHECK THIS OUT FOR A HANDFUL TEST!
OUGMPFF!
OOOH! SWOLLEN! THAT'S THE GLANDFUL TEST!
AWWW! NURSE!

BURGER HILL

I was already late by twenty minutes. I reached the summit of the hill and turned left into the burger bar car park. My usual parking space was occupied, so I had to drive all the way to the very end. I parked the tank and trudged wearily back towards the entrance. The weather was blustery and wet; the place was unusually packed for such a crappy day.

I pressed my face against the window, it was steamed up inside by the masses of damp, hot bodies. I could just make out Booga, sitting by himself in the corner, wolfing down the final remnants of his triple-decker burger.

Shit. Too late. I'd spoilt our romantic dinner for two again. When would I ever get it right?

Booga licked the traces of relish from the corners of his burger carton. I watched him through the condensation as he belched silently. He was beautiful that day. I berated myself for my shoddy time-keeping.

Booga started picking his nose. "I'd better get in there," I thought. I was still a hungry gal.

I queued for ten minutes until I finally received my veggie-sloppy-special. I took it over to Booga's table and slumped myself down in the plastic chair.

Booga smiled at me lovingly. "What took you so long?" he asked, without a hint of malice.

"Man," I sighed, "loads of shit. And I had a real tough time driving the tank up the hill."

"Really?" he replied with genuine concern, "What gear were you in?"

"My green track-suit and orange trainers."

THE YELLOW GUN

Going for a burger?
You'd better think of bloody murder.
Think of screaming cattle,
Think of body bags after a battle.
And think of a world with no air,
After all the forests have been cleared.

Because I'll be watching you.

And with my yellow gun
I'll shoot you bloody dead
In your sad little single bed.

Going for a burger?
Go for a walk instead.

Fucker.

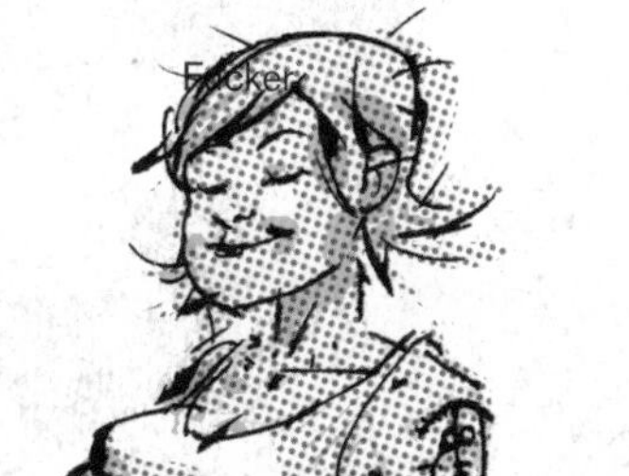

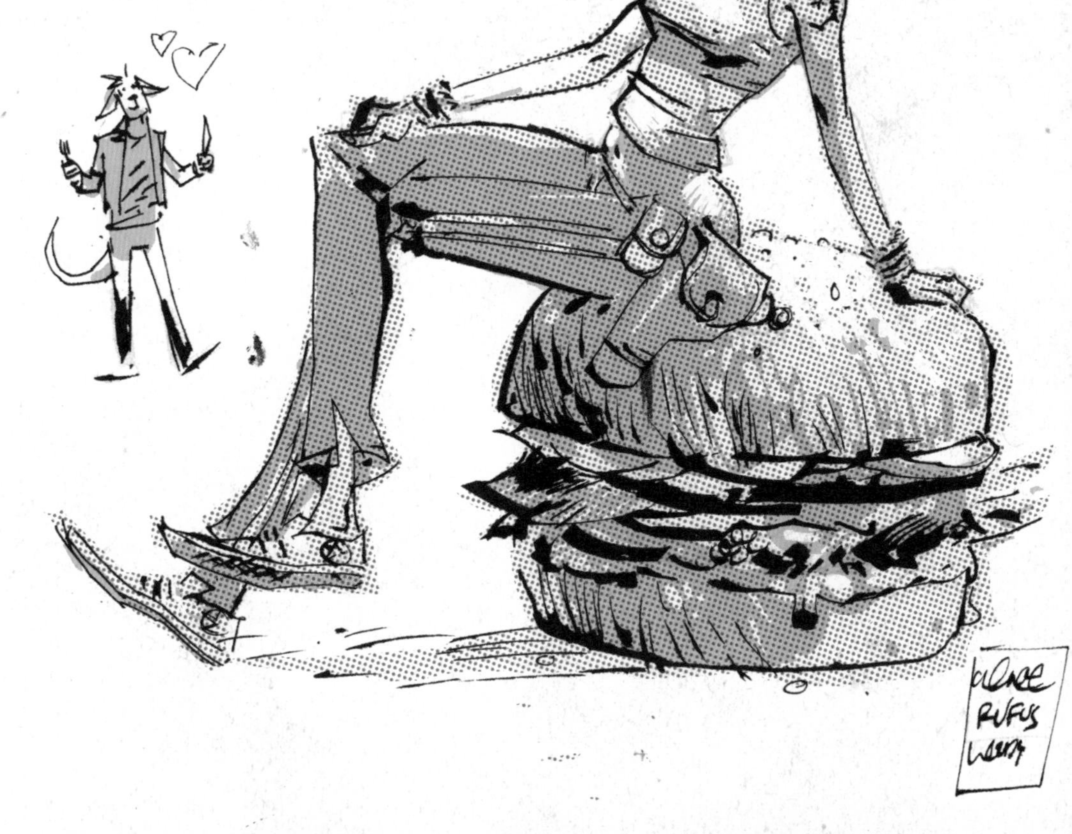

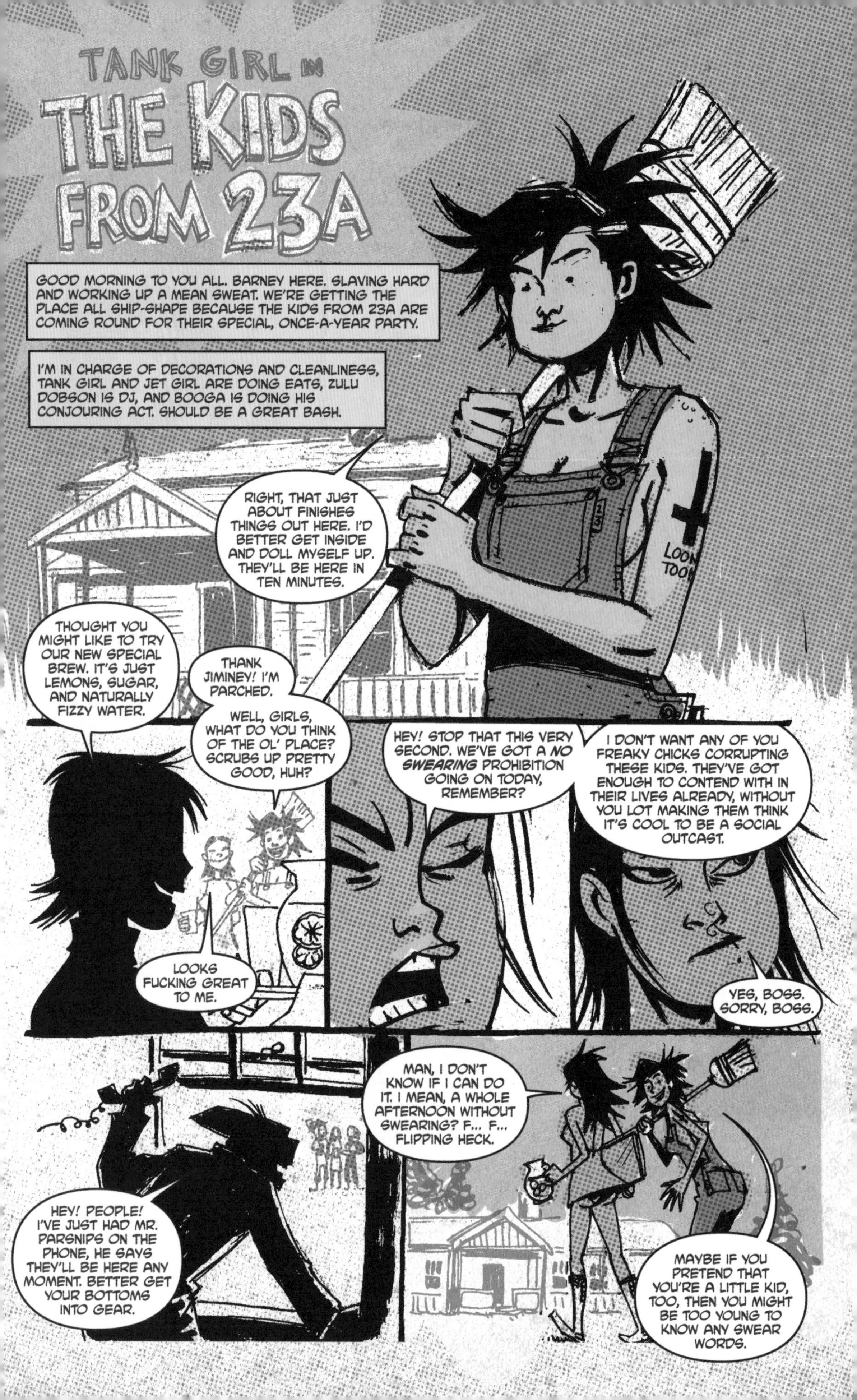
TANK GIRL IN
THE KIDS FROM 23A
GOOD MORNING TO YOU ALL. BARNEY HERE. SLAVING HARD AND WORKING UP A MEAN SWEAT. WE'RE GETTING THE PLACE ALL SHIP-SHAPE BECAUSE THE KIDS FROM 23A ARE COMING ROUND FOR THEIR SPECIAL, ONCE-A-YEAR PARTY.
I'M IN CHARGE OF DECORATIONS AND CLEANLINESS, TANK GIRL AND JET GIRL ARE DOING EATS, ZULU DOBSON IS DJ, AND BOOGA IS DOING HIS CONJOURING ACT. SHOULD BE A GREAT BASH.
RIGHT, THAT JUST ABOUT FINISHES THINGS OUT HERE. I'D BETTER GET INSIDE AND DOLL MYSELF UP. THEY'LL BE HERE IN TEN MINUTES.
LOON TOO
THOUGHT YOU MIGHT LIKE TO TRY OUR NEW SPECIAL BREW. IT'S JUST LEMONS, SUGAR, AND NATURALLY FIZZY WATER.
THANK JIMINEY! I'M PARCHED.
WELL, GIRLS, WHAT DO YOU THINK OF THE OL' PLACE? SCRUBS UP PRETTY GOOD, HUH?
LOOKS FUCKING GREAT TO ME.
HEY! STOP THAT THIS VERY SECOND. WE'VE GOT A *NO SWEARING* PROHIBITION GOING ON TODAY, REMEMBER?
I DON'T WANT ANY OF YOU FREAKY CHICKS CORRUPTING THESE KIDS. THEY'VE GOT ENOUGH TO CONTEND WITH IN THEIR LIVES ALREADY, WITHOUT YOU LOT MAKING THEM THINK IT'S COOL TO BE A SOCIAL OUTCAST.
YES, BOSS. SORRY, BOSS.
HEY! PEOPLE! I'VE JUST HAD MR. PARSNIPS ON THE PHONE, HE SAYS THEY'LL BE HERE ANY MOMENT. BETTER GET YOUR BOTTOMS INTO GEAR.
MAN, I DON'T KNOW IF I CAN DO IT. I MEAN, A WHOLE AFTERNOON WITHOUT SWEARING? F... F... FLIPPING HECK.
MAYBE IF YOU PRETEND THAT YOU'RE A LITTLE KID, TOO, THEN YOU MIGHT BE TOO YOUNG TO KNOW ANY SWEAR WORDS.

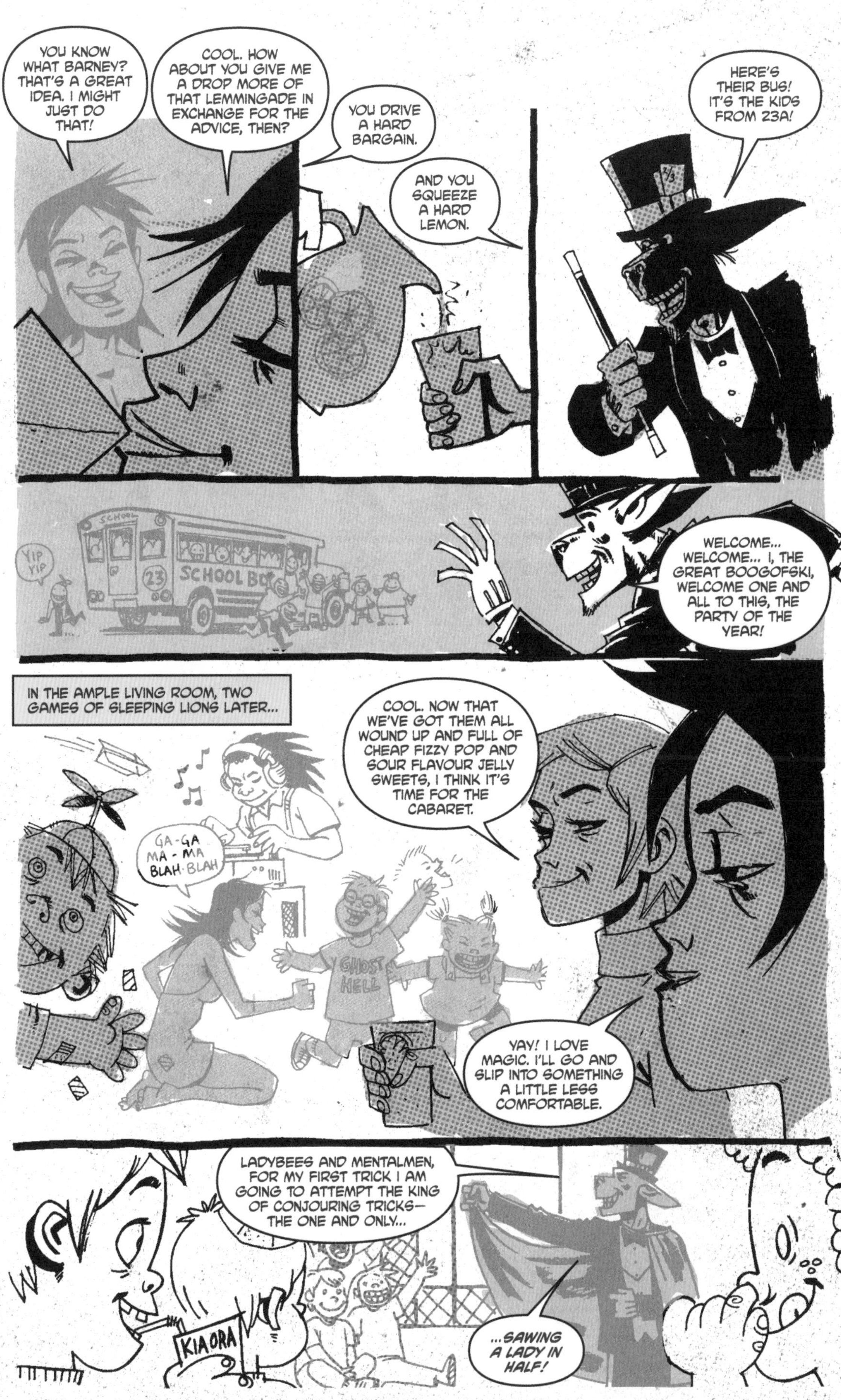
YOU KNOW WHAT BARNEY? THAT'S A GREAT IDEA. I MIGHT JUST DO THAT!
COOL. HOW ABOUT YOU GIVE ME A DROP MORE OF THAT LEMMINGADE IN EXCHANGE FOR THE ADVICE, THEN?
YOU DRIVE A HARD BARGAIN.
AND YOU SQUEEZE A HARD LEMON.
HERE'S THEIR BUS! IT'S THE KIDS FROM 23A!
YIP YIP
SCHOOL
23
SCHOOL BU
WELCOME... WELCOME... I, THE GREAT BOOGOFSKI, WELCOME ONE AND ALL TO THIS, THE PARTY OF THE YEAR!
IN THE AMPLE LIVING ROOM, TWO GAMES OF SLEEPING LIONS LATER...
COOL. NOW THAT WE'VE GOT THEM ALL WOUND UP AND FULL OF CHEAP FIZZY POP AND SOUR FLAVOUR JELLY SWEETS, I THINK IT'S TIME FOR THE CABARET.
GA-GA MA-MA BLAH-BLAH
GHOST HELL
YAY! I LOVE MAGIC. I'LL GO AND SLIP INTO SOMETHING A LITTLE LESS COMFORTABLE.
LADYBEES AND MENTALMEN, FOR MY FIRST TRICK I AM GOING TO ATTEMPT THE KING OF CONJOURING TRICKS— THE ONE AND ONLY...
KIA ORA
...SAWING A LADY IN HALF!

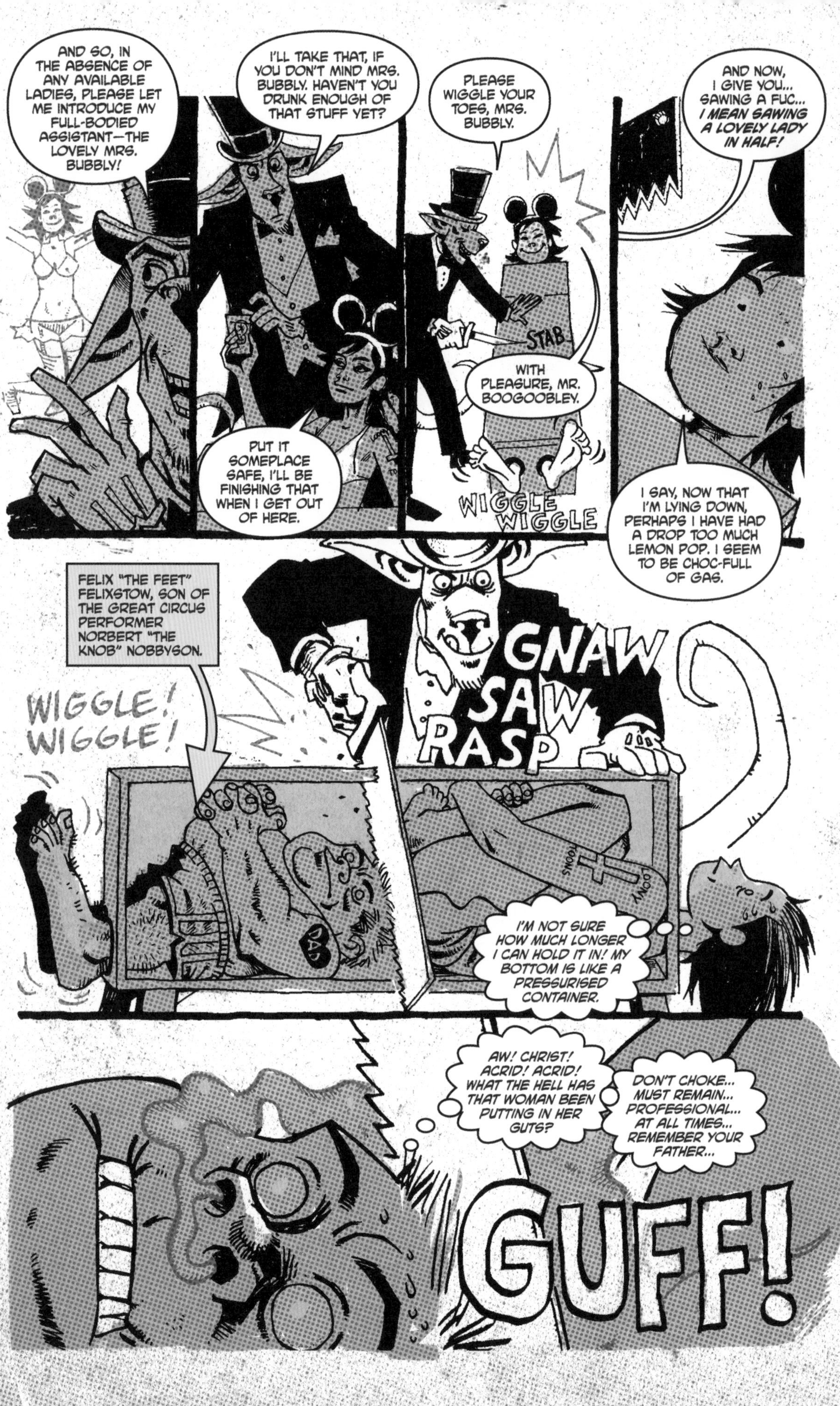
AND SO, IN THE ABSENCE OF ANY AVAILABLE LADIES, PLEASE LET ME INTRODUCE MY FULL-BODIED ASSISTANT—THE LOVELY MRS. BUBBLY!
I'LL TAKE THAT, IF YOU DON'T MIND MRS. BUBBLY. HAVEN'T YOU DRUNK ENOUGH OF THAT STUFF YET?
PUT IT SOMEPLACE SAFE, I'LL BE FINISHING THAT WHEN I GET OUT OF HERE.
PLEASE WIGGLE YOUR TOES, MRS. BUBBLY.
STAB
WITH PLEASURE, MR. BOOGOOBLEY.
WIGGLE WIGGLE
AND NOW, I GIVE YOU... SAWING A FUC... I MEAN SAWING A LOVELY LADY IN HALF!
I SAY, NOW THAT I'M LYING DOWN, PERHAPS I HAVE HAD A DROP TOO MUCH LEMON POP. I SEEM TO BE CHOC-FULL OF GAS.
FELIX "THE FEET" FELIXSTOW, SON OF THE GREAT CIRCUS PERFORMER NORBERT "THE KNOB" NOBBYSON.
WIGGLE! WIGGLE!
GNAW SAW RASP
I'M NOT SURE HOW MUCH LONGER I CAN HOLD IT IN! MY BOTTOM IS LIKE A PRESSURISED CONTAINER.
AW! CHRIST! ACRID! ACRID! WHAT THE HELL HAS THAT WOMAN BEEN PUTTING IN HER GUTS?
DON'T CHOKE... MUST REMAIN... PROFESSIONAL... AT ALL TIMES... REMEMBER YOUR FATHER...
GUFF!

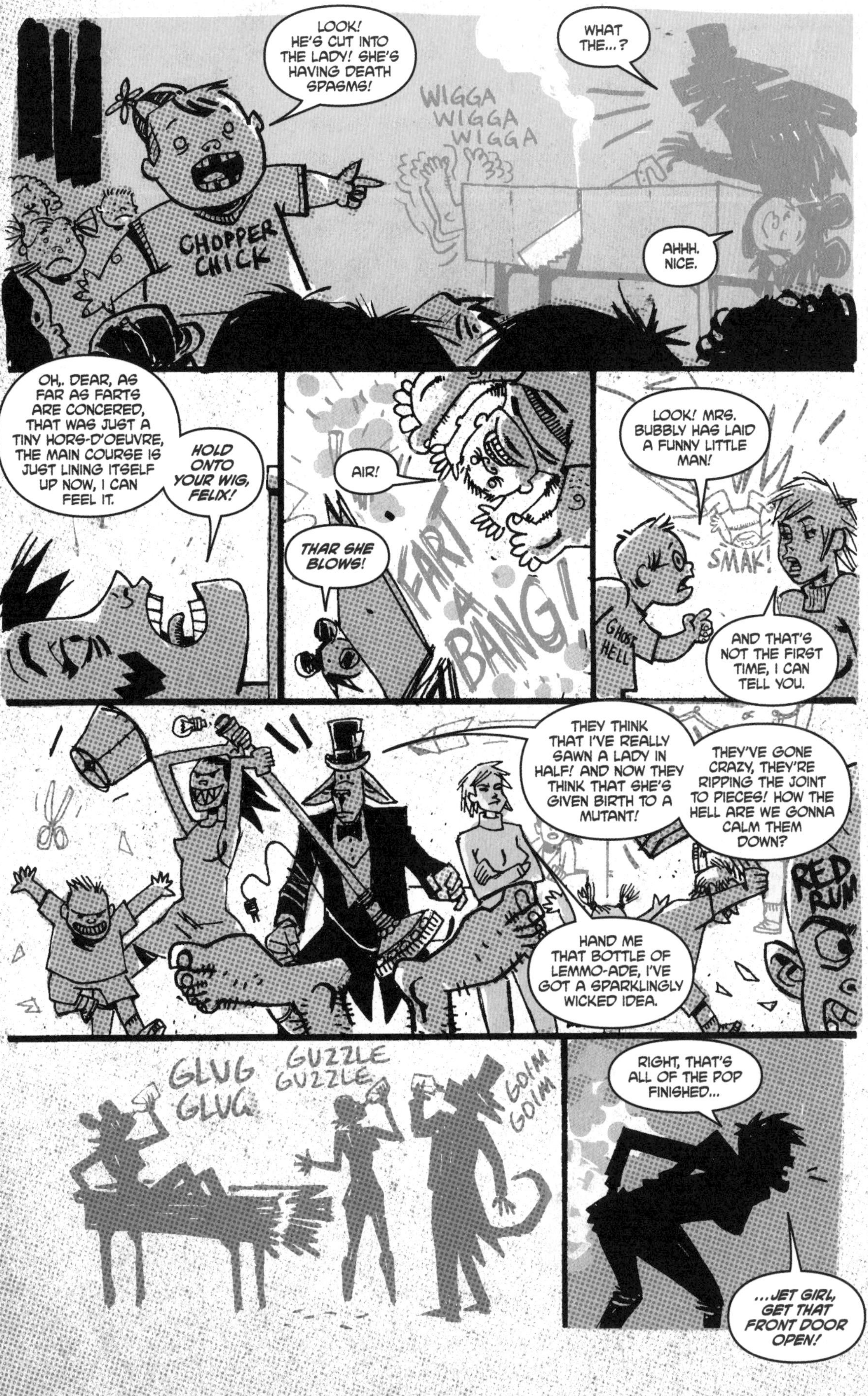
LOOK! HE'S CUT INTO THE LADY! SHE'S HAVING DEATH SPASMS!
WHAT THE...?
WIGGA WIGGA WIGGA
CHOPPER CHICK
AHHH. NICE.
OH,. DEAR, AS FAR AS FARTS ARE CONCERED, THAT WAS JUST A TINY HORS-D'OEUVRE, THE MAIN COURSE IS JUST LINING ITSELF UP NOW, I CAN FEEL IT.
HOLD ONTO YOUR WIG, FELIX!
AIR!
THAR SHE BLOWS!
FART A BANG!
LOOK! MRS. BUBBLY HAS LAID A FUNNY LITTLE MAN!
SMAK!
GHOST HELL
AND THAT'S NOT THE FIRST TIME, I CAN TELL YOU.
THEY THINK THAT I'VE REALLY SAWN A LADY IN HALF! AND NOW THEY THINK THAT SHE'S GIVEN BIRTH TO A MUTANT!
THEY'VE GONE CRAZY, THEY'RE RIPPING THE JOINT TO PIECES! HOW THE HELL ARE WE GONNA CALM THEM DOWN?
RED RUM
HAND ME THAT BOTTLE OF LEMMO-ADE, I'VE GOT A SPARKLINGLY WICKED IDEA.
GLUG GLUG
GUZZLE GUZZLE
GDIM GDIM
RIGHT, THAT'S ALL OF THE POP FINISHED...
...JET GIRL, GET THAT FRONT DOOR OPEN!

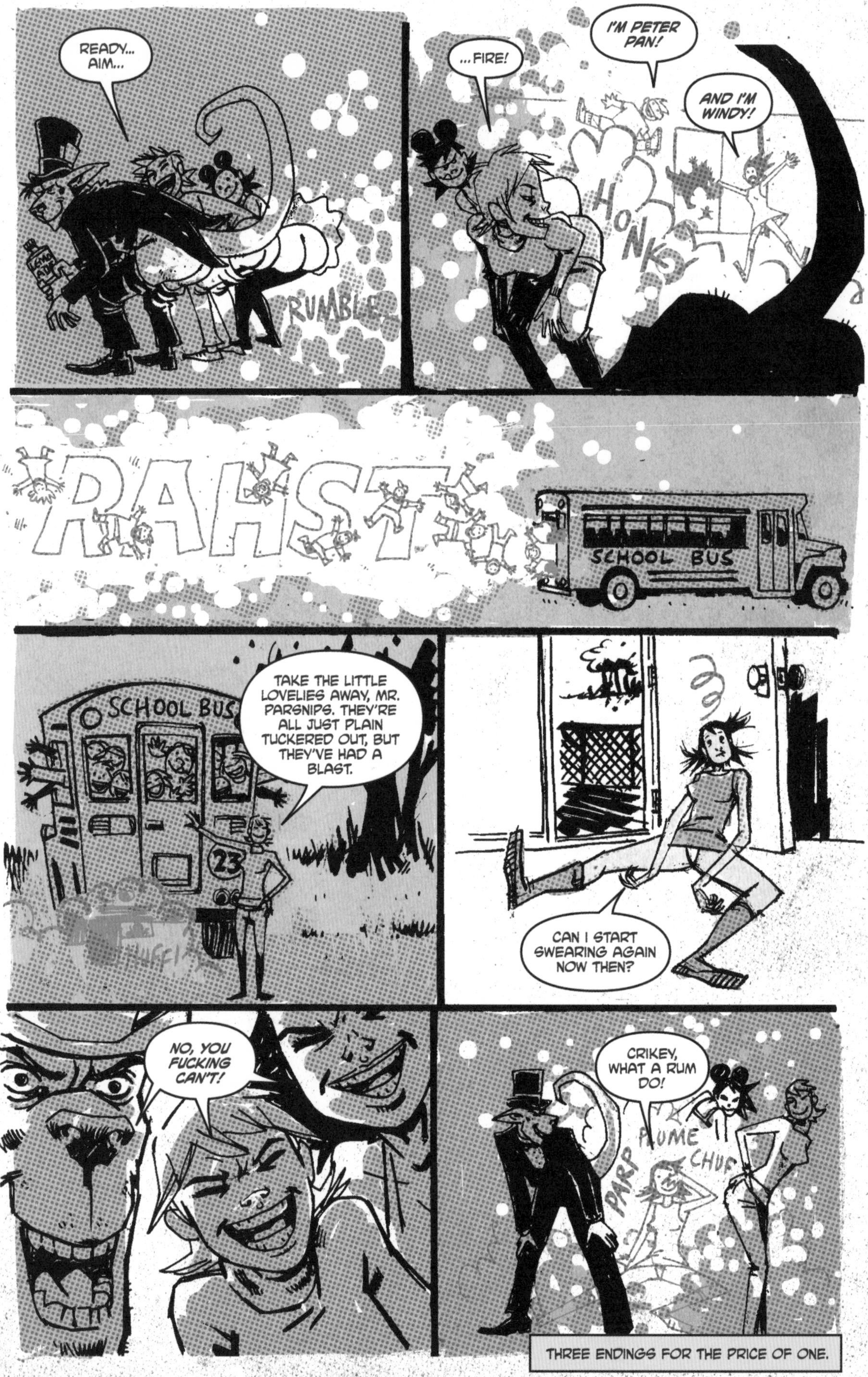
READY... AIM...
RUMBLE
...FIRE!
I'M PETER PAN!
AND I'M WINDY!
HONK
RAHST
SCHOOL BUS
SCHOOL BUS
TAKE THE LITTLE LOVELIES AWAY, MR. PARSNIPS. THEY'RE ALL JUST PLAIN TUCKERED OUT, BUT THEY'VE HAD A BLAST.
23
CAN I START SWEARING AGAIN NOW THEN?
NO, YOU FUCKING CAN'T!
CRIKEY, WHAT A RUM DO!
PARP
PLUME
CHUF
THREE ENDINGS FOR THE PRICE OF ONE.

HELP ME BRING THIS WENDY HOUSE DOWN.

I'm bummed
Chums
Moulded myself into a stupor
Like a plastic stormtrooper

I'm living in a dream
And I'm living in a bubble
That's the source of all my woes
That's a geyser of fuckin' trouble

The real world is beyond me
A childlike haze is upon me
And I'm paralysed with the fear
That an unknown force is gonna get me

Everyone around me is evolving
Maturing gracefully, problem solving
But I'm regressing into infancy
As an evil plan is unfolding

My prison walls are made of cotton
The outside world I have forgotten
So before my dreams turn rotten

Won't you please, please

Help me bring this Wendy House down

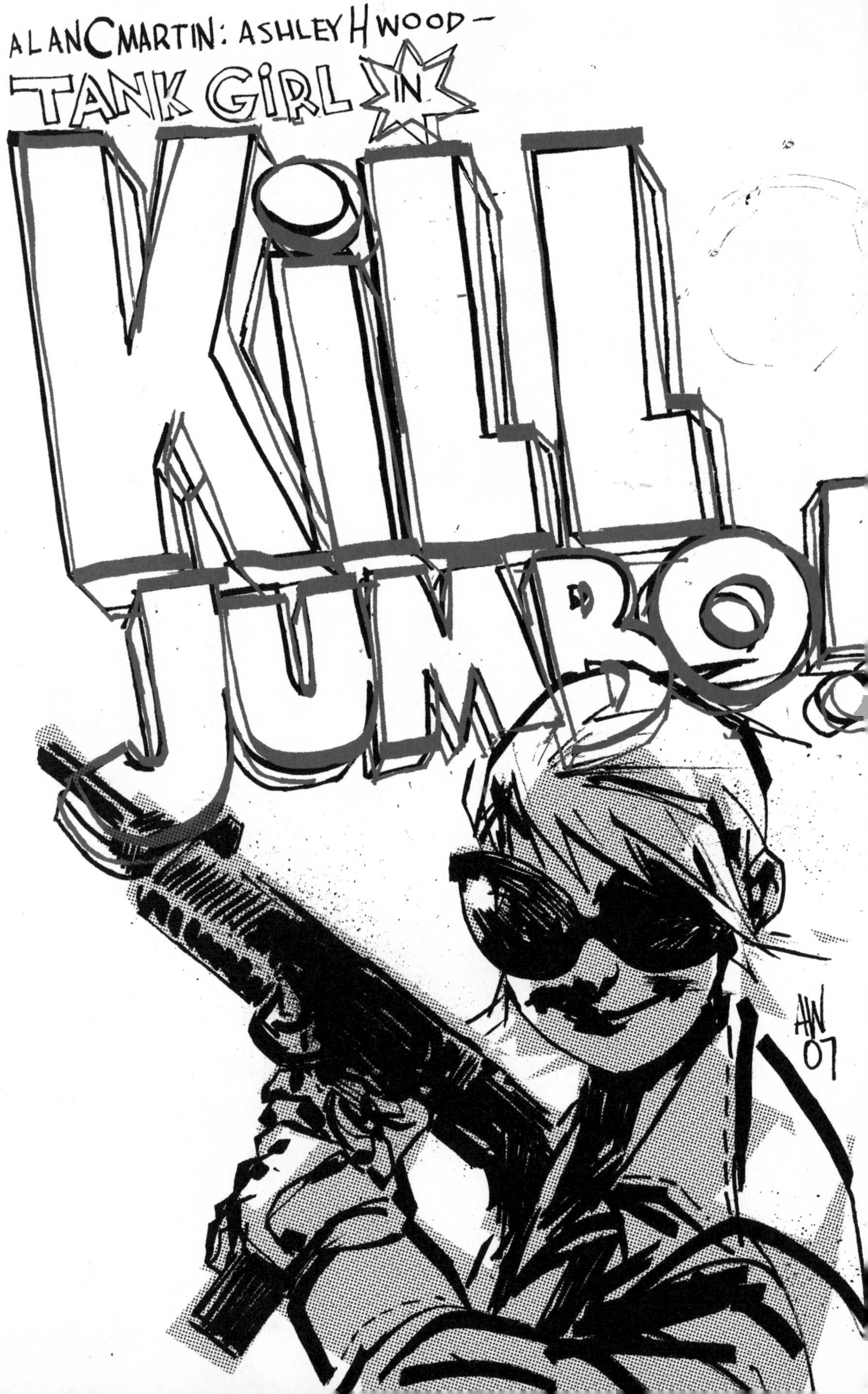
ALANCMARTIN: ASHLEYHWOOD -
TANK GIRL IN
KILL JUMBO!
AW 07

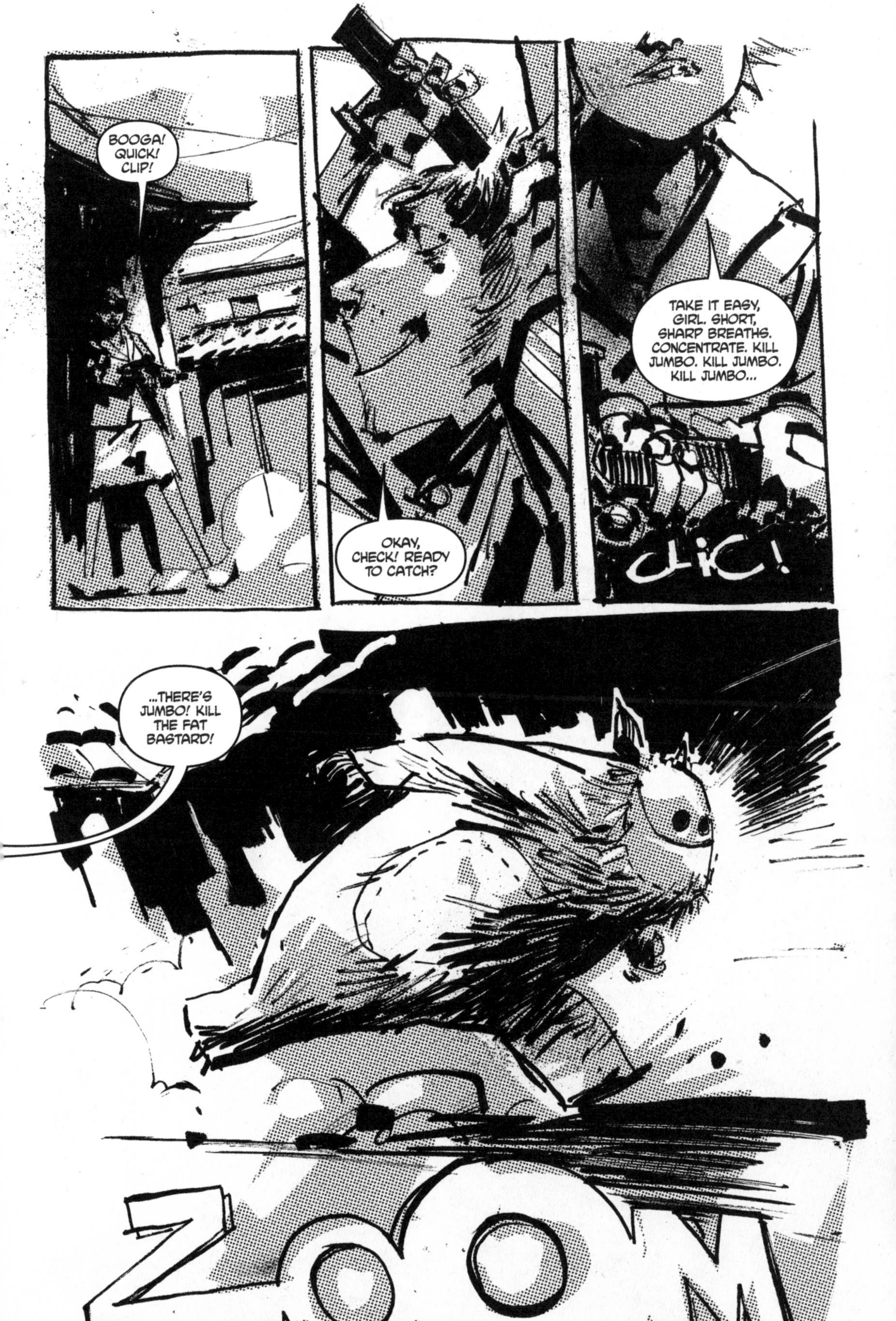
BOOGA! QUICK! CLIP!
OKAY, CHECK! READY TO CATCH?
TAKE IT EASY, GIRL. SHORT, SHARP BREATHS. CONCENTRATE. KILL JUMBO. KILL JUMBO. KILL JUMBO...
CLIC!
...THERE'S JUMBO! KILL THE FAT BASTARD!
ZOOM

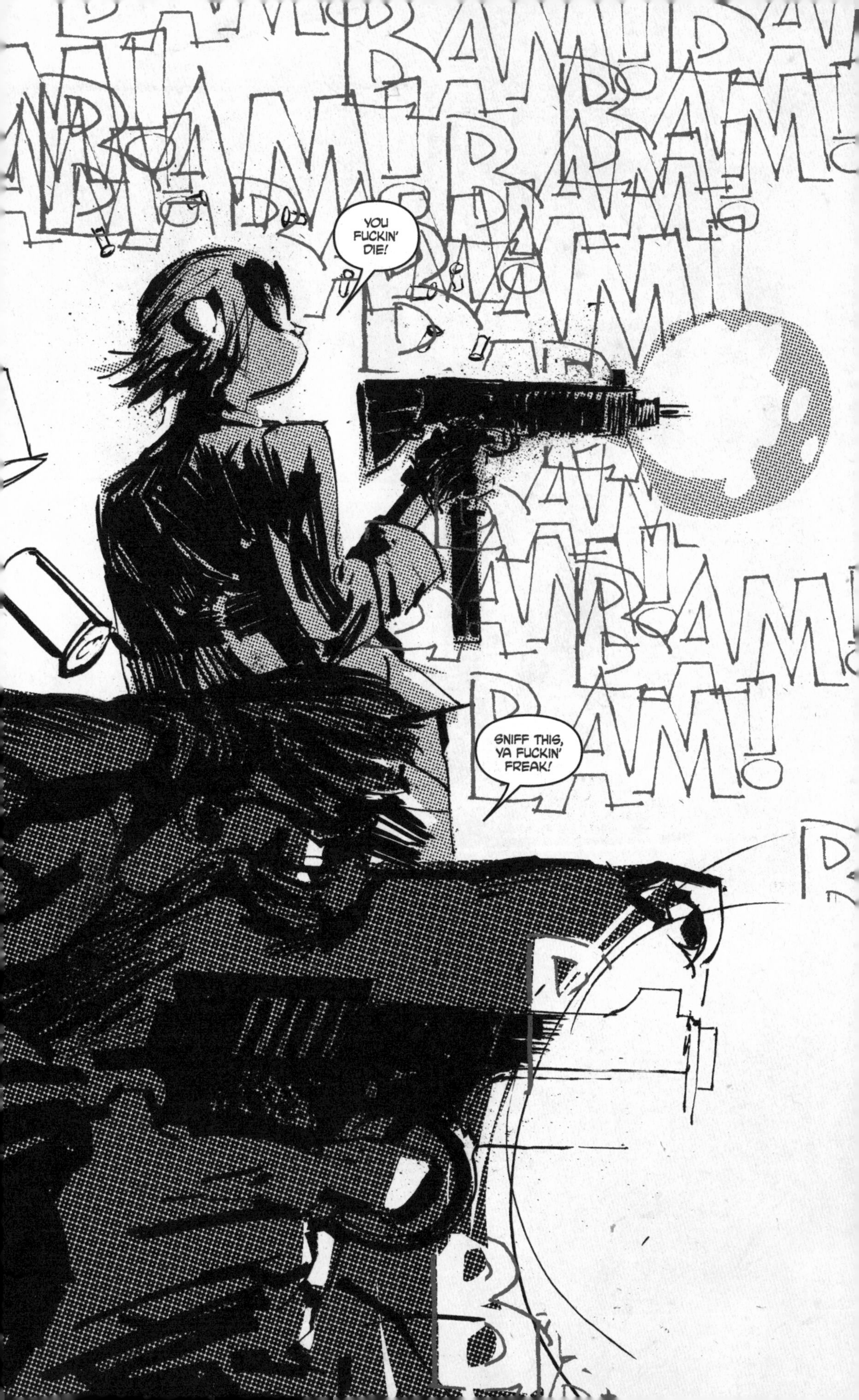
YOU FUCKIN' DIE!
SNIFF THIS, YA FUCKIN' FREAK!

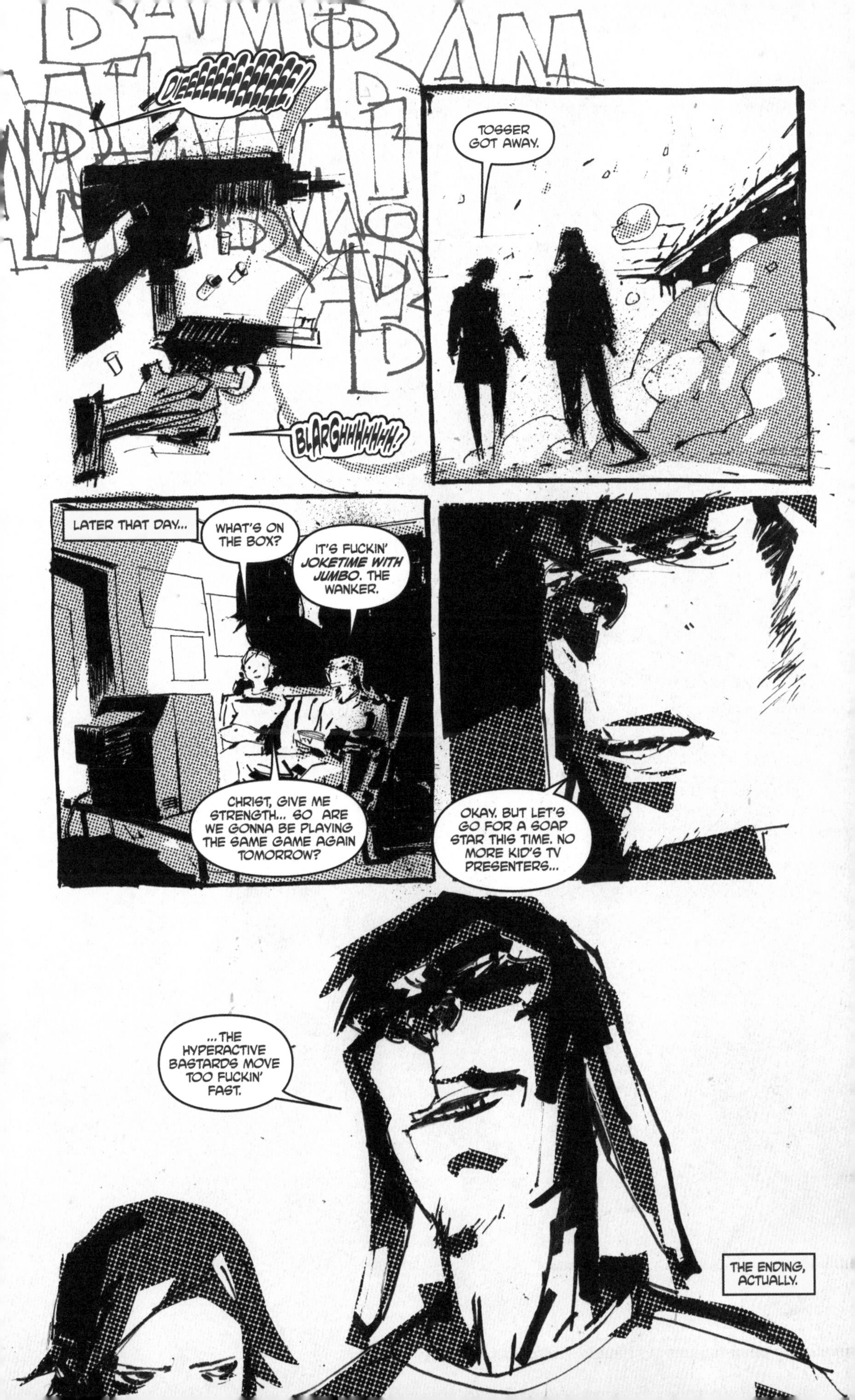
DIEEEEEEEEEEEEE!
BLARGHHHHHH!
TOSSER GOT AWAY.
LATER THAT DAY...
WHAT'S ON THE BOX?
IT'S FUCKIN' *JOKETIME WITH JUMBO*. THE WANKER.
CHRIST, GIVE ME STRENGTH... SO ARE WE GONNA BE PLAYING THE SAME GAME AGAIN TOMORROW?
OKAY. BUT LET'S GO FOR A SOAP STAR THIS TIME. NO MORE KID'S TV PRESENTERS...
...THE HYPERACTIVE BASTARDS MOVE TOO FUCKIN' FAST.
THE ENDING, ACTUALLY.

THERE'S A COMMON MISCONCEPTION GOING AROUND, THAT HAPPY MEMORIES COME IN VERY SMALL DOSES. F'RINSTANCE, TAKE A LOOK AT THE FRAMED PHOTOS IN AN AVERAGE GRANDMOTHER'S HOME... THEY'LL BE OF A LIMITED AMOUNT OF SOCIALLY ACCEPTABLE SITUATIONS...

...FOR EXAMPLE: KIDS IN UNCOMFORTABLY STIFF CLOTHING AT FORMAL FAMILY FUNCTIONS; YOUTHS LEAVING SCHOOL/COLLEGE; ADULTS RECEIVING AWARDS/GETTING MARRIED/HAVING MORE KIDS, ETC.

IT WOULD SEEM THAT THE ONLY MEMORIES WORTH KEEPING HOLD OF ARE THE ONES THAT WE FEEL PROUD OF—THE ONES THAT WE CAN SHOW OFF TO THE NEIGHBOURS. THESE PEAK MOMENTS ARE ALREADY BURNT INTO OUR BRAINS. MAYBE WE DON'T NEED PICTURE EVIDENCE OF THE MOST MEMORABLE TIMES OF OUR LIVES.

SOMEHOW THE TIME IN BETWEEN THE PEAKS SLIPS INTO INSIGNIFICANCE. I MEAN YOU'D NEVER FIND AN OLD WOMAN WITH A PHOTO ON HER BEDSIDE TABLE OF HER GRANDSON PICKING HIS NOSE AND SCRATCHING HIS BALLS, WOULD YOU, EH?

THIS IS MY POINT—IT'S THE TIMES THAT DON'T STAND OUT THAT ARE THE REAL GOLD DUST OF MEMORY. THE MINUTES, THE HOURS, THE DAYS AND THE YEARS OF MUNDANE ROUTINE, TIMES THAT ARE LONG-FORGOTTEN BECAUSE OF THEIR LACK OF DISTINCTION, THAT'S WHERE THE HEART OF LIFE IS TO BE FOUND.

TAKE A STEP BACK IN TIME... REVISIT A HOUSE YOU ONCE LIVED IN, A PLACE YOU WORKED IN, A SCHOOL YOU STUDIED IN, AN ALBUM YOU PLAYED TO DEATH... FIND SOME OF THOSE MOMENTS... THE POWER OF MEMORY IS ALWAYS ENOUGH TO BRING ABOUT A PARADIGM SHIFT IN CONCIOUSNESS.

ACTIONS OF THIS NATURE ARE MORE THAN NECCESSARY IF MANKIND IS TO PROGRESS OUT OF ITS CURRENT DEATHLY SLUMBER...

...COME BACK WITH ME NOW AS I REVISIT ONE SUCH NON-DISTINCT, ACTION-FREE MOMENT FROM MY OWN PAST...

TANK GIRL IN THE CHOCOLATE HANDSHAKE

WHOM TO BLAME... ALAN + RUFUS

SPECIAL THANKS DEPT... ALICE BIRD, GARRY LEACH, SIMON MORSE, DAVID TULLOCH, MICHELE PERRY, FINLAY AND THE RAMONES ♥

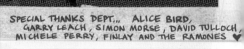

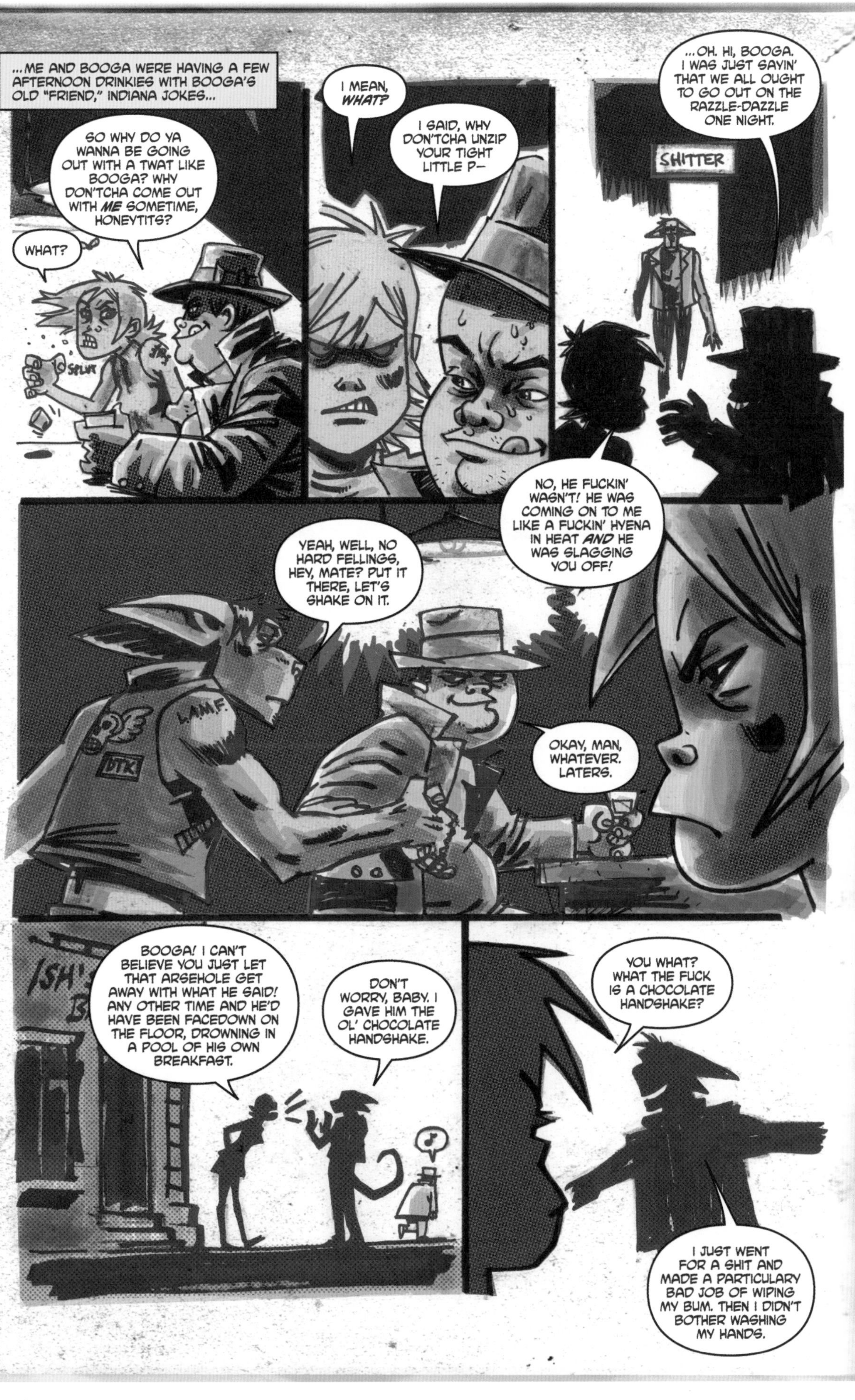
...ME AND BOOGA WERE HAVING A FEW AFTERNOON DRINKIES WITH BOOGA'S OLD "FRIEND," INDIANA JOKES...
SO WHY DO YA WANNA BE GOING OUT WITH A TWAT LIKE BOOGA? WHY DON'TCHA COME OUT WITH ***ME*** SOMETIME, HONEYTITS?
WHAT?
SPLUT
I MEAN, ***WHAT?***
I SAID, WHY DON'TCHA UNZIP YOUR TIGHT LITTLE P–
...OH. HI, BOOGA. I WAS JUST SAYIN' THAT WE ALL OUGHT TO GO OUT ON THE RAZZLE-DAZZLE ONE NIGHT.
SHITTER
NO, HE FUCKIN' WASN'T! HE WAS COMING ON TO ME LIKE A FUCKIN' HYENA IN HEAT ***AND*** HE WAS SLAGGING YOU OFF!
YEAH, WELL, NO HARD FELLINGS, HEY, MATE? PUT IT THERE, LET'S SHAKE ON IT.
L.A.M.F.
DTK
OKAY, MAN, WHATEVER. LATERS.
BOOGA! I CAN'T BELIEVE YOU JUST LET THAT ARSEHOLE GET AWAY WITH WHAT HE SAID! ANY OTHER TIME AND HE'D HAVE BEEN FACEDOWN ON THE FLOOR, DROWNING IN A POOL OF HIS OWN BREAKFAST.
DON'T WORRY, BABY. I GAVE HIM THE OL' CHOCOLATE HANDSHAKE.
YOU WHAT? WHAT THE FUCK IS A CHOCOLATE HANDSHAKE?
I JUST WENT FOR A SHIT AND MADE A PARTICULARY BAD JOB OF WIPING MY BUM. THEN I DIDN'T BOTHER WASHING MY HANDS.

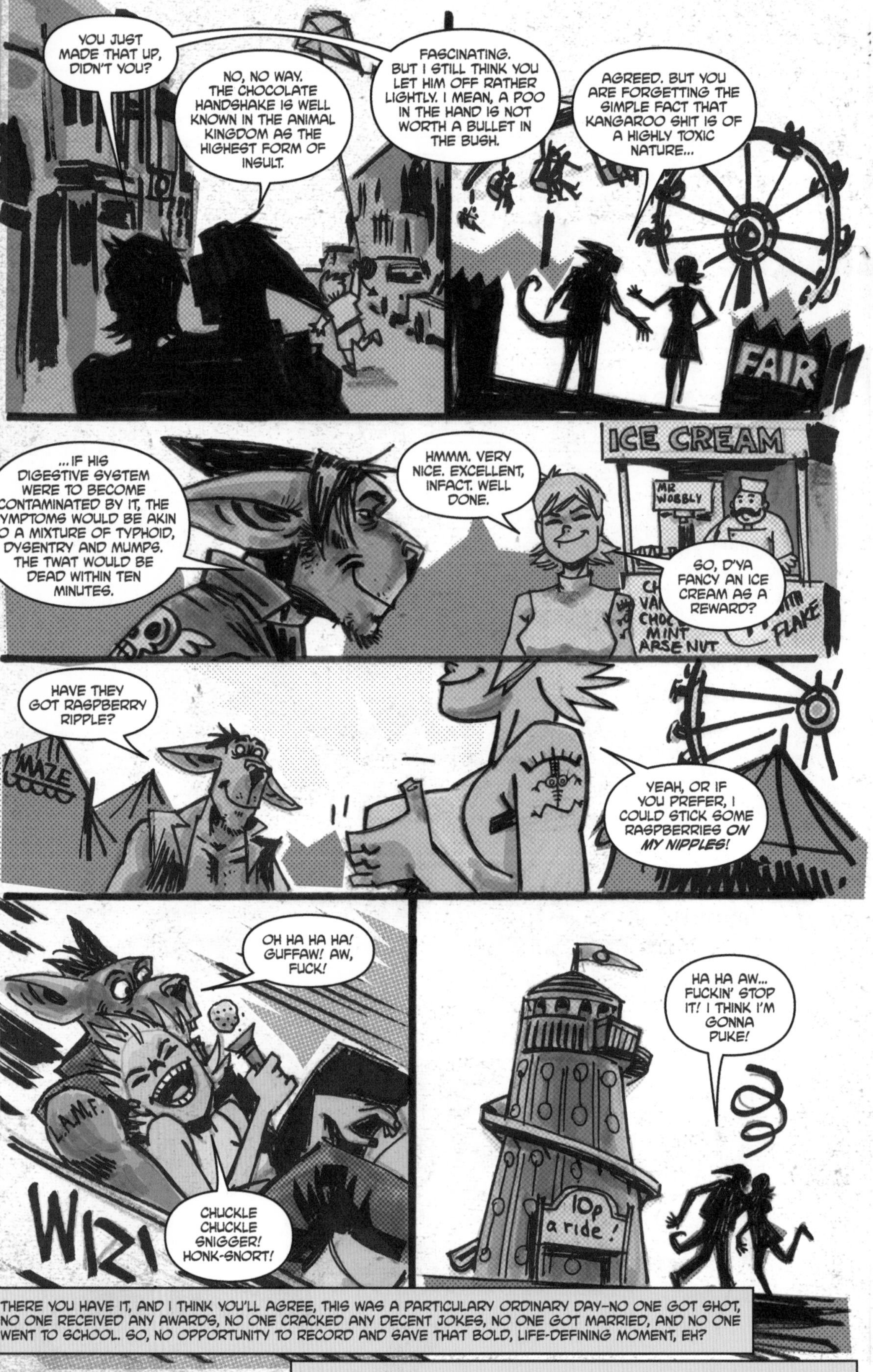
YOU JUST MADE THAT UP, DIDN'T YOU?
NO, NO WAY. THE CHOCOLATE HANDSHAKE IS WELL KNOWN IN THE ANIMAL KINGDOM AS THE HIGHEST FORM OF INSULT.
FASCINATING. BUT I STILL THINK YOU LET HIM OFF RATHER LIGHTLY. I MEAN, A POO IN THE HAND IS NOT WORTH A BULLET IN THE BUSH.
AGREED. BUT YOU ARE FORGETTING THE SIMPLE FACT THAT KANGAROO SHIT IS OF A HIGHLY TOXIC NATURE...
FAIR
ICE CREAM
MR WOBBLY
...IF HIS DIGESTIVE SYSTEM WERE TO BECOME CONTAMINATED BY IT, THE SYMPTOMS WOULD BE AKIN TO A MIXTURE OF TYPHOID, DYSENTRY AND MUMPS. THE TWAT WOULD BE DEAD WITHIN TEN MINUTES.
HMMM. VERY NICE. EXCELLENT, INFACT. WELL DONE.
SO, D'YA FANCY AN ICE CREAM AS A REWARD?
MINT
ARSE NUT
FLAKE
HAVE THEY GOT RASPBERRY RIPPLE?
MAZE
YEAH, OR IF YOU PREFER, I COULD STICK SOME RASPBERRIES *ON MY NIPPLES*!
OH HA HA HA! GUFFAW! AW, FUCK!
L.A.M.F.
CHUCKLE CHUCKLE SNIGGER! HONK-SNORT!
HA HA AW... FUCKIN' STOP IT! I THINK I'M GONNA PUKE!
10p a ride!
THERE YOU HAVE IT, AND I THINK YOU'LL AGREE, THIS WAS A PARTICULARY ORDINARY DAY–NO ONE GOT SHOT, NO ONE RECEIVED ANY AWARDS, NO ONE CRACKED ANY DECENT JOKES, NO ONE GOT MARRIED, AND NO ONE WENT TO SCHOOL. SO, NO OPPORTUNITY TO RECORD AND SAVE THAT BOLD, LIFE-DEFINING MOMENT, EH?
WELL, THINK AGAIN... LET US ZERO-IN ON ONE TINY SECOND OF THAT MEMORY...

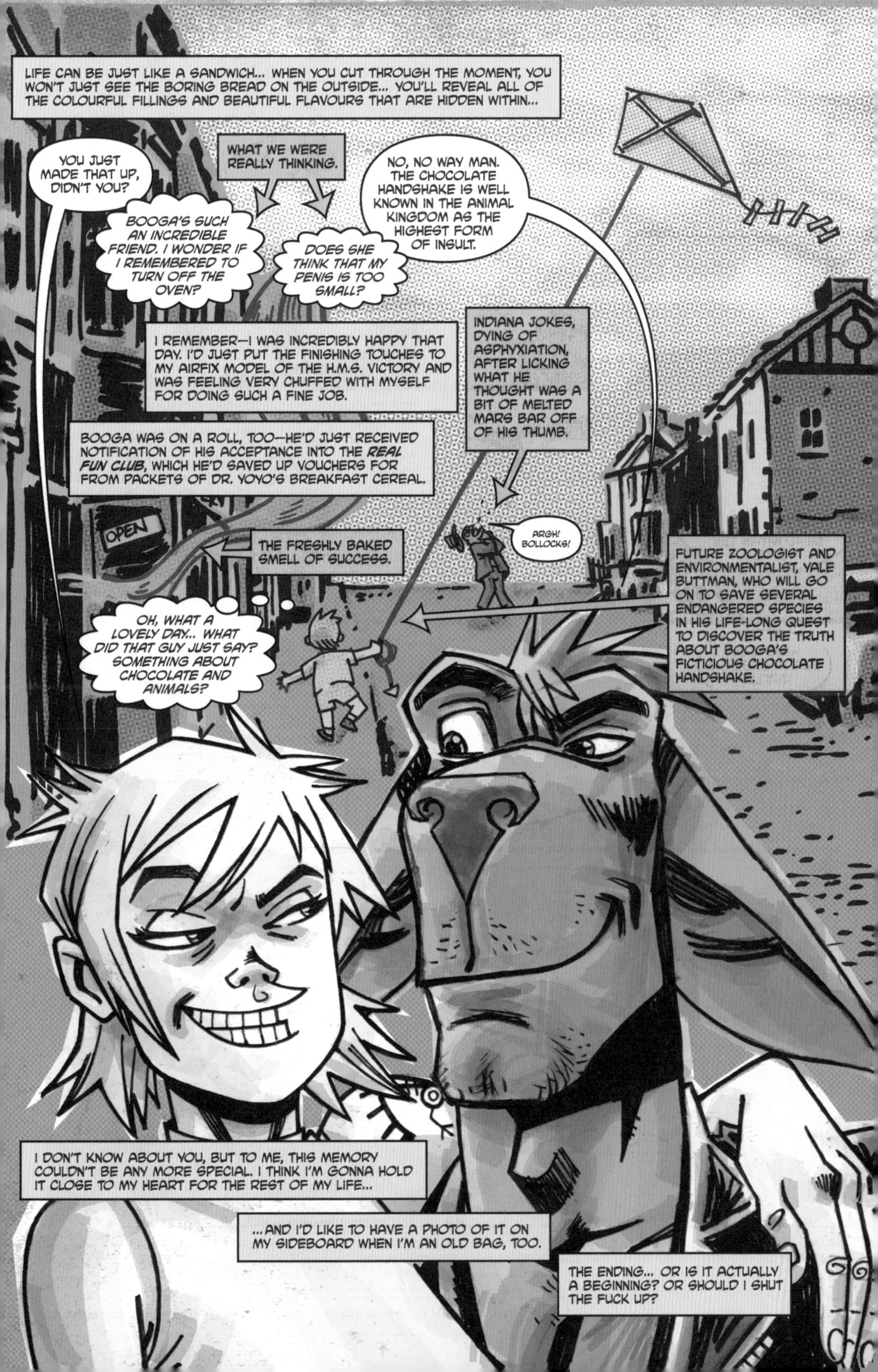
LIFE CAN BE JUST LIKE A SANDWICH... WHEN YOU CUT THROUGH THE MOMENT, YOU WON'T JUST SEE THE BORING BREAD ON THE OUTSIDE... YOU'LL REVEAL ALL OF THE COLOURFUL FILLINGS AND BEAUTIFUL FLAVOURS THAT ARE HIDDEN WITHIN...
YOU JUST MADE THAT UP, DIDN'T YOU?
WHAT WE WERE REALLY THINKING.
BOOGA'S SUCH AN INCREDIBLE FRIEND. I WONDER IF I REMEMBERED TO TURN OFF THE OVEN?
DOES SHE THINK THAT MY PENIS IS TOO SMALL?
NO, NO WAY MAN. THE CHOCOLATE HANDSHAKE IS WELL KNOWN IN THE ANIMAL KINGDOM AS THE HIGHEST FORM OF INSULT.
I REMEMBER—I WAS INCREDIBLY HAPPY THAT DAY. I'D JUST PUT THE FINISHING TOUCHES TO MY AIRFIX MODEL OF THE H.M.S. VICTORY AND WAS FEELING VERY CHUFFED WITH MYSELF FOR DOING SUCH A FINE JOB.
INDIANA JOKES, DYING OF ASPHYXIATION, AFTER LICKING WHAT HE THOUGHT WAS A BIT OF MELTED MARS BAR OFF OF HIS THUMB.
BOOGA WAS ON A ROLL, TOO—HE'D JUST RECEIVED NOTIFICATION OF HIS ACCEPTANCE INTO THE *REAL FUN CLUB*, WHICH HE'D SAVED UP VOUCHERS FOR FROM PACKETS OF DR. YOYO'S BREAKFAST CEREAL.
OPEN
THE FRESHLY BAKED SMELL OF SUCCESS.
ARGH! BOLLOCKS!
FUTURE ZOOLOGIST AND ENVIRONMENTALIST, YALE BUTTMAN, WHO WILL GO ON TO SAVE SEVERAL ENDANGERED SPECIES IN HIS LIFE-LONG QUEST TO DISCOVER THE TRUTH ABOUT BOOGA'S FICTICIOUS CHOCOLATE HANDSHAKE.
OH, WHAT A LOVELY DAY... WHAT DID THAT GUY JUST SAY? SOMETHING ABOUT CHOCOLATE AND ANIMALS?
I DON'T KNOW ABOUT YOU, BUT TO ME, THIS MEMORY COULDN'T BE ANY MORE SPECIAL. I THINK I'M GONNA HOLD IT CLOSE TO MY HEART FOR THE REST OF MY LIFE...
...AND I'D LIKE TO HAVE A PHOTO OF IT ON MY SIDEBOARD WHEN I'M AN OLD BAG, TOO.
THE ENDING... OR IS IT ACTUALLY A BEGINNING? OR SHOULD I SHUT THE FUCK UP?

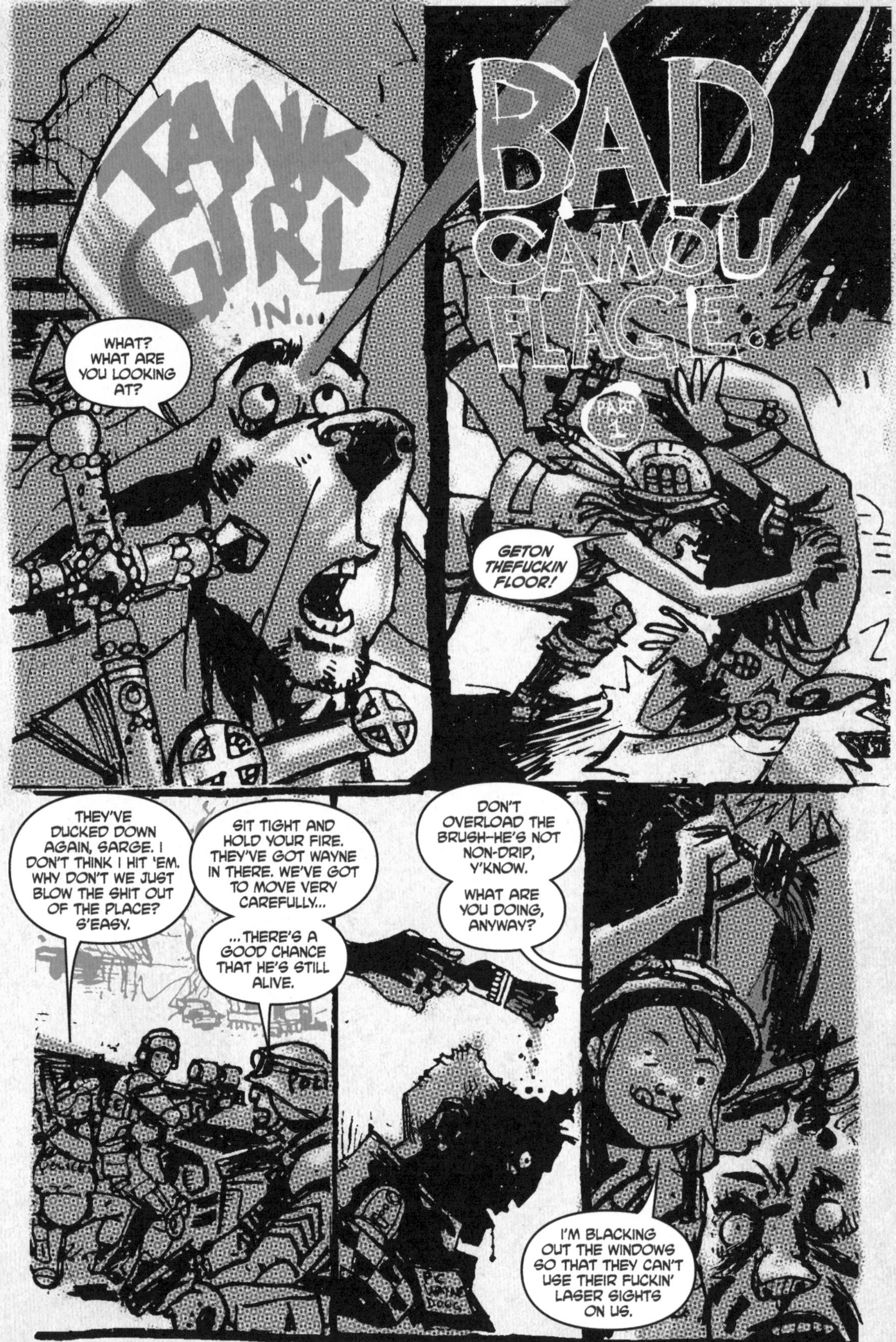
TANK GIRL IN...
BAD CAMOUFLAGE
PART 1
WHAT? WHAT ARE YOU LOOKING AT?
GETON THEFUCKIN FLOOR!
THEY'VE DUCKED DOWN AGAIN, SARGE. I DON'T THINK I HIT 'EM. WHY DON'T WE JUST BLOW THE SHIT OUT OF THE PLACE? S'EASY.
SIT TIGHT AND HOLD YOUR FIRE. THEY'VE GOT WAYNE IN THERE. WE'VE GOT TO MOVE VERY CAREFULLY...
...THERE'S A GOOD CHANCE THAT HE'S STILL ALIVE.
DON'T OVERLOAD THE BRUSH–HE'S NOT NON-DRIP, Y'KNOW.
WHAT ARE YOU DOING, ANYWAY?
I'M BLACKING OUT THE WINDOWS SO THAT THEY CAN'T USE THEIR FUCKIN' LASER SIGHTS ON US.

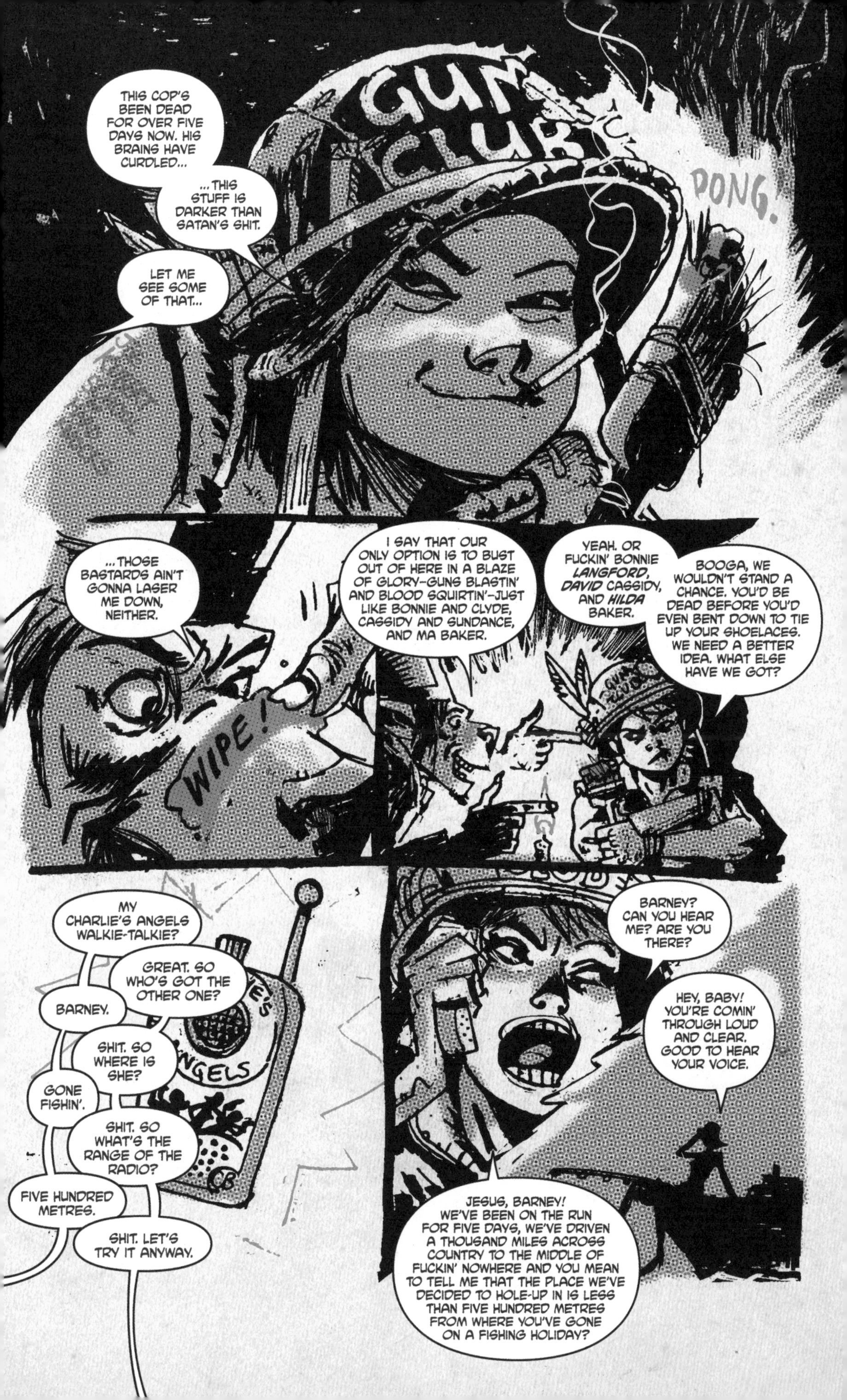

THIS COP'S BEEN DEAD FOR OVER FIVE DAYS NOW. HIS BRAINS HAVE CURDLED...
...THIS STUFF IS DARKER THAN SATAN'S SHIT.
LET ME SEE SOME OF THAT...
GUM CLUB
PONG!
...THOSE BASTARDS AIN'T GONNA LASER ME DOWN, NEITHER.
WIPE!
I SAY THAT OUR ONLY OPTION IS TO BUST OUT OF HERE IN A BLAZE OF GLORY—GUNS BLASTIN' AND BLOOD SQUIRTIN'—JUST LIKE BONNIE AND CLYDE, CASSIDY AND SUNDANCE, AND MA BAKER.
YEAH. OR FUCKIN' BONNIE *LANGFORD*, *DAVID* CASSIDY, AND *HILDA* BAKER.
BOOGA, WE WOULDN'T STAND A CHANCE. YOU'D BE DEAD BEFORE YOU'D EVEN BENT DOWN TO TIE UP YOUR SHOELACES. WE NEED A BETTER IDEA. WHAT ELSE HAVE WE GOT?
MY CHARLIE'S ANGELS WALKIE-TALKIE?
GREAT. SO WHO'S GOT THE OTHER ONE?
BARNEY.
SHIT. SO WHERE IS SHE?
GONE FISHIN'.
SHIT. SO WHAT'S THE RANGE OF THE RADIO?
FIVE HUNDRED METRES.
SHIT. LET'S TRY IT ANYWAY.
BARNEY? CAN YOU HEAR ME? ARE YOU THERE?
HEY, BABY! YOU'RE COMIN' THROUGH LOUD AND CLEAR. GOOD TO HEAR YOUR VOICE.
JESUS, BARNEY! WE'VE BEEN ON THE RUN FOR FIVE DAYS, WE'VE DRIVEN A THOUSAND MILES ACROSS COUNTRY TO THE MIDDLE OF FUCKIN' NOWHERE AND YOU MEAN TO TELL ME THAT THE PLACE WE'VE DECIDED TO HOLE-UP IN IS LESS THAN FIVE HUNDRED METRES FROM WHERE YOU'VE GONE ON A FISHING HOLIDAY?

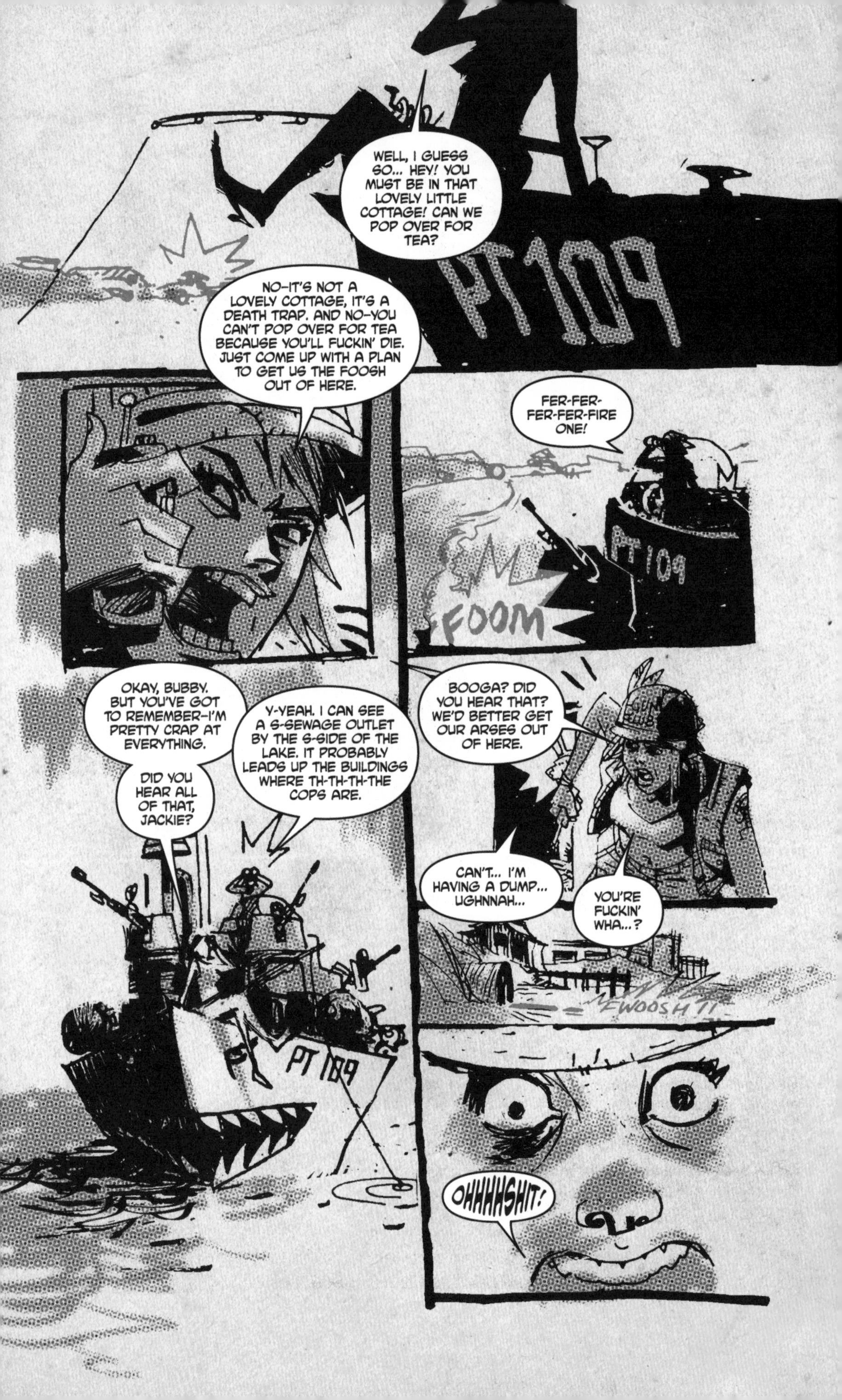
WELL, I GUESS SO... HEY! YOU MUST BE IN THAT LOVELY LITTLE COTTAGE! CAN WE POP OVER FOR TEA?
PT 109
NO–IT'S NOT A LOVELY COTTAGE, IT'S A DEATH TRAP. AND NO–YOU CAN'T POP OVER FOR TEA BECAUSE YOU'LL FUCKIN' DIE. JUST COME UP WITH A PLAN TO GET US THE FOOSH OUT OF HERE.
FER-FER-FER-FER-FIRE ONE!
PT 109
FOOM
OKAY, BUBBY. BUT YOU'VE GOT TO REMEMBER–I'M PRETTY CRAP AT EVERYTHING.
DID YOU HEAR ALL OF THAT, JACKIE?
Y-YEAH. I CAN SEE A S-SEWAGE OUTLET BY THE S-SIDE OF THE LAKE. IT PROBABLY LEADS UP THE BUILDINGS WHERE TH-TH-TH-THE COPS ARE.
PT 109
BOOGA? DID YOU HEAR THAT? WE'D BETTER GET OUR ARSES OUT OF HERE.
CAN'T... I'M HAVING A DUMP... UGHNNAH...
YOU'RE FUCKIN' WHA...?
FWOOSH!!
OHHHHSHIT!

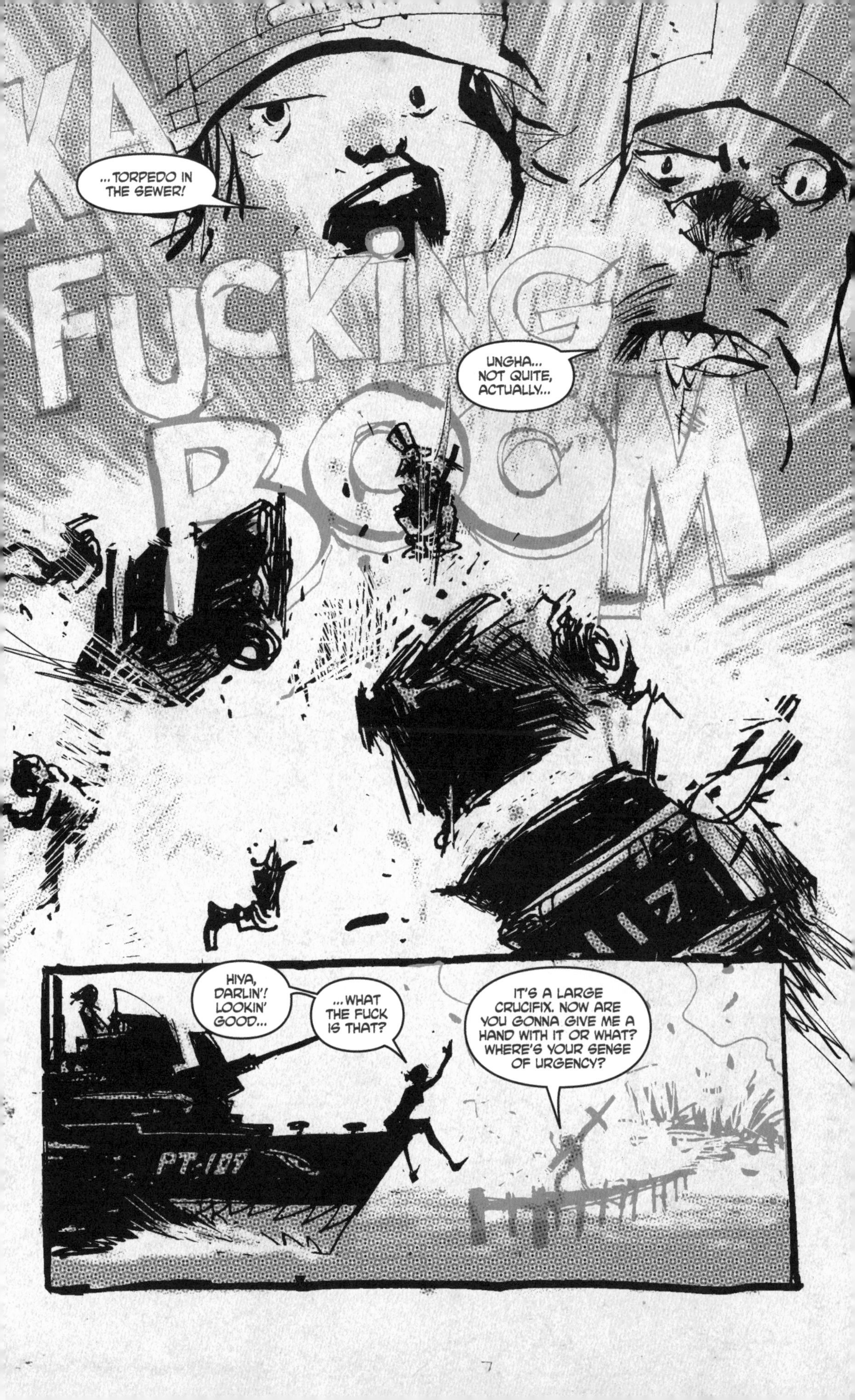
KA
...TORPEDO IN THE SEWER!
FUCKING
UNGHA... NOT QUITE, ACTUALLY...
BOOM
HIYA, DARLIN'! LOOKIN' GOOD...
...WHAT THE FUCK IS THAT?
IT'S A LARGE CRUCIFIX. NOW ARE YOU GONNA GIVE ME A HAND WITH IT OR WHAT? WHERE'S YOUR SENSE OF URGENCY?
PT-107

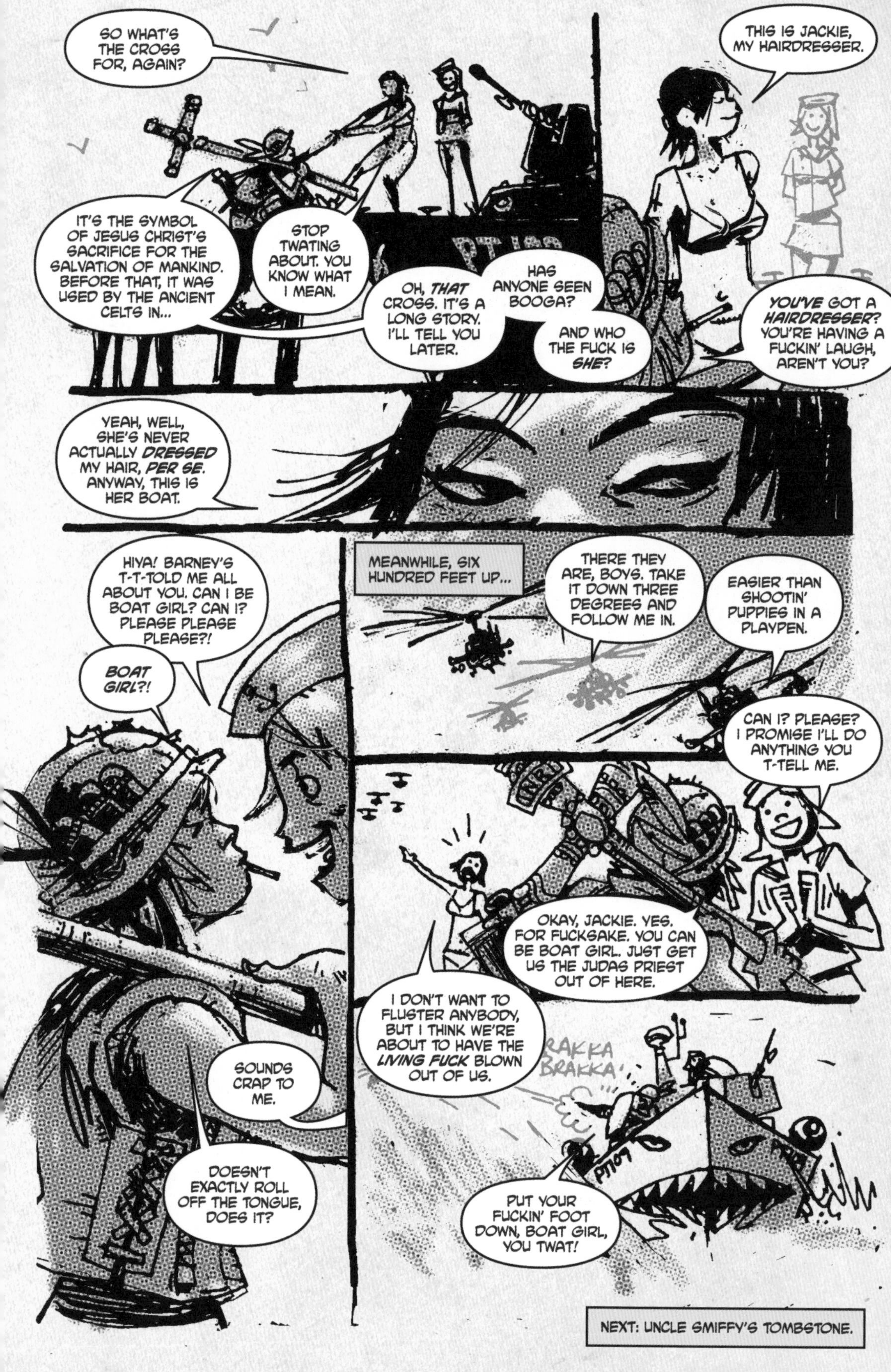
SO WHAT'S THE CROSS FOR, AGAIN?
IT'S THE SYMBOL OF JESUS CHRIST'S SACRIFICE FOR THE SALVATION OF MANKIND. BEFORE THAT, IT WAS USED BY THE ANCIENT CELTS IN...
STOP TWATING ABOUT. YOU KNOW WHAT I MEAN.
OH, THAT CROSS. IT'S A LONG STORY. I'LL TELL YOU LATER.
HAS ANYONE SEEN BOOGA?
AND WHO THE FUCK IS SHE?
THIS IS JACKIE, MY HAIRDRESSER.
YOU'VE GOT A HAIRDRESSER? YOU'RE HAVING A FUCKIN' LAUGH, AREN'T YOU?
YEAH, WELL, SHE'S NEVER ACTUALLY DRESSED MY HAIR, PER SE. ANYWAY, THIS IS HER BOAT.
HIYA! BARNEY'S T-T-TOLD ME ALL ABOUT YOU. CAN I BE BOAT GIRL? CAN I? PLEASE PLEASE PLEASE?!
BOAT GIRL?!
SOUNDS CRAP TO ME.
DOESN'T EXACTLY ROLL OFF THE TONGUE, DOES IT?
MEANWHILE, SIX HUNDRED FEET UP...
THERE THEY ARE, BOYS. TAKE IT DOWN THREE DEGREES AND FOLLOW ME IN.
EASIER THAN SHOOTIN' PUPPIES IN A PLAYPEN.
CAN I? PLEASE? I PROMISE I'LL DO ANYTHING YOU T-TELL ME.
OKAY, JACKIE. YES. FOR FUCKSAKE. YOU CAN BE BOAT GIRL. JUST GET US THE JUDAS PRIEST OUT OF HERE.
I DON'T WANT TO FLUSTER ANYBODY, BUT I THINK WE'RE ABOUT TO HAVE THE LIVING FUCK BLOWN OUT OF US.
BRAKKA BRAKKA
PT107
PUT YOUR FUCKIN' FOOT DOWN, BOAT GIRL, YOU TWAT!
NEXT: UNCLE SMIFFY'S TOMBSTONE.

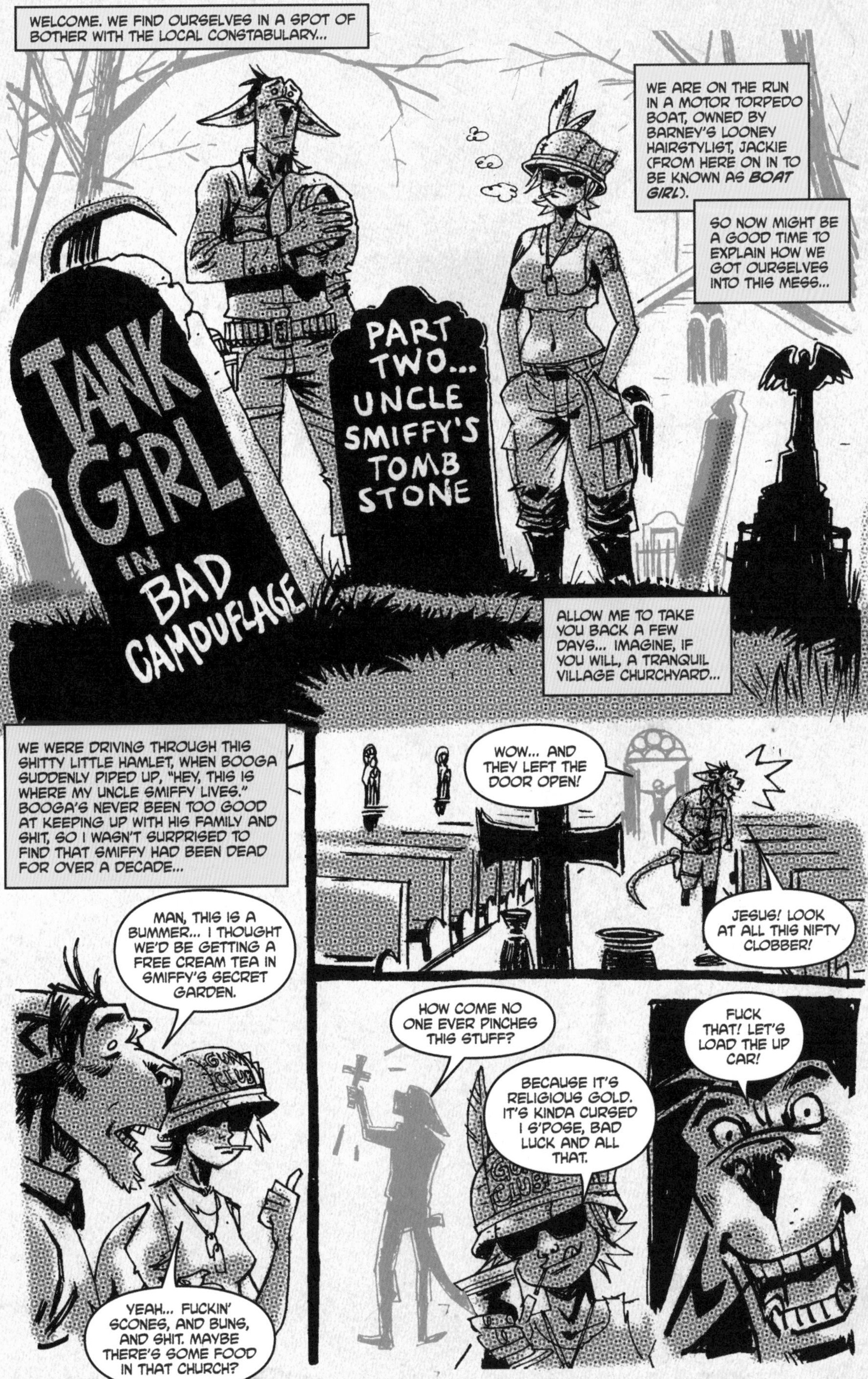
WELCOME. WE FIND OURSELVES IN A SPOT OF BOTHER WITH THE LOCAL CONSTABULARY...
WE ARE ON THE RUN IN A MOTOR TORPEDO BOAT, OWNED BY BARNEY'S LOONEY HAIRSTYLIST, JACKIE (FROM HERE ON IN TO BE KNOWN AS *BOAT GIRL*).
SO NOW MIGHT BE A GOOD TIME TO EXPLAIN HOW WE GOT OURSELVES INTO THIS MESS...
TANK GIRL IN BAD CAMOUFLAGE
PART TWO... UNCLE SMIFFY'S TOMB STONE
ALLOW ME TO TAKE YOU BACK A FEW DAYS... IMAGINE, IF YOU WILL, A TRANQUIL VILLAGE CHURCHYARD...
WE WERE DRIVING THROUGH THIS SHITTY LITTLE HAMLET, WHEN BOOGA SUDDENLY PIPED UP, "HEY, THIS IS WHERE MY UNCLE SMIFFY LIVES." BOOGA'S NEVER BEEN TOO GOOD AT KEEPING UP WITH HIS FAMILY AND SHIT, SO I WASN'T SURPRISED TO FIND THAT SMIFFY HAD BEEN DEAD FOR OVER A DECADE...
MAN, THIS IS A BUMMER... I THOUGHT WE'D BE GETTING A FREE CREAM TEA IN SMIFFY'S SECRET GARDEN.
GUN CLUB
YEAH... FUCKIN' SCONES, AND BUNS, AND SHIT. MAYBE THERE'S SOME FOOD IN THAT CHURCH?
WOW... AND THEY LEFT THE DOOR OPEN!
JESUS! LOOK AT ALL THIS NIFTY CLOBBER!
HOW COME NO ONE EVER PINCHES THIS STUFF?
BECAUSE IT'S RELIGIOUS GOLD. IT'S KINDA CURSED I S'POSE, BAD LUCK AND ALL THAT.
FUCK THAT! LET'S LOAD THE UP CAR!

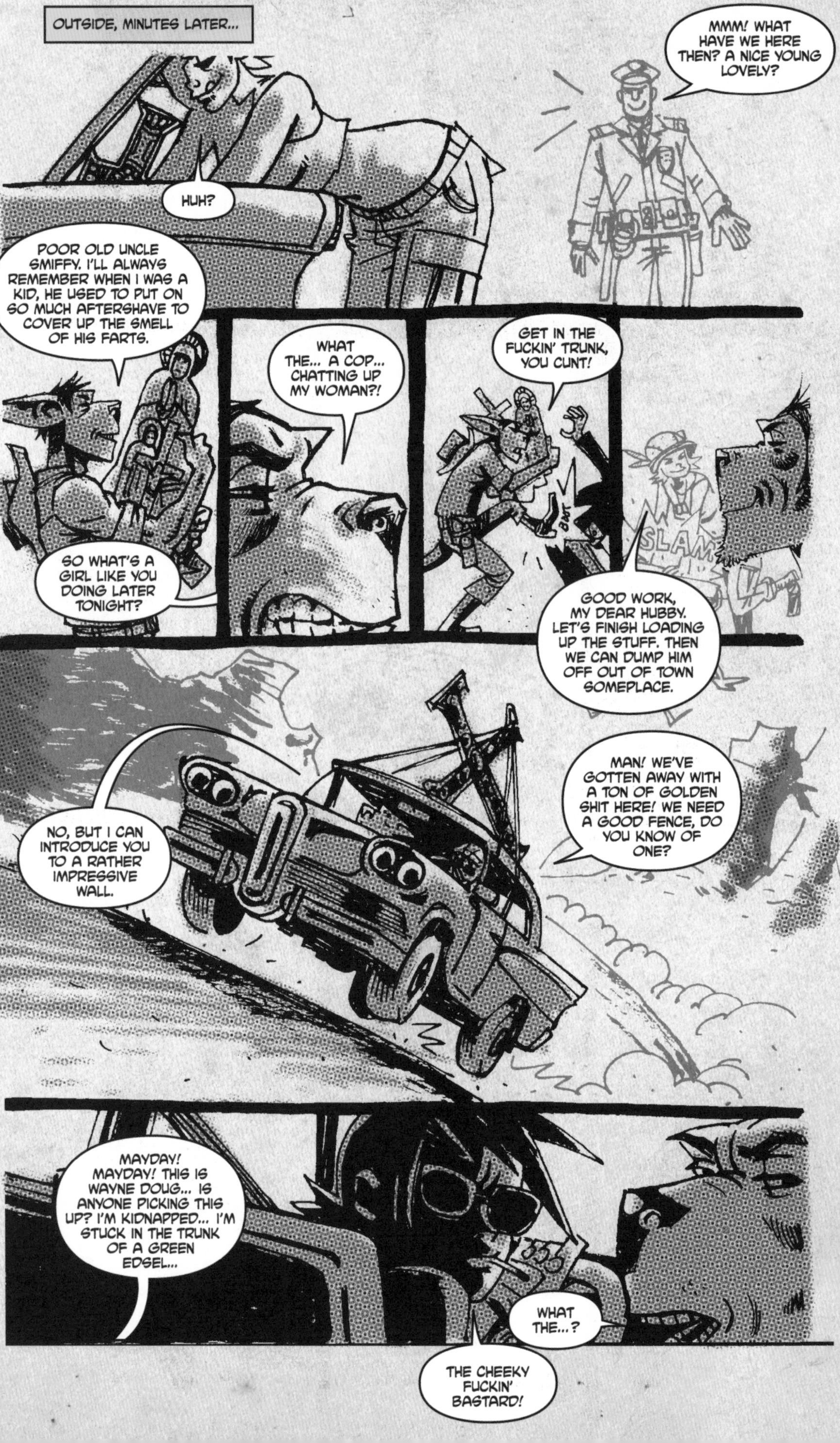
OUTSIDE, MINUTES LATER...
MMM! WHAT HAVE WE HERE THEN? A NICE YOUNG LOVELY?
HUH?
POOR OLD UNCLE SMIFFY. I'LL ALWAYS REMEMBER WHEN I WAS A KID, HE USED TO PUT ON SO MUCH AFTERSHAVE TO COVER UP THE SMELL OF HIS FARTS.
SO WHAT'S A GIRL LIKE YOU DOING LATER TONIGHT?
NO, BUT I CAN INTRODUCE YOU TO A RATHER IMPRESSIVE WALL.
WHAT THE... A COP... CHATTING UP MY WOMAN?!
GET IN THE FUCKIN' TRUNK, YOU CUNT!
SLAM
GOOD WORK, MY DEAR HUBBY. LET'S FINISH LOADING UP THE STUFF. THEN WE CAN DUMP HIM OFF OUT OF TOWN SOMEPLACE.
MAN! WE'VE GOTTEN AWAY WITH A TON OF GOLDEN SHIT HERE! WE NEED A GOOD FENCE, DO YOU KNOW OF ONE?
MAYDAY! MAYDAY! THIS IS WAYNE DOUG... IS ANYONE PICKING THIS UP? I'M KIDNAPPED... I'M STUCK IN THE TRUNK OF A GREEN EDSEL...
WHAT THE...?
THE CHEEKY FUCKIN' BASTARD!

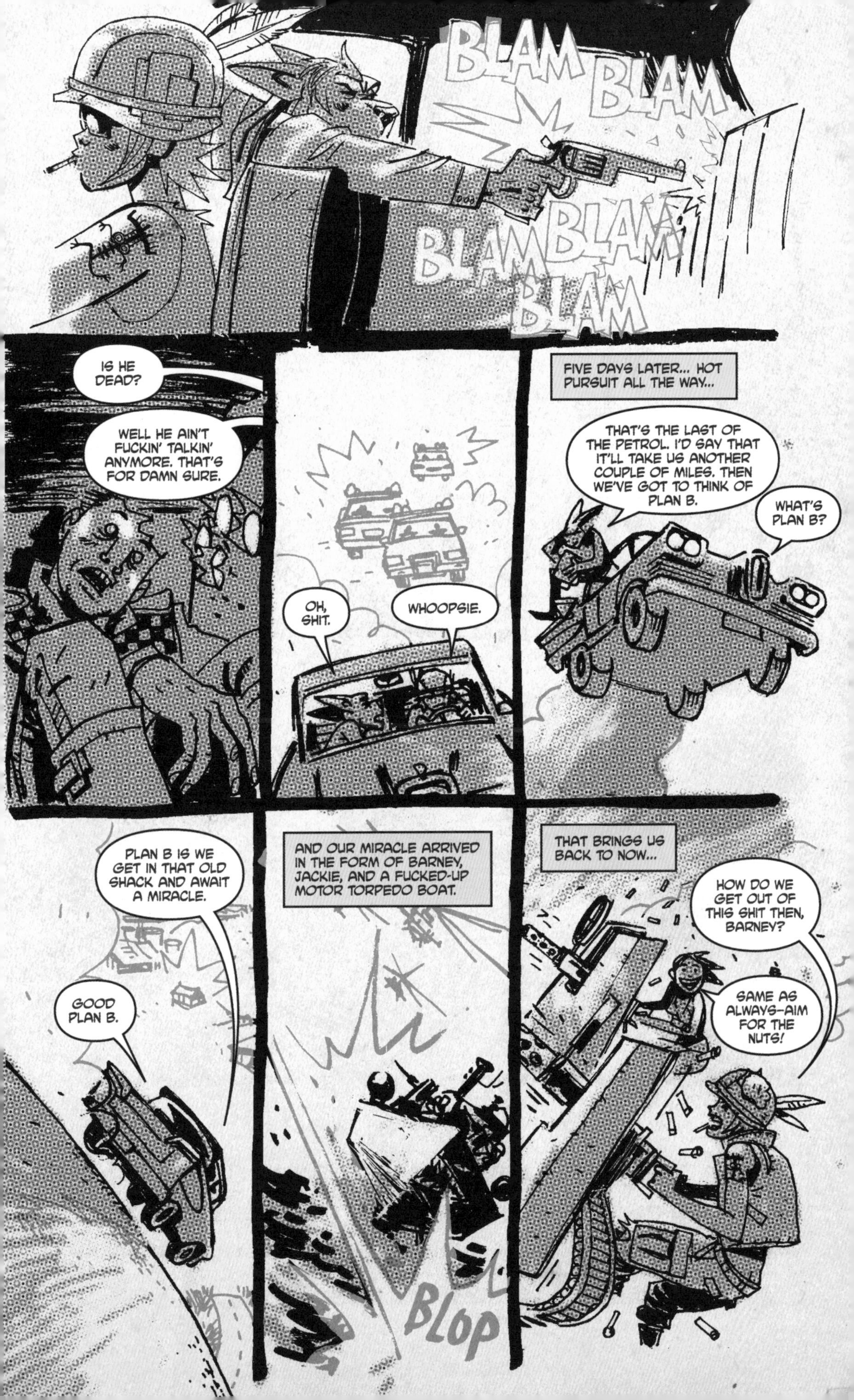
BLAM BLAM
BLAM BLAM
BLAM
IS HE DEAD?
WELL HE AIN'T FUCKIN' TALKIN' ANYMORE. THAT'S FOR DAMN SURE.
OH, SHIT.
WHOOPSIE.
FIVE DAYS LATER... HOT PURSUIT ALL THE WAY...
THAT'S THE LAST OF THE PETROL. I'D SAY THAT IT'LL TAKE US ANOTHER COUPLE OF MILES. THEN WE'VE GOT TO THINK OF PLAN B.
WHAT'S PLAN B?
PLAN B IS WE GET IN THAT OLD SHACK AND AWAIT A MIRACLE.
GOOD PLAN B.
AND OUR MIRACLE ARRIVED IN THE FORM OF BARNEY, JACKIE, AND A FUCKED-UP MOTOR TORPEDO BOAT.
BLOP
THAT BRINGS US BACK TO NOW...
HOW DO WE GET OUT OF THIS SHIT THEN, BARNEY?
SAME AS ALWAYS—AIM FOR THE NUTS!

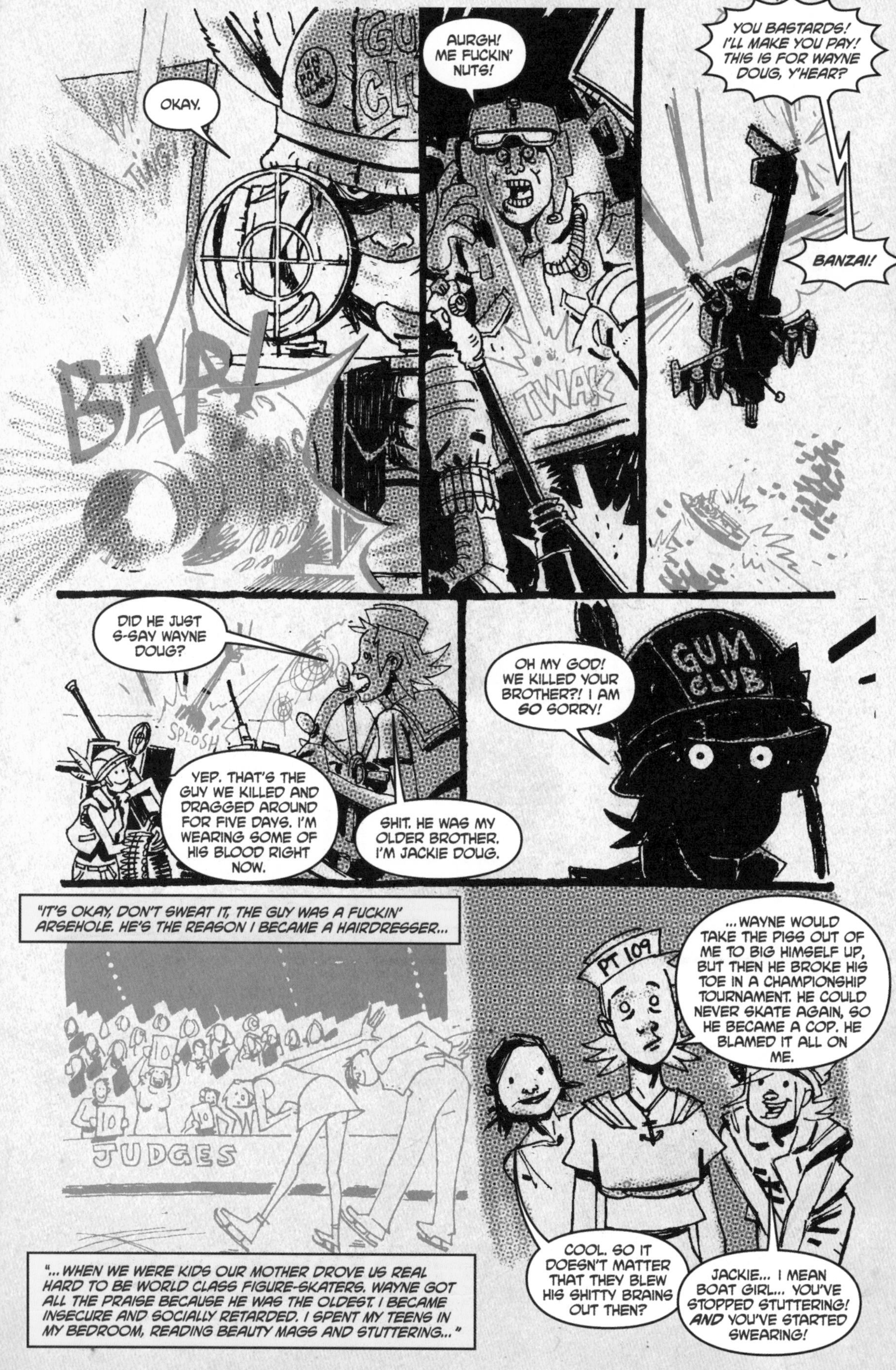
OKAY.
TING!
BAP!
AURGH! ME FUCKIN' NUTS!
TWAK
YOU BASTARDS! I'LL MAKE YOU PAY! THIS IS FOR WAYNE DOUG, Y'HEAR?
BANZAI!
DID HE JUST S-SAY WAYNE DOUG?
SPLOSH
YEP. THAT'S THE GUY WE KILLED AND DRAGGED AROUND FOR FIVE DAYS. I'M WEARING SOME OF HIS BLOOD RIGHT NOW.
SHIT. HE WAS MY OLDER BROTHER. I'M JACKIE DOUG.
GUM CLUB
OH MY GOD! WE KILLED YOUR BROTHER?! I AM SO SORRY!
"IT'S OKAY, DON'T SWEAT IT, THE GUY WAS A FUCKIN' ARSEHOLE. HE'S THE REASON I BECAME A HAIRDRESSER...
JUDGES
"... WHEN WE WERE KIDS OUR MOTHER DROVE US REAL HARD TO BE WORLD CLASS FIGURE-SKATERS. WAYNE GOT ALL THE PRAISE BECAUSE HE WAS THE OLDEST. I BECAME INSECURE AND SOCIALLY RETARDED. I SPENT MY TEENS IN MY BEDROOM, READING BEAUTY MAGS AND STUTTERING..."
PT 109
...WAYNE WOULD TAKE THE PISS OUT OF ME TO BIG HIMSELF UP, BUT THEN HE BROKE HIS TOE IN A CHAMPIONSHIP TOURNAMENT. HE COULD NEVER SKATE AGAIN, SO HE BECAME A COP. HE BLAMED IT ALL ON ME.
COOL. SO IT DOESN'T MATTER THAT THEY BLEW HIS SHITTY BRAINS OUT THEN?
JACKIE... I MEAN BOAT GIRL... YOU'VE STOPPED STUTTERING! AND YOU'VE STARTED SWEARING!

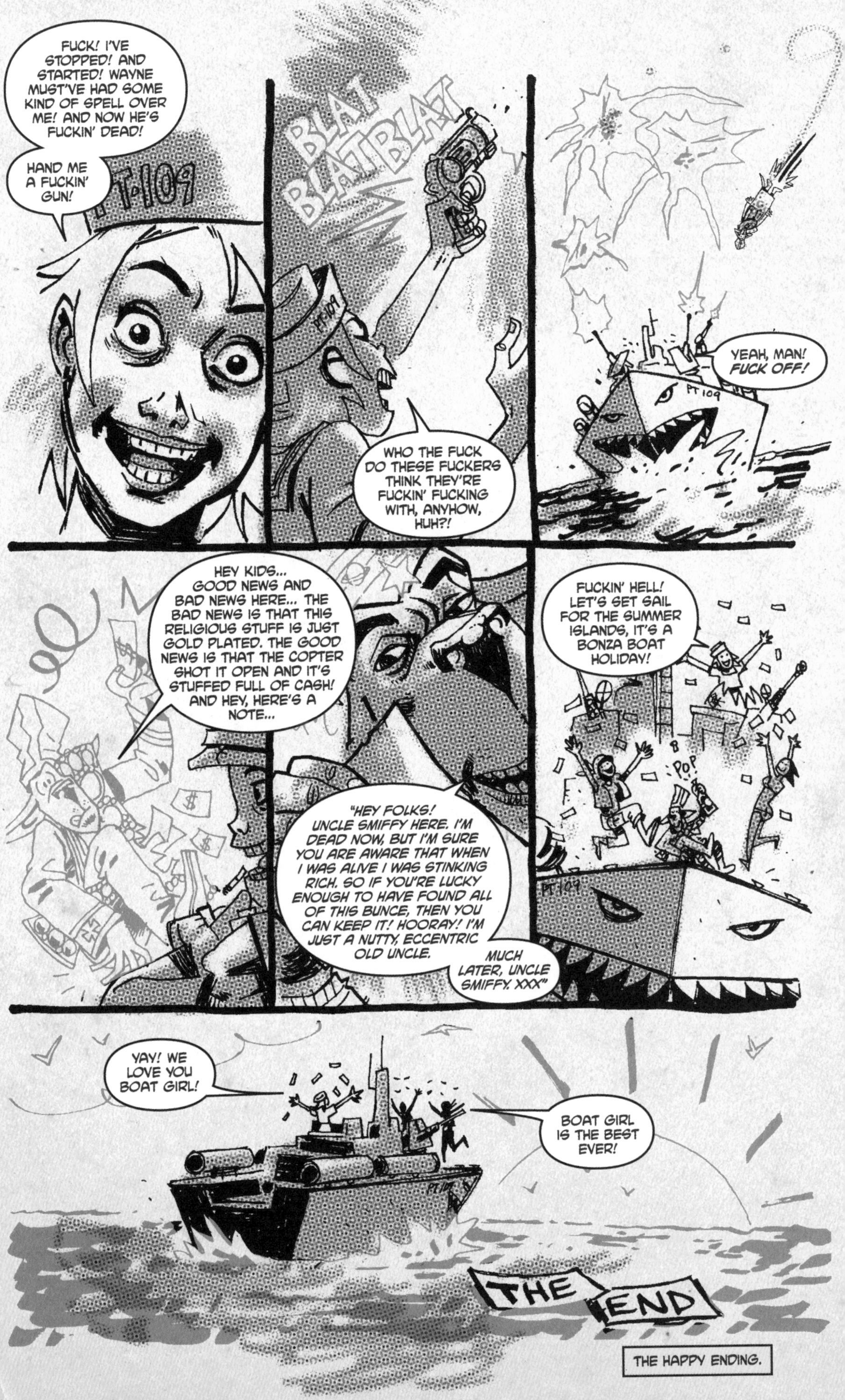
FUCK! I'VE STOPPED! AND STARTED! WAYNE MUST'VE HAD SOME KIND OF SPELL OVER ME! AND NOW HE'S FUCKIN' DEAD!
HAND ME A FUCKIN' GUN!
PT-109
BLAT BLATBLAT
WHO THE FUCK DO THESE FUCKERS THINK THEY'RE FUCKIN' FUCKING WITH, ANYHOW, HUH?!
YEAH, MAN! *FUCK OFF!*
PT 109
HEY KIDS... GOOD NEWS AND BAD NEWS HERE... THE BAD NEWS IS THAT THIS RELIGIOUS STUFF IS JUST GOLD PLATED. THE GOOD NEWS IS THAT THE COPTER SHOT IT OPEN AND IT'S STUFFED FULL OF CASH! AND HEY, HERE'S A NOTE...
"HEY FOLKS! UNCLE SMIFFY HERE. I'M DEAD NOW, BUT I'M SURE YOU ARE AWARE THAT WHEN I WAS ALIVE I WAS STINKING RICH. SO IF YOU'RE LUCKY ENOUGH TO HAVE FOUND ALL OF THIS BUNCE, THEN YOU CAN KEEP IT! HOORAY! I'M JUST A NUTTY, ECCENTRIC OLD UNCLE.
MUCH LATER, UNCLE SMIFFY. XXX"
FUCKIN' HELL! LET'S SET SAIL FOR THE SUMMER ISLANDS, IT'S A BONZA BOAT HOLIDAY!
POP
PT 109
YAY! WE LOVE YOU BOAT GIRL!
BOAT GIRL IS THE BEST EVER!
THE END
THE HAPPY ENDING.

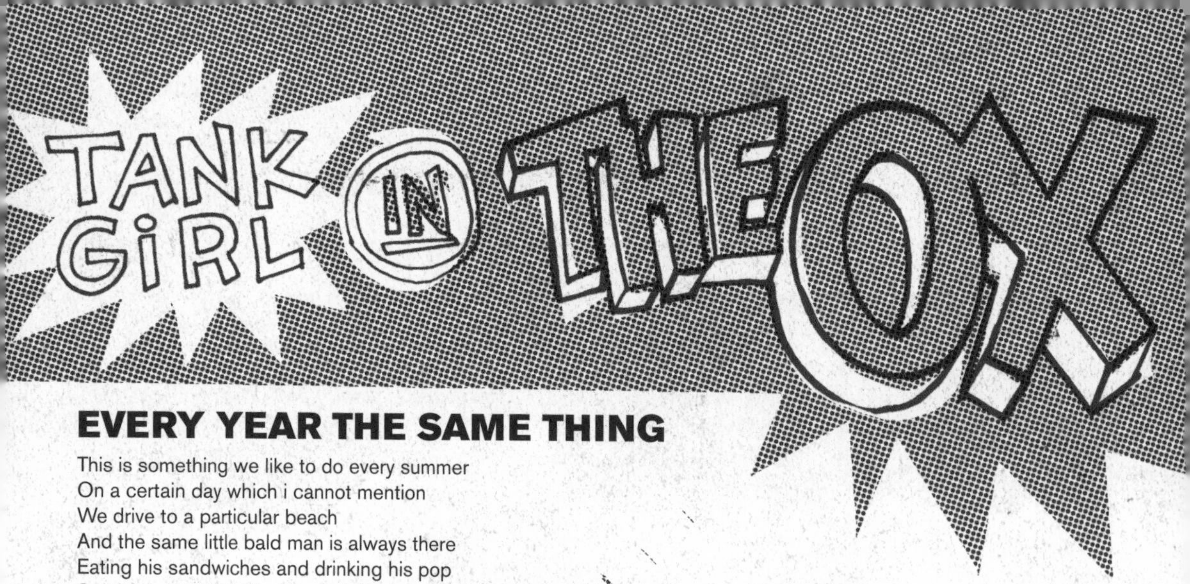
TANK GIRL
IN
THE O.X

EVERY YEAR THE SAME THING

This is something we like to do every summer
On a certain day which i cannot mention
We drive to a particular beach
And the same little bald man is always there
Eating his sandwiches and drinking his pop
So we chase the fucker up and down the sand
Screaming
Honking
And firing guns
And every year
We stop just short of giving him a heart attack

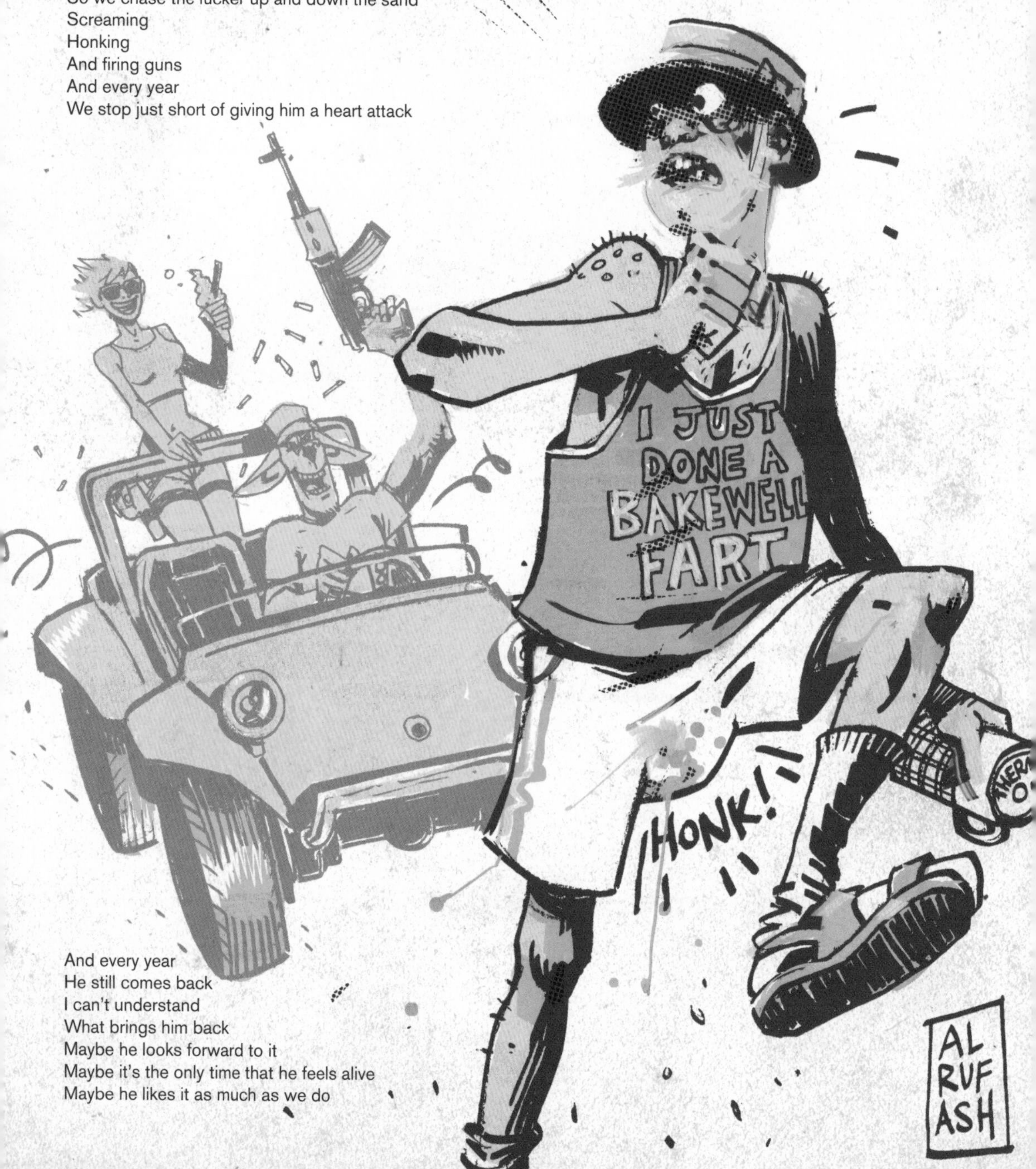
I JUST DONE A BAKEWELL FART
HONK!
AL RUF ASH

And every year
He still comes back
I can't understand
What brings him back
Maybe he looks forward to it
Maybe it's the only time that he feels alive
Maybe he likes it as much as we do

LIKE A ROAST POTATO IN A PICK-UP TRUCK

No one's happy any more
They're all chasing something
A memory of a golden sunset
A dream of happiness yesterday
A spectre of the past
Searching for something that never was
And never shall be
With their shopping trolleys
And fat wallets
And big cars
And chubby families
I'm here to tell them
That it never existed in the first place
It was never there
Only in their waking dreams
As they watched their televisions
And ate their snacks
It never was

And

Like a roast potato in a pick-up truck

They wouldn't've wanted it anyway

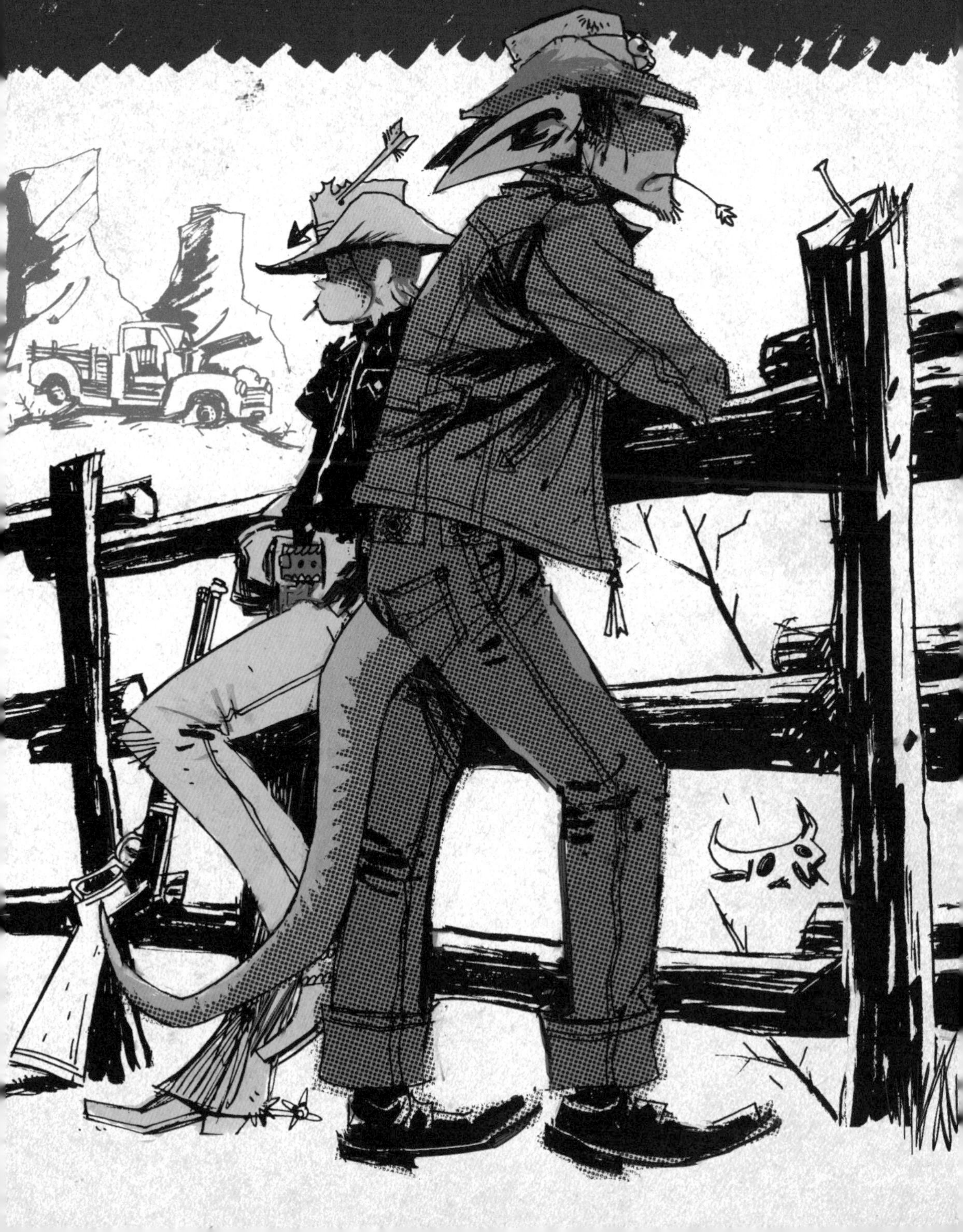

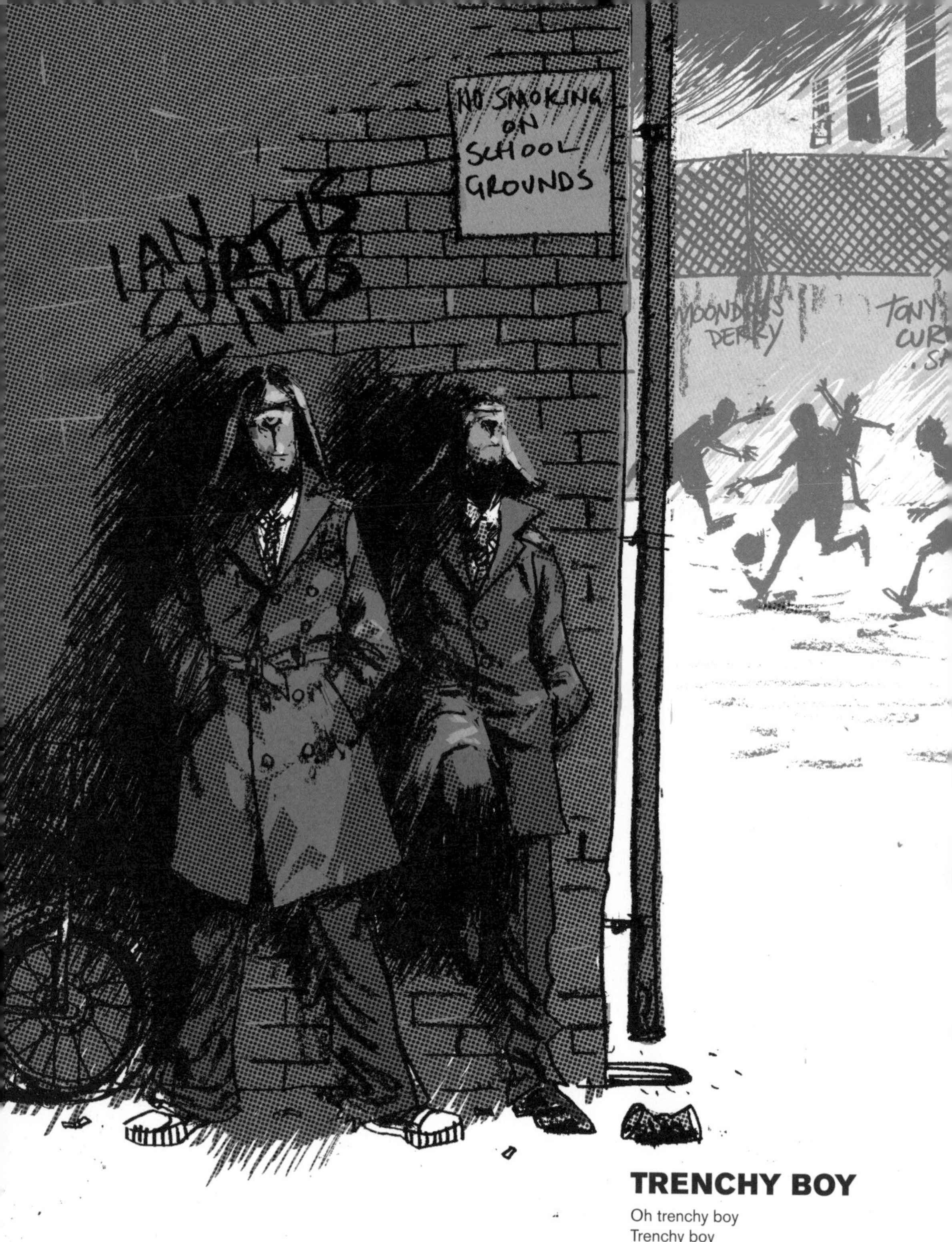
NO SMOKING ON SCHOOL GROUNDS

TRENCHY BOY

Oh trenchy boy
Trenchy boy
Do you recall?
When our trench coats flowed
And we did our hair
With a trench digger
And our rallying call
Was "over the top"
My dear, dear trenchy boy
Now
The past has filled in
And poppies have grown over
But those happy days
Are entrenched in my memory
Until the day
That peace comes to stay

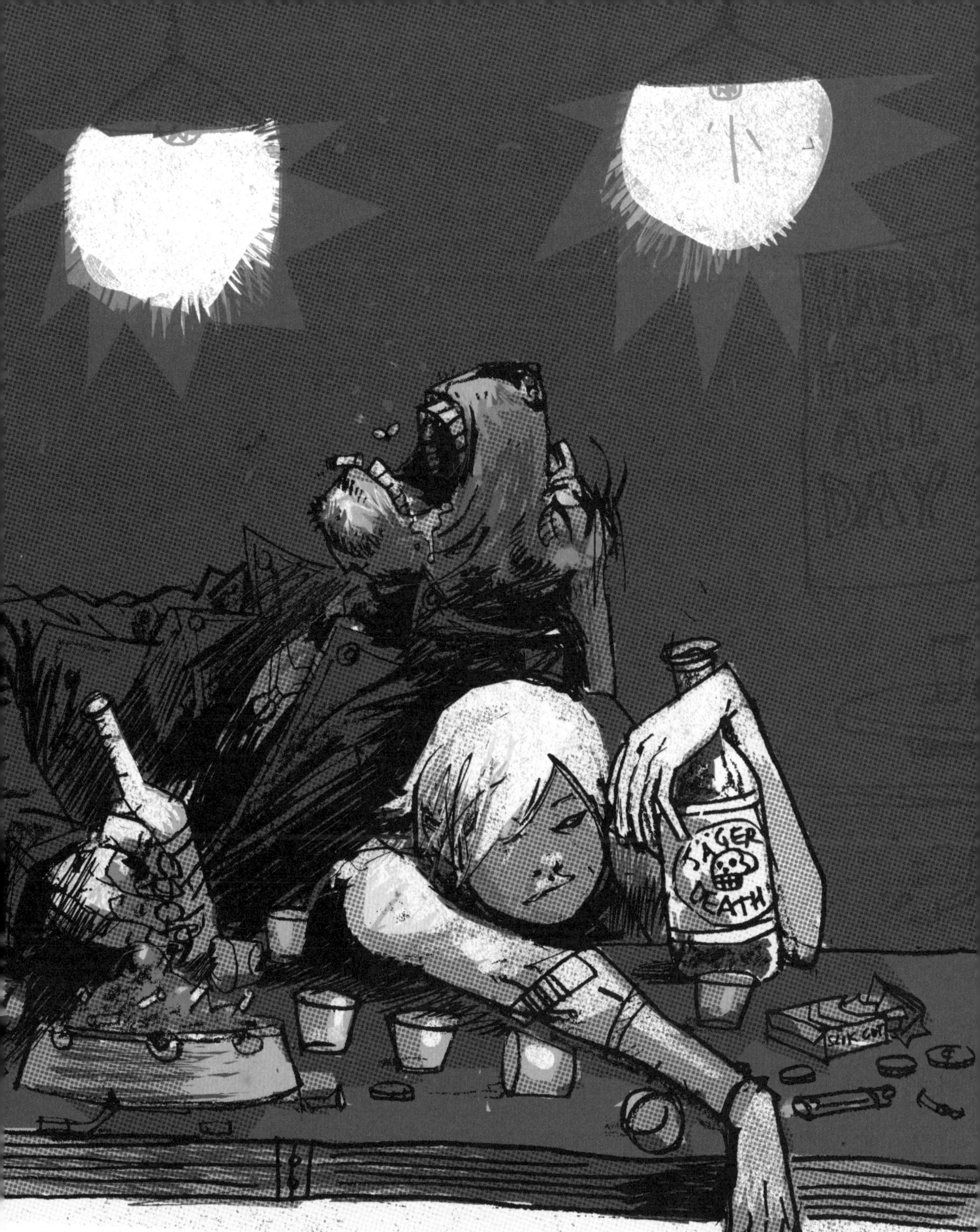
JÄGER DEATH
SILK CUT

SUSTAINABLE DAMAGE

Life
Keeps coming at me
And it's in the fuckin' balls
Every fuckin' time

Dreams
Burst like perishing balloons
Rubber shrapnel in my eyes
I can't see you anymore

Death
Clings to my back
A fuckin' rucksack full of lead
I've got to drag for one more mile

Peace
What we always talked of
A place so far away
We ain't never gonna get there

Love
The only thing left
The touch of a hairy hand
Smothering my empty thoughts
Lifting
And caressing my weary soul

THE OX

THE OX

The truth is staring you right in the face
Remember?
A strange village, a long way away
A play
Me as the mother
Barney as the shepherd
The pearson brothers as the three wise men
And booga as the ox
It could've all been so beautiful
The party was set for after the performance
Everyone was in high spirits
The trestle-tables were loaded with nosh
The cucumber sandwiches were cut
The scones were baked
The oranges had been squashed
Love bound us all together
And the villagers were our friends

But the ox
The ox sneaked away
Just as the baby was being born
And scoffed the fuckin' lot

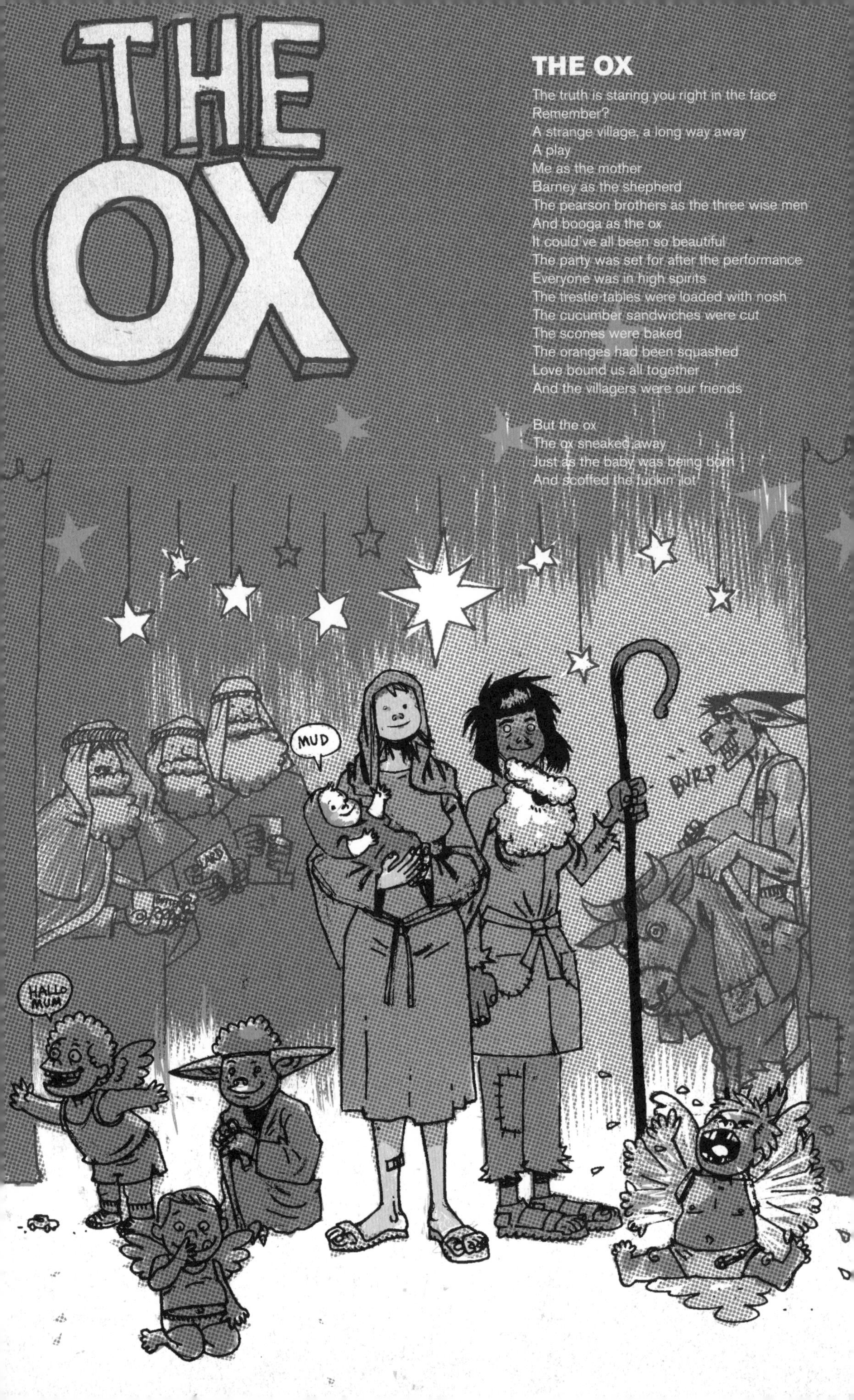
MUD
BURP
HALLO MUM

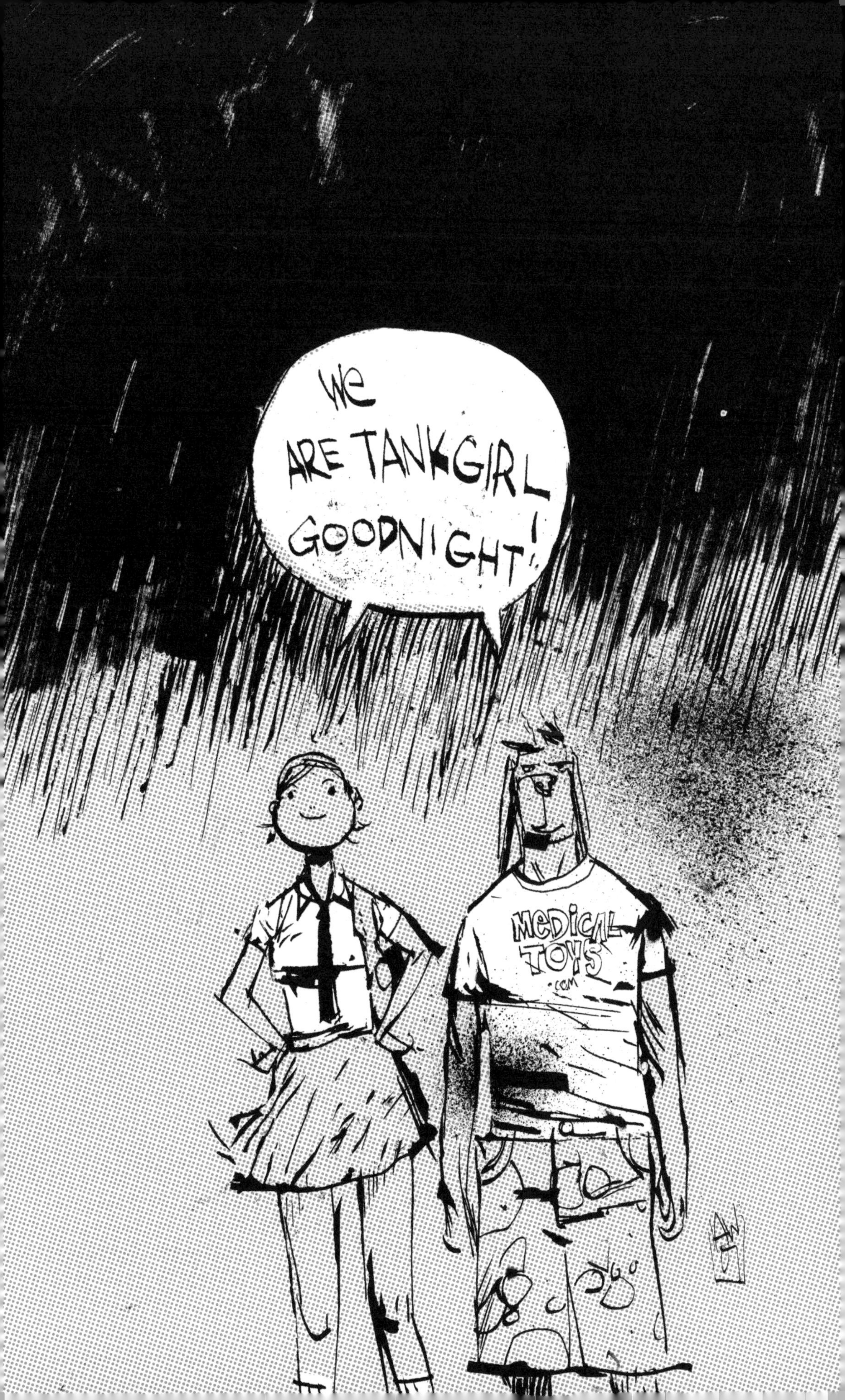
WE ARE TANKGIRL GOODNIGHT!
MEDICAL TOYS .COM

TANK GIRL ART GALLERY BY ASHLEY WOOD

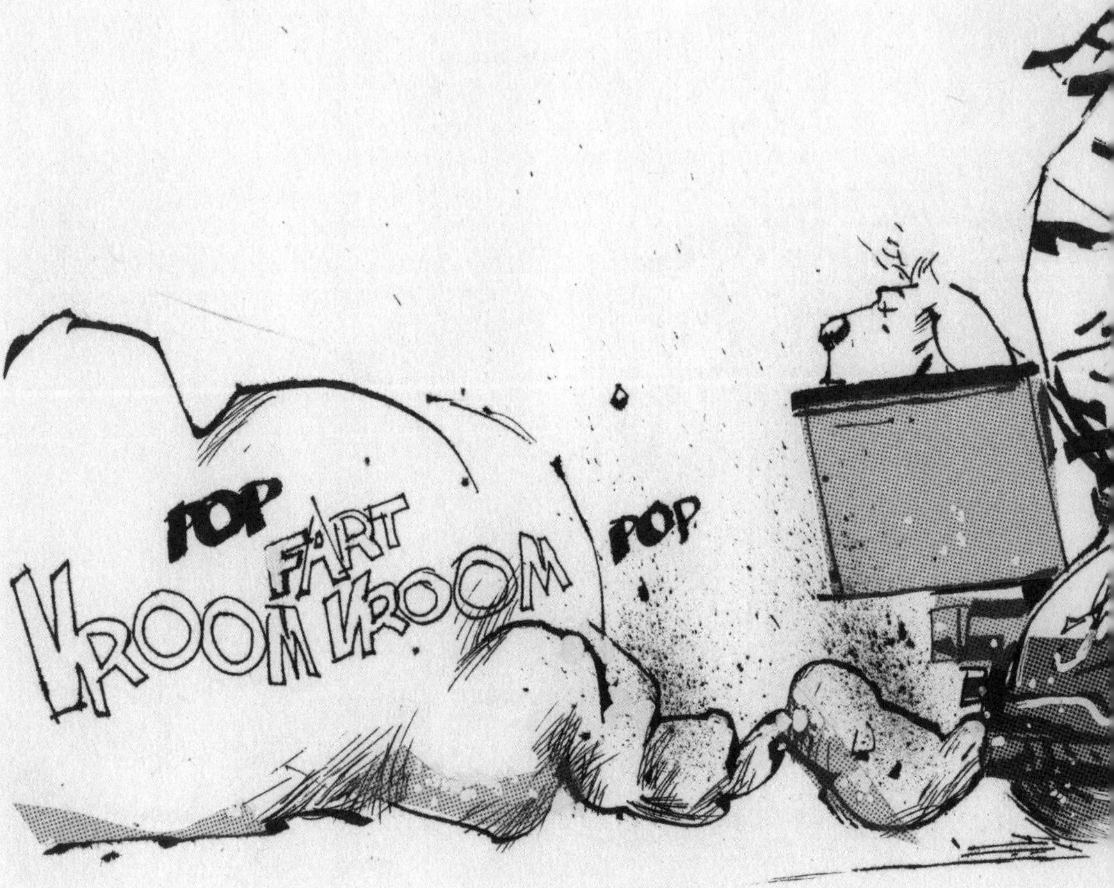

POP
FART
POP
KROOM KROOM

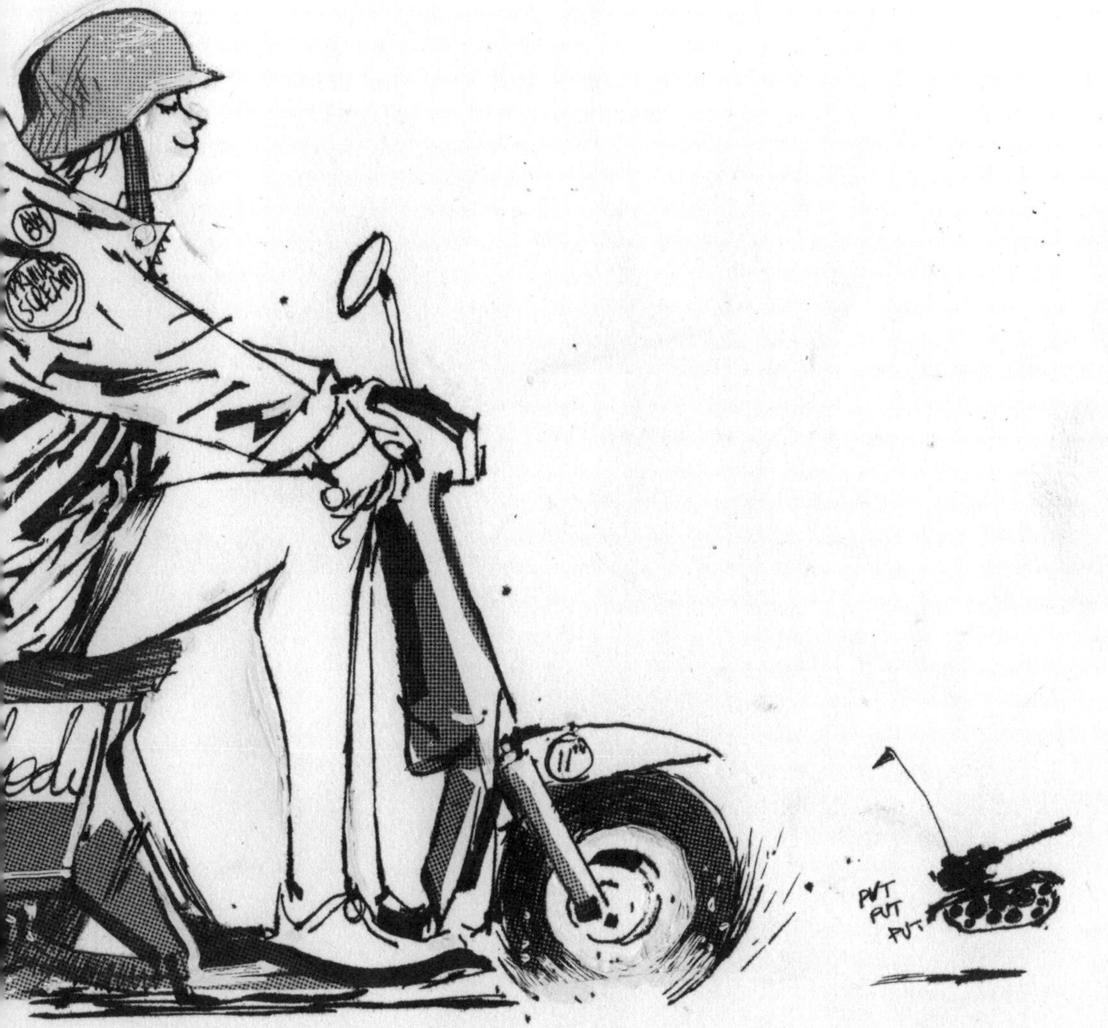
PUT
PUT
PUT

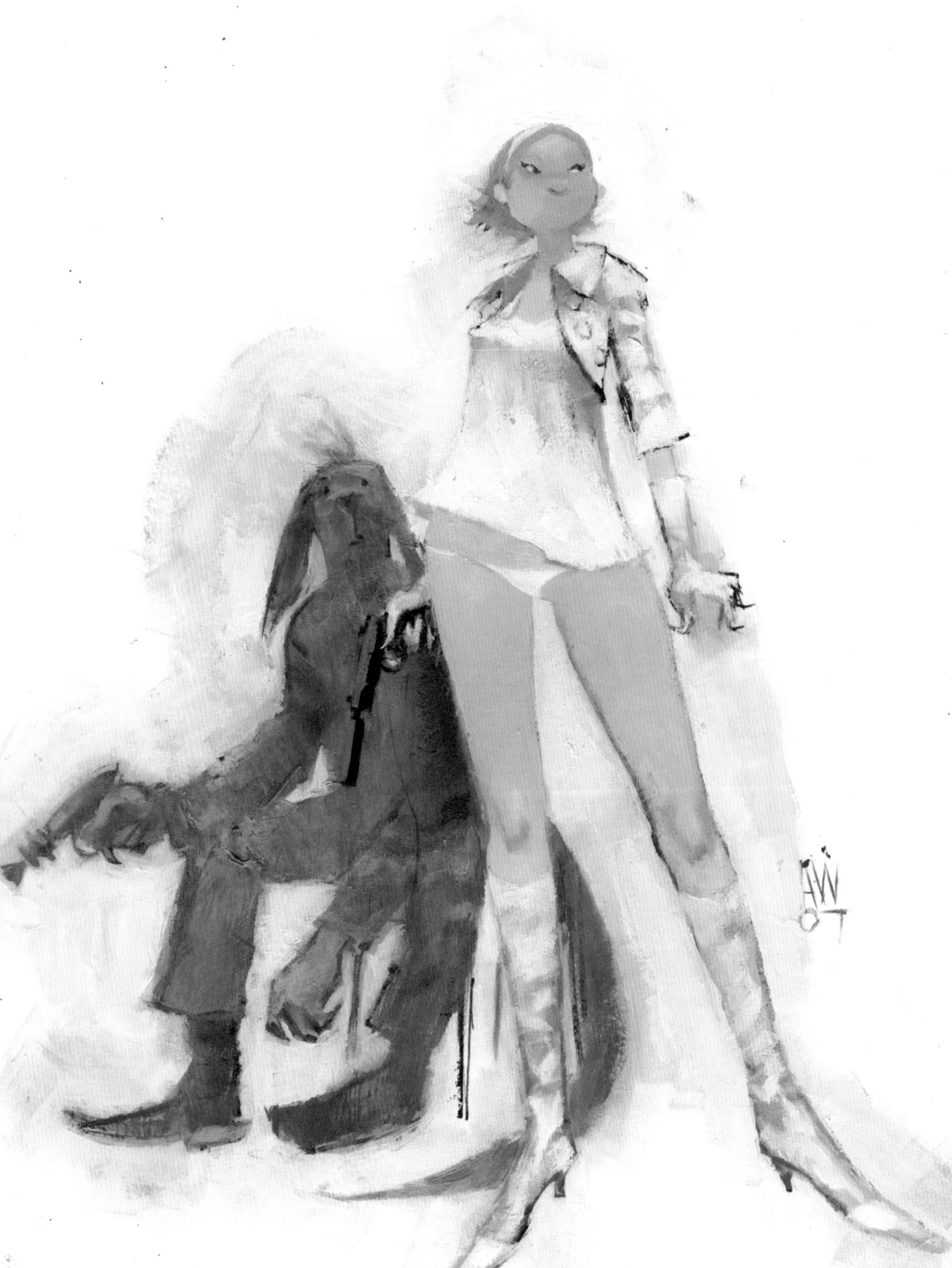

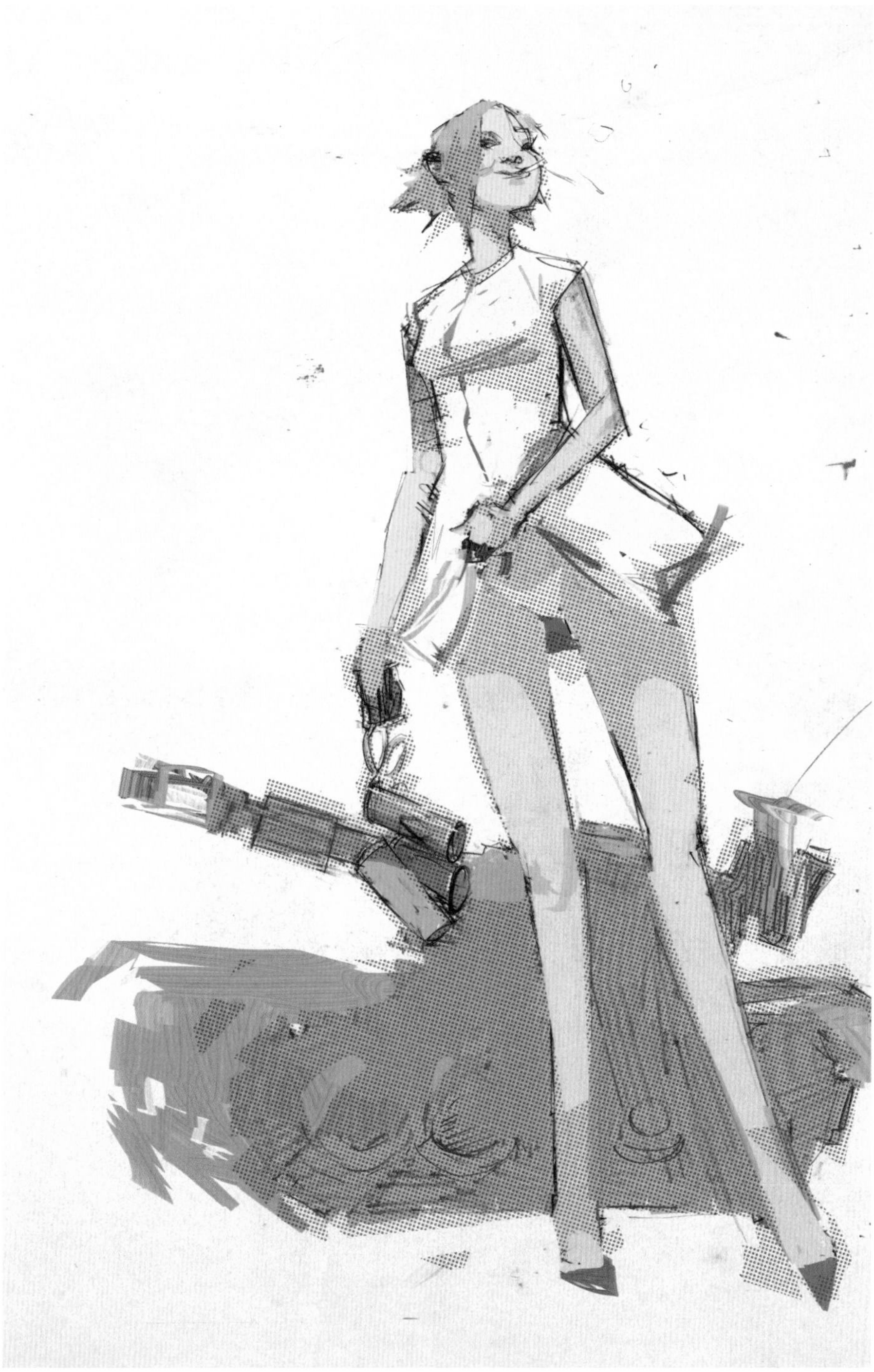

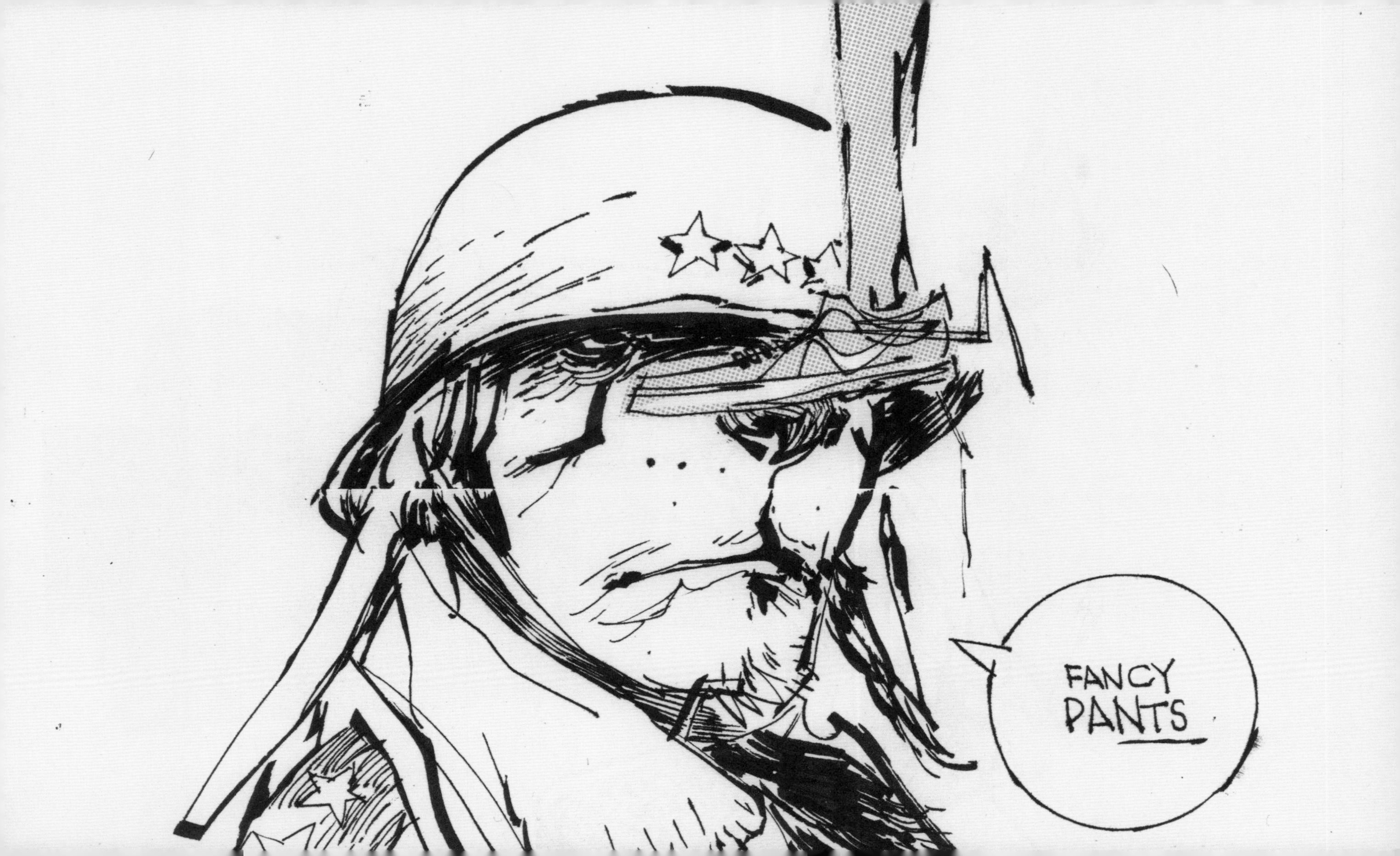
FANCY PANTS

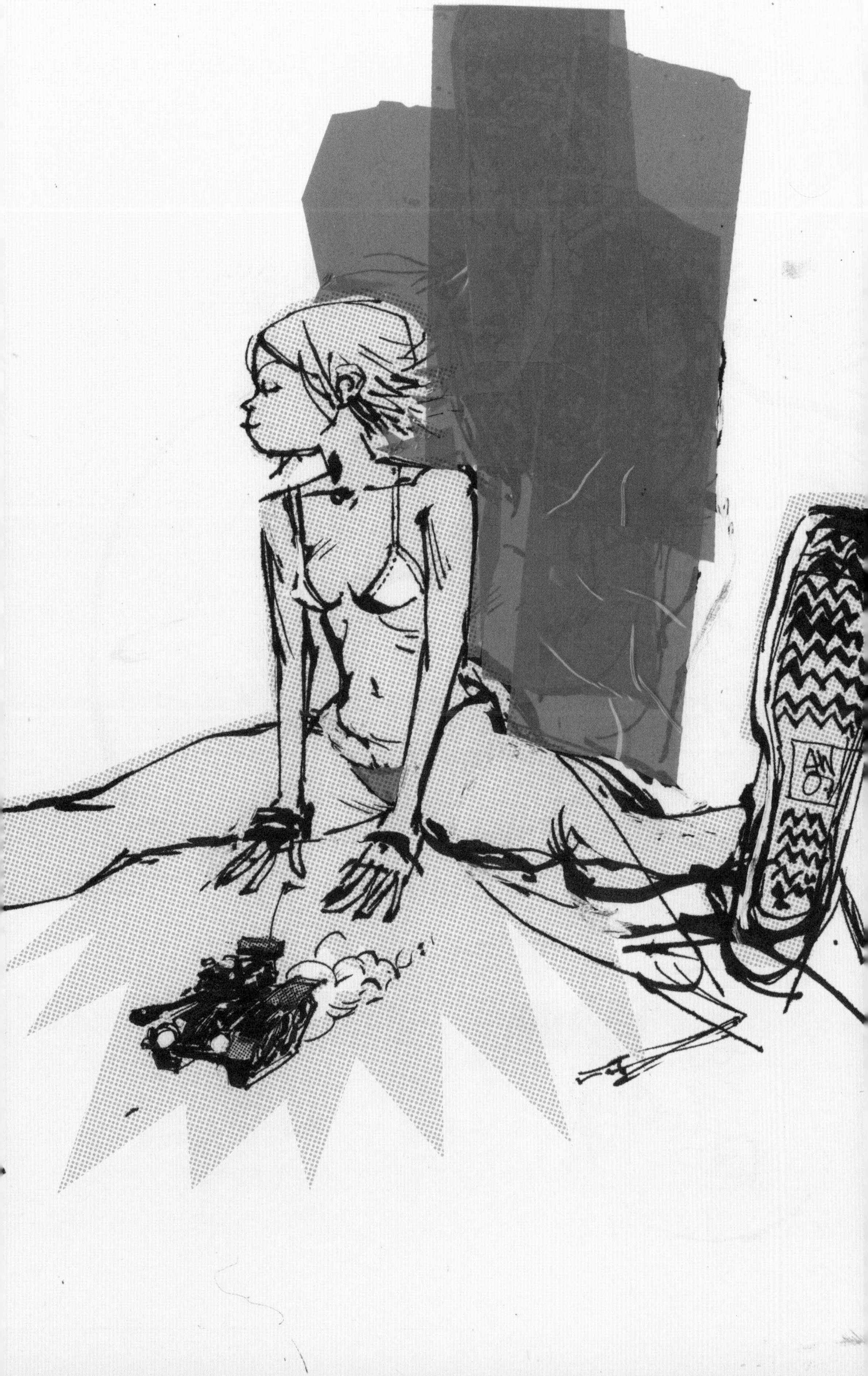

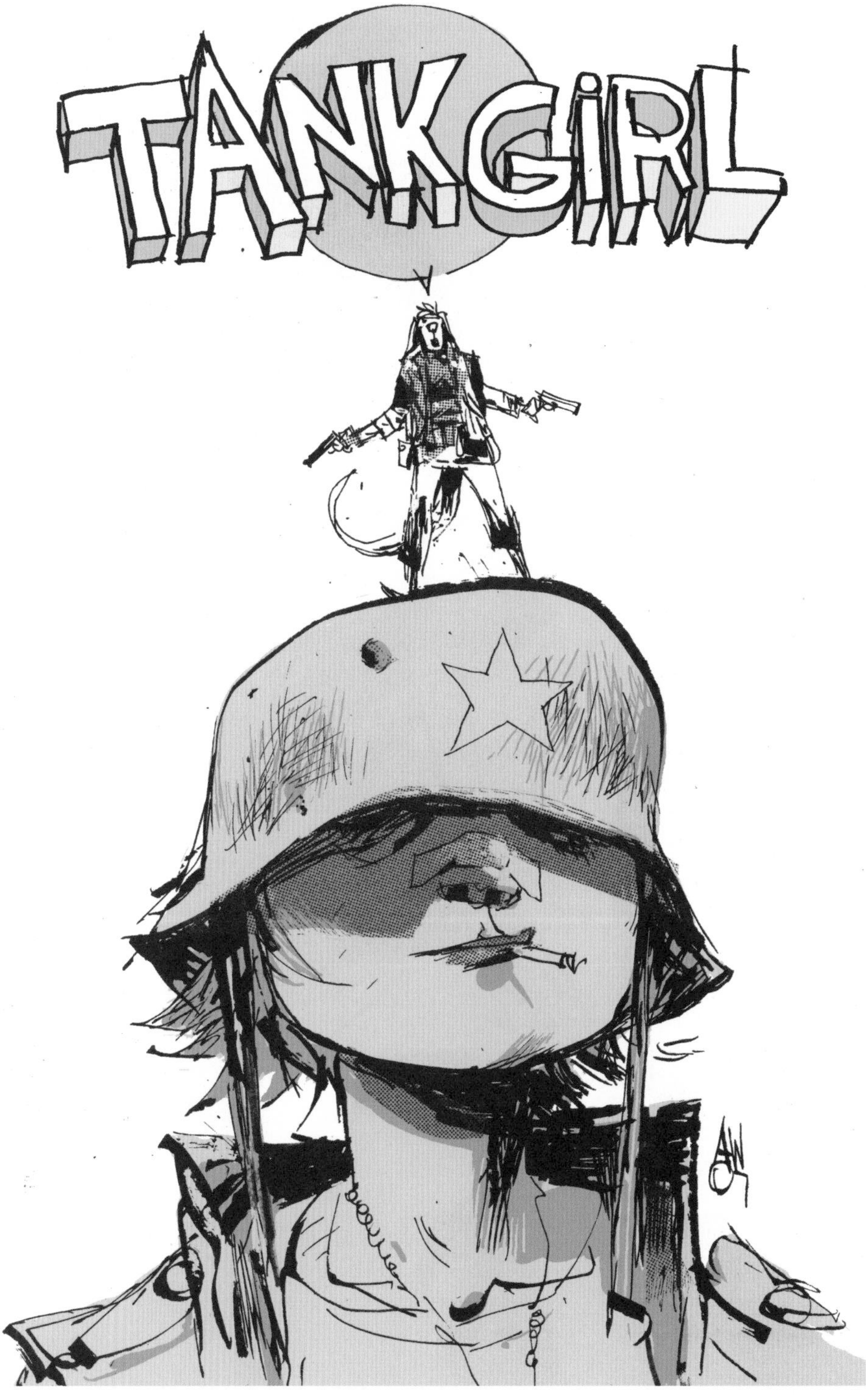
TANKGIRL

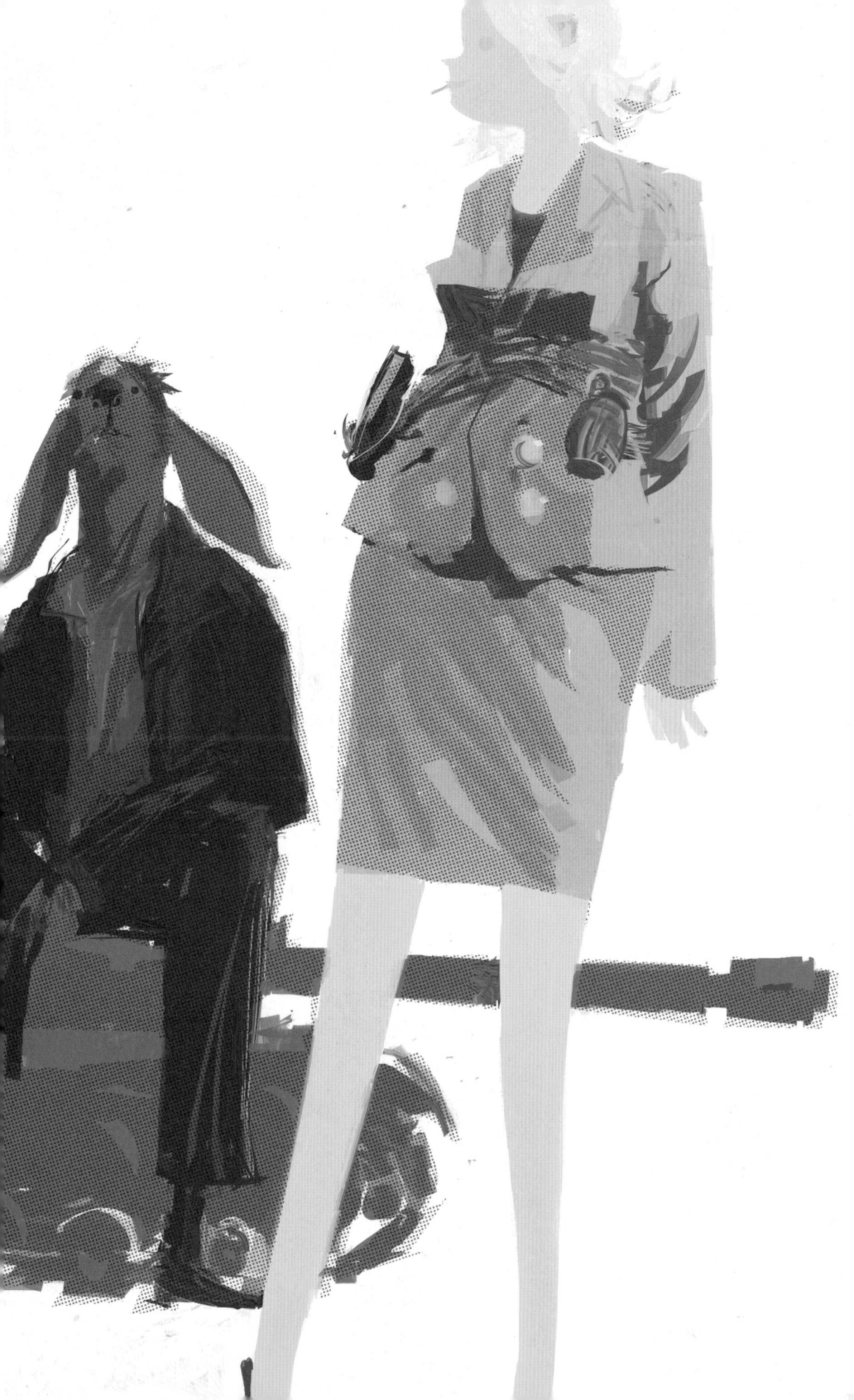

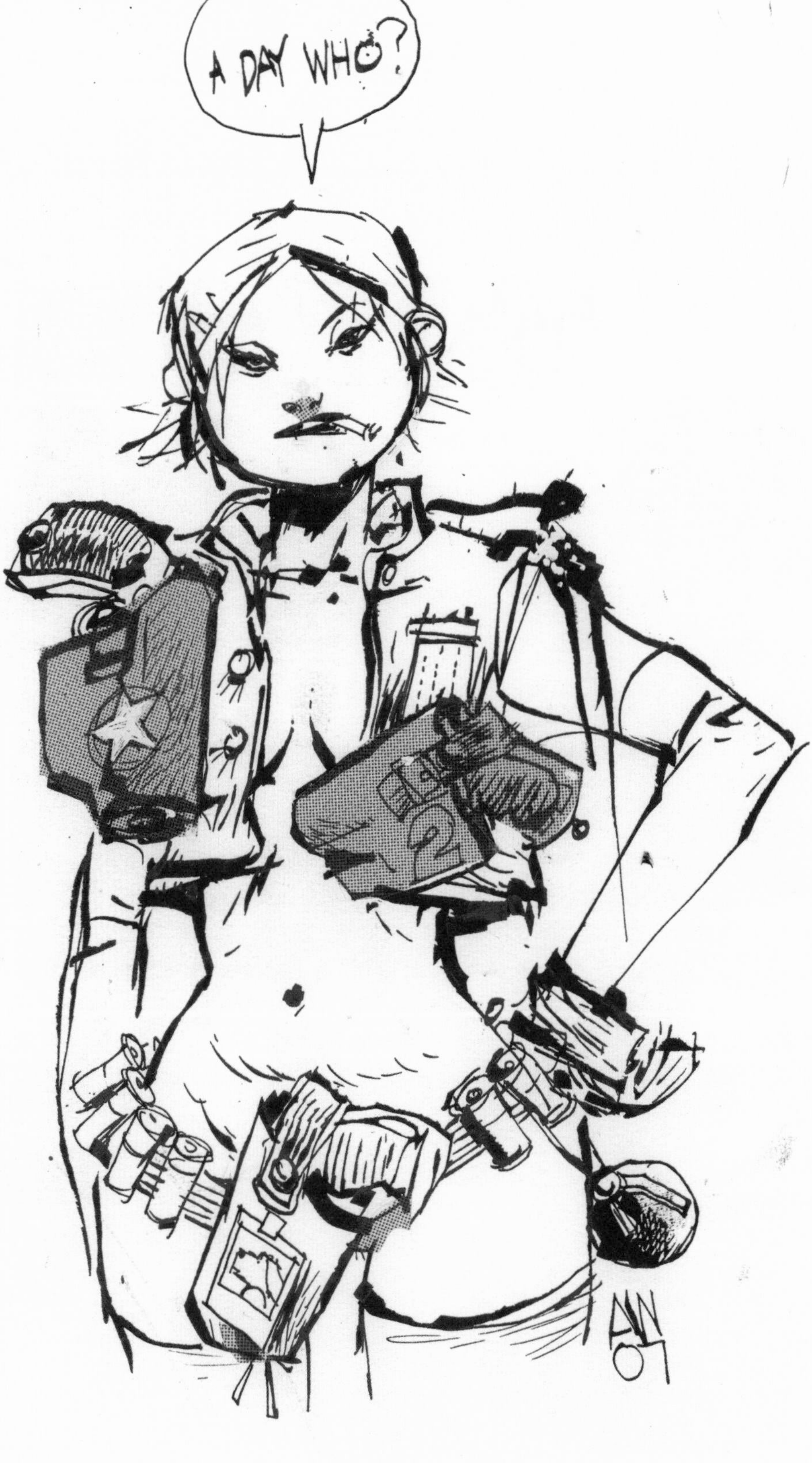
A DAY WHO?

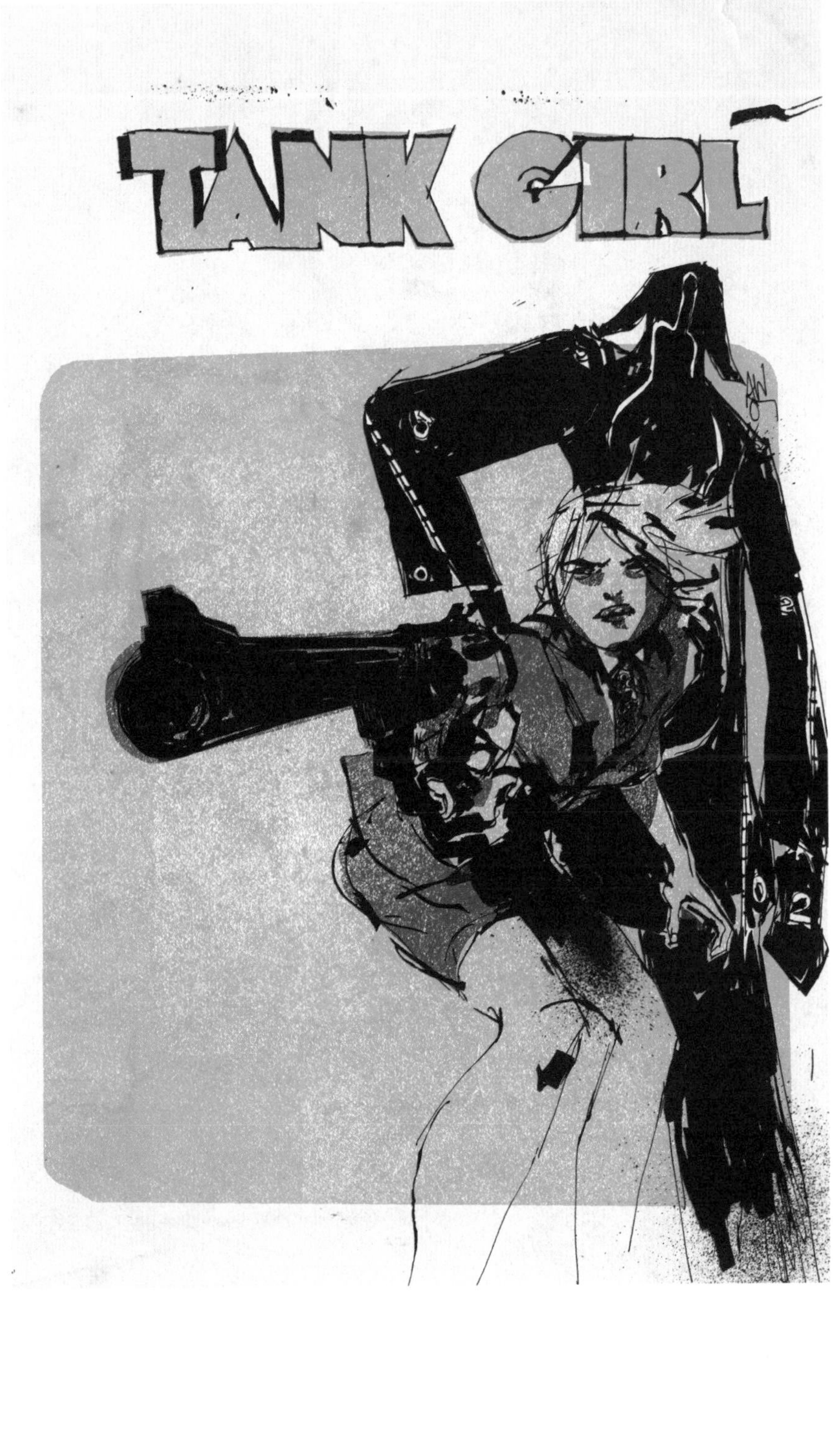
TANK GIRL

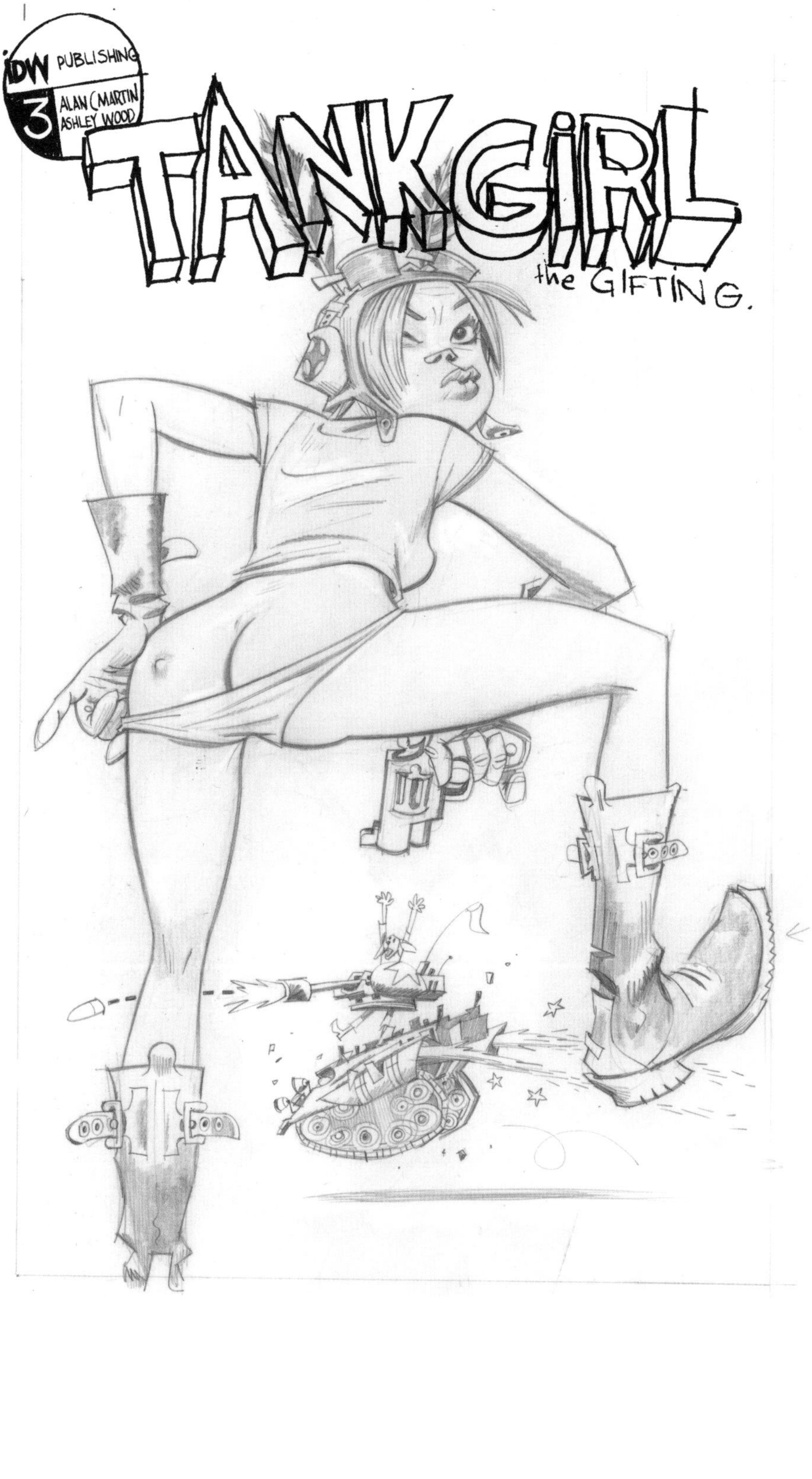
IDW PUBLISHING
3
ALAN C MARTIN
ASHLEY WOOD
TANKGIRL
the GIFTING.

art by jamie hewlett, colors by ashley wood

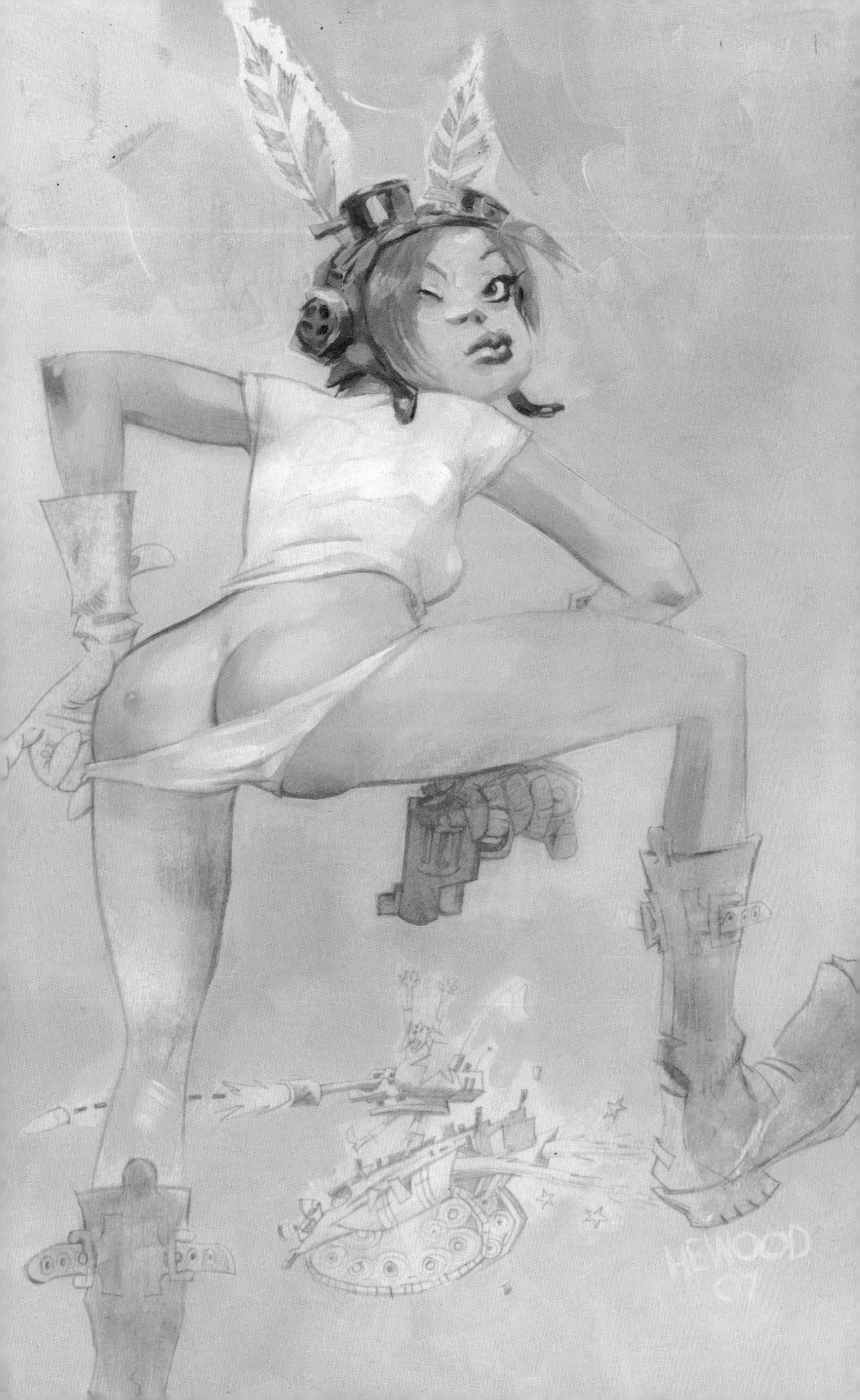

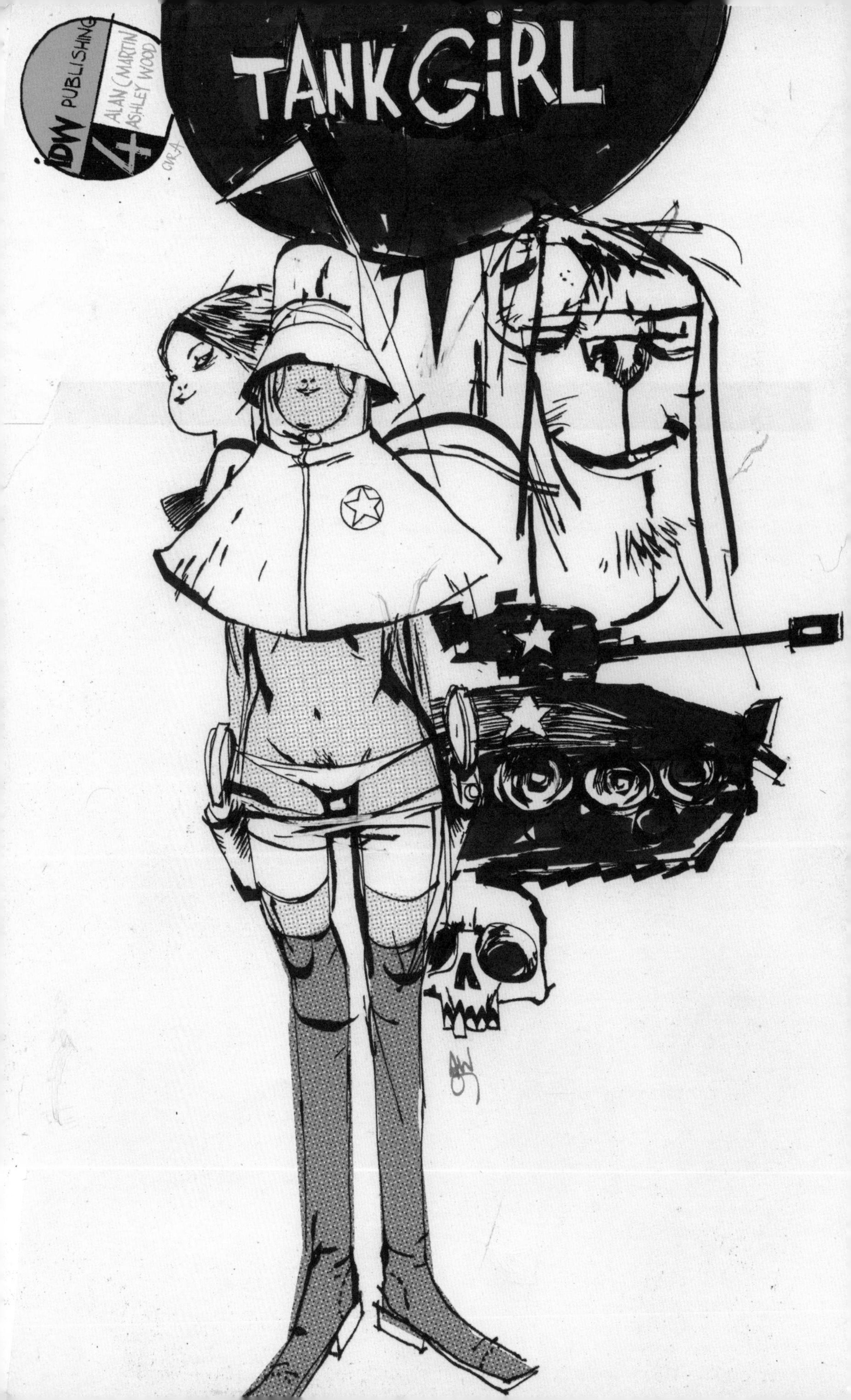
TANK GiRL
IDW PUBLISHING
4
ALAN C MARTIN
ASHLEY WOOD